# SCHOOLING

## and

HE

Sir William Turne

# Equality

# fact, concept
# and policy

Edited by
# DAVE HILL    MIKE COLE

RoutledgeFalmer
Taylor & Francis Group

LONDON AND NEW YORK

First published in 2001
By RoutledgeFalmer

Reprinted 2004
By RoutledgeFalmer
2 Park Square, Milton Park,
Abingdon, Oxon, OX14 4RN

Transferred to Digital Printing 2005

*Routledge is an imprint of the Taylor & Francis Group*

---

**British Library Cataloguing in Publication Data**

A CIP record for this book is available from the British Library.

ISBN 0 7494 3370 1 (hardback)
ISBN 0 7494 3369 8 (paperback)

---

Typeset by JS Typesetting, Wellingborough, Northants

# Contents

# Contributors

*Mike Cole* is Senior Lecturer in Education, and Education Research and Publications Mentor in the Faculty of Education and Sport at the University of Brighton. He has written extensively on equality issues – in particular, equality and education. In more recent years he has engaged in critiques of post-modernism, globalization and education. With Dave Hill he co-founded the Hillcole Group of Radical Left Educators in England. He edited *Bowles and Gintis Revisited* (Falmer Press, 1988*), Education for Equality* (Routledge, 1989) and *The Social Contexts of Schooling* (Falmer Press, 1989). His most recent publications include the co-written (with the Hillcole Group) *Rethinking Education and Democracy* (Tufnell Press, 1997) and the edited collections, *Promoting Equality in Primary Schools*) (Cassell, 1997), *Promoting Equality in Secondary Schools* (Cassell, 1999), *Professional Issues for Teachers and Student Teachers* (David Fulton, 1999), *Migrant Labour in the European Union* (Berg, 1999), and *Education, Equality and Human Rights; Issues of Gender, 'Race', Sexuality, Special Needs and Social Class* (Routledge/Falmer, 2000). With Dave Hill, Peter McLaren and Glenn Rikowski he wrote *Red Chalk: On schooling, capitalism and politics* (Institute for Education Policy Studies, 2001).

*Kenneth Dunkwu* is Social Inclusion and Diversity Co-ordinator, BUILD, Nottingham Mentor Programme, Nottingham. His MPhil is from Nottingham Trent University and his PhD on *Attitudes and Perceptions of Pupils towards School Exclusion* from Manchester University. Kenneth has published on this in Simms and Showumni (eds) *Teachers for the Future* (Trentham Books, 1995). He has participated in a number of research projects. These include 'Recruitment Barriers for Black Teachers', a HEFCE funded project, and 'Overseas Qualifica-tions of Black and Ethnic Minority Groups in Manchester' for the Progress Trust. He is currently researching principles for education and social justice for the British Educational Research Association special interest group, 'Social Justice', for publication in the *British Journal of Education Research*.

*Chris Gaine* is Reader in the Sociology of Education at University College Chichester, where he was for some years responsible for 'equalities' courses in initial teacher education. Formerly he was Head of Humanities in a Wiltshire comprehensive. He has written extensively on 'race' and education – in particular *No Problem Here* (Hutchinson, 1991), *Still No Problem Here* (Trentham, 1995) and (with Rosalyn George) *Gender, 'Race' and Class in Schooling* (Falmer, 1999), with forthcoming chapters in books in Italian and German. He was also one of the group that produced the Runnymede Trust's *Equality Assurance* (Trentham, 1993) and Longman's *Training for Equality* (1993). He wrote the anti-racist Web site www.britkid.org.

*Ian Grosvenor* lectures in the School of Education, University of Birmingham. He was previously Head of History at Newman College and Educational Research Co-ordinator at University College Northampton. He has taught in primary, secondary and special schools, worked on local authority anti-racist initiatives, and worked in equal opportunities programmes. He has published articles on the teaching of history, the writing of history, and post-1945 British education policy. He is the author of *Assimilating Identities: Racism and education policy in post-1945 Britain* (Lawrence & Wishart, 1997), edited *An Introduction to the Study of Education* (David Fulton, 1999) with David Matheson and edited *Silences and Images: The social history of the classroom* (Peter Lang, 1999) with Martin Lawn and Kate Rousmaniere. His current research interests include 19th- and 20th-century urban education and children and the dynamics of social exclusion.

*Dave Hill* teaches at University College Northampton, having also taught at Chichester Institute of Higher Education and at Tower Hamlets College and Stockwell Manor School in inner London. He is a former Labour Parliamentary candidate (in 1979 and 1987), former Labour Group Leader on East Sussex County Council, and regional higher education Chair of NATFHE, the lecturers' union. Formerly he was a building worker. He has advised the Labour Party on teacher education from a radical Left perspective. With Mike Cole, in 1989, he co-founded the Hillcole Group of Radical Left Educators. He has written a number of Hillcole Group booklets on Teacher Education, co-wrote *Practical Ideas for Multicultural Learning and Teaching in the Primary Classroom* with Ruth Hessari (Routledge, 1989), has co-written the two Hillcole Group books *Changing the Future: Redprint for education* (Tufnell Press, 1991) and *Rethinking Education and Democracy* (Tufnell Press, 1997), has co-edited *Promoting Equality in Primary Schools* and *Promoting Equality in Secondary Schools* (Cassell, 1997, 1999) and *Postmodernism and Education: Towards a politics of human resistance* (Tufnell Press, 1999). He is editing *Education, Education, Education: Capitalism, Socialism and 'the Third Way'* (forthcoming), and co-wrote *Red Chalk: On schooling, capitalism and politics* (2001), with Mike Cole, Peter McLaren and Glenn Rikowski. He directs the Institute for Education Policy Studies, an independent radical Left education institute.

*Rachel Hill* was formerly a mathematics teacher at a comprehensive school in the north-east of England. She is now an educational psychologist.

*Kate Hirom* has taught in schools in the London area for over 20 years and has also been an associate lecturer with the Open University. She is now English Co-ordinator in the School of Education at University College Northampton and also teaches and researches in the field of discourse analysis.

*Kevin Myers* teaches British social history and the history of education at the University of Birmingham, Westhill. His recently completed doctoral thesis examines the settlement and education of refugee children in Britain between 1937 and 1945 and he has published numerous articles in this area. A member of the History of Education Society Committee, he is currently working on aspects of refugee schooling in 20th-century Britain.

*Leena Helavaara Robertson* teaches at University College Northampton. She teaches professional English teacher education courses and early childhood studies courses. She was formerly an early years teacher in multi-ethnic schools in Watford and specializes and researches into literacy, and bilingual and bicultural education. She is involved in a number of national research projects on home literacy, children's emergent literacy, and community learning experiences. She guest lectures and advises on these, and on multiculturalism and education, in Finland, with education authorities and in higher education. She is Finnish and bilingual/bicultural herself and was involved in organizing Finnish/English bilingual education provision in England.

*Richard Rose* is Head of the Centre for Special Needs Education and Research (CeSNER) at University College Northampton. He has previously worked as a teacher, head teacher and LEA inspector in several parts of the UK. He has published widely in the field of special education and has presented papers at several national and international conferences. He is research editor for the British Journal of Special Education. His most recent book, *Promoting Inclusive Practice*, written in collaboration with Christina Tilstone and Lani Florian, and published by Routledge, won the NASEN/TES Academic Book of the Year Award for 1999. Richard's research interests are in the areas of inclusive education, pupil involvement in their own assessment and learning procedures and children's rights.

*Tim Waller* is Early Years Coordinator in the School of Education at University College Northampton. He teaches on a range of undergraduate and postgraduate courses and is course leader for the BA (Hons) Early Childhood Studies. He taught in nursery, infant and primary schools in London and has also worked in the United States. His research interests include early literacy, information and communication technology and equality, and he has been investigating the use of computers by young children for over six years. His most recent publications concern the application of ICT in the teaching and learning of literacy and he is also involved in an international research project comparing young children's computer use at home and school, in Sweden and the UK. His contribution to this book is dedicated to the students and staff at John Lea Comprehensive School, Wellingborough, Northants. The unnecessary and unwelcome closure of this school, he feels, is a sad indictment of both Conservative and Labour education policy.

*Iain Williamson* is lecturer in psychology at University College Northampton. Formerly he taught sociology and psychology in further education for eight years and was head of psychology at Oldham Sixth Form College. He is currently carrying out research into eating disturbance among gay men and the educational experience of young offenders.

# Acknowledgements

We would like to acknowledge the tremendous support, encouragement and editorial advice given to us by Jonathan Simpson at Kogan Page, throughout the project of co-writing and co-editing this book. We have valued very much his diligence, professionalism and commitment.

We would also like to thank Christine Fox, of Running Heads Editorial Services, Brighton, for her acute, humorous and knowledgeable expertise in working with us on the book.

*Dave Hill*
*Mike Cole*
*July 2001*

# Introduction

## Dave Hill

This book is intended to demonstrate and analyse the persistent inequalities in the education system in England and Wales. Schools – and the education system more widely – have been systematically restructured in the last quarter of a century both by Conservative governments (1979–97) and New Labour governments elected in two electoral landslides in May 1997 and June 2001. These policies have had a major impact on inequalities in society.

Chapter 1, by Dave Hill, sets out the various types of education (and wider) policies pursued by different types of government in Britain. It examines the main characteristics of different ideologies underlying the education policies, and also looks at the effects of (for example) socialist/Marxist ideas, social democratic ideas, Conservative (neo-liberal and neo-conservative) ideas and New Labour ideas and policies on equality of opportunity and equality. The chapter concludes with an assessment of the ideology informing New Labour in government.

In Chapter 2, Dave Hill locates the policy developments discussed in Chapter 1 within the wider policy context of neo-liberalism, which emphasizes privatization and competitive markets in education and in social and welfare policy more generally. Neo-liberalism is also identified as a global phenomenon – similar restructuring of schooling and education has taken place across the globe. The chapter proceeds to examine the effects of neo-liberal policies in increasing inequalities in Britain and in other states. The chapter concludes by constructing a critique of neo-liberalism – making a number of trenchant theoretical criticisms of neo-liberalism, for example in the work of British neo-liberal propagandist James Tooley. It concludes the wide-ranging critique of neo-liberalism by looking forward to critical transformative education for equality.

In Chapter 3, Kenneth Dunkwu looks at the role of research in the quest for equal opportunities and equality. He uncovers the uses and misuses of educational research for political purposes, discusses research into the effects of 'league tables' and market forces in education policy, and considers a political role for educational research in the achievement of social justice, and for what he terms 'diversity without disempowerment'. Dunkwu examines significant post-war examples such as the assimilationist approaches to the children of immigrant communities during the 1950s and 1960s, the Education Reform Act of 1988, aspects of the contemporary National Curriculum and the reorganization of research. He uses these to illustrate the limits imposed on egalitarianism by legislation for education that carries with it social and economic forms of discrimination

Chapter 4, by Leena Helevaara Robertson and Rachel Hill, considers the inequalities suffered by 'the excluded' within the education system. The chapter listens to the voices of the excluded and places these voices – from Pahari/Mirpuri-speaking young children in Watford to white working-class teenagers in north-east England – within the broader family, cultural and policy contexts. The chapter identifies different types of exclusion – from physical exclusion from school, to self-exclusion from school, to wider social exclusion. It draws distinctions between the more inclusive Early Years curriculum in England and Wales and the more exclusive 5–16 National Curriculum.

Chapter 5, by Dave Hill, analyses how the subject curriculum and the hidden curriculum serve to exclude particular social types/groups of children and to reproduce and confirm inequalities in education and society. The chapter makes use of principles derived from Althusser and Bourdieu. These concepts – of schools as ideological state apparatuses, and of cultural capital – are used to analyse curriculum knowledge that has been selected, and cultural behaviours privileged and rewarded through both the formal and the hidden curricula. The chapter also identifies the mixture of gains and losses created by the National Curriculum in terms of educational equality regarding 'race', gender, special needs, sexual diversity and social class.

In Chapter 6, Chris Gaine discusses the historical development, strengths and weaknesses of equal opportunities policies in local education authorities (LEAs) and in schools. He focuses on how to embed and secure effective equal opportunities policies in the face of various types of resistance to them. He therefore concentrates on the management of change – on the support systems in schools (the processes and personnel) that are required if the policies are to be implemented thoroughly and completely. The chapter maps the crucial areas where policy has failed to effect change in the past and where it can succeed in the future, particularly in relation to equality. Chris Gaine points out that 'Policies legitimate certain concerns, provide resources to further them, and provide a basis for evaluation and refinement.'

The next five chapters highlight particular inequalities within the education 'system' – within schools, the wider education system and within society. In Chapter 7, Dave Hill and Mike Cole examine social class; in Chapter 8, Tim Waller, Dave Hill and Mike Cole look at 'race'; Kate Hirom deals with gender in Chapter 9; Chapter 10, by Iain Williamson, looks at sexuality and Chapter 11, by Richard Rose, examines special educational needs.

Each of these five chapters sets out factual evidence about equality in education and in society, about inequalities and about recent trends. The various authors also evaluate various explanations for the inequalities. The extent of the persistent discrimination against particular groups of young people in schools may surprise some readers. Each chapter defines key concepts. The authors regard 'nomenclature' – what we call people – as important. Each chapter also examines in detail how various government policies on schools and education have affected particular groups and how these education policies relate to wider areas of government policy and ideology.

In Chapter 12, Kevin Myers and Ian Grosvenor address the question of why prejudice against ostracized groups such as immigrants and asylum seekers still exists in our society. Myers and Grosvenor use an historical perspective to chart a 'chronology of exclusion' in the political rhetoric, education policy and practical treatment of 'outsider' children and their communities in Britain, throughout the 20th century – for Jewish children in the 1930s through to the children of refugees and asylum seekers in 2000. Foreshadowing some of the conclusions of the book, they also highlight the tradition of resistance to social, political and cultural alienation, most notably in the development of positive and progressive education systems.

Part I

# Policy

1

# Equality, ideology and education policy

*Dave Hill*

## Editors' introduction

*Whether equality becomes a fact of life depends on how it is valued, on whether it is seen as an improving or destructive force within social, cultural and economic relationships. Dave Hill gives an account of how equality in the provision of education is assessed within the competing value systems, or ideologies, advocated from the different political positions across the arena of modern British politics. From Left to Right, the main criteria of social policy for socialism, social democracy, liberal-progressivism and conservatism are broadly defined, so that their influence – discriminatory or egalitarian – can be seen in the background history of education policy in England and Wales from 1880. The discussion then tightens into detailed analysis of political principles and post-war education policy, especially the recent evaluations of equality within radical Left and radical Right-wing agendas. Acknowledging the complex and shifting relationship between ideology and policy making, typified by the fracture of neo-liberal and neo-conservative ideologies within the radical Right, the chapter leads to an incisive assessment of the ideology informing New Labour in government.*

## Introduction

This chapter examines a number of the ideologies in education that have most influenced education policy and debate in England and Wales, from the Second World War to New Labour.

As political positions differ on the desirability of social and economic equality, so they differ on the need for equality and the equality of opportunity within education. Consequently, the policies that more or less flow from the different ideas and values that compose these ideologies are often explicitly framed in terms of their intention to promote either equality and equality of opportunity, or elitism and an unequal hierarchy of schooling.

The first section of the chapter begins with a definition of ideology. The second section, an historical overview, briefly describes key aspects of the ideologies that have clearly affected education policy from 1945 to the mid-1970s (particularly the ideologies of social democracy, of liberal progressivism and of the radical Left). The third section examines in more depth the political principles of the various ideologies underlying education policy.

The fourth section examines the more recent influence of radical Right ideology on Conservative education policies during the three Thatcher governments of 1979–83, 1983–87 and 1987–90, the two Major administrations of 1990–92 and 1992–97, and policy under the leadership of William Hague.

Since the election of New Labour to government in 1997, has radical Right ideology ceased to inform education policy? In the final section, this question is directly addressed in the analysis of New Labour education policy, and its impact on equality.

## The concept of ideology

Ideology can be understood as a more-or-less coherent set of beliefs and attitudes that is regarded as self-evidently true, as 'common sense' in opposition to other belief systems. Examples of ideologies are socialism, conservatism, feminism, racism, and theism.

When people and political parties disagree about how society, schooling or the economy should be organized, they justify their views with a particular version of what is right and what is wrong (with a particular version of what is 'common sense').

The influence of an ideology can be overwhelming. As Eagleton puts it, 'What persuades men and women to mistake each other from time to time for gods or vermin is ideology' (Eagleton, 1991: xiii). Althusser (1971) observes how individuals and groups are 'interpellated' or 'called out to' by different ideologies. In the ideological 'Culture Wars', in the battle over ideas about what is right and what is wrong, people are 'hailed' both by dominant ideologies and by oppositional ideologies, each with their variously constructed notions of 'common sense'.

As an aspect of subjectivity, ideology is contested and commonly inconsistent, arising from multiple forces within different social experiences and histories. Ideological perspectives – and the resulting opinions – derive from and are structured by social class position and from factors such as sexuality, disability, 'race', gender, 'nation', religion. Ideologies arise substantially from individual and group histories and experiences of material, social and economic relations and conditions.

## Ideology as true or false consciousness

There are two main perceptions of ideology in critical thought. The first is negative, viewing ideology as distorted consciousness. The other is positive, where ideology can be the positive expression of the interests and world view or *weltangschaaung* of a class-located person or group. Such an ideology would be 'class conscious'.

Firstly, as a negative concept, 'Ideology may be conceived in eminently negative terms as a critical concept which means a form of false consciousness or necessary deception which somehow distorts men's (sic) understanding of social reality' so that 'the cognitive value of ideas affected by ideology is called into question' (Larrain, 1979: 13–14). For Marx, ideology is in some respects a distorted consciousness. It conceals social contradictions and conflict (the class struggle) and it does so in the interests of a dominant class (Larrain, 1979: 48). In this sense, ideology can create 'false consciousness' because it fools people into going along with an exploitative and oppressive system, into thinking, for example, that competitive individualism, consumerism and capitalism are 'only natural' (see Chapter 5 of this volume for more examples, drawn from the work of Bourdieu and of Althusser).

Secondly, Marx (and Lukacs, the Hungarian Marxist) also define, in contrast, a fundamentally positive aspect of ideology, which renders it more akin to 'true consciousness'. Consciousness results from material conditions of existence, people's everyday conditions of living and working, so the 'mode of production of material life conditions the social, political and intellectual life process in general. . . (therefore). . . [i]t is not the consciousness of men that determines their being, but, on the contrary, their social being that determines their consciousness' (Marx, 1962: 362 in Eagleton, 1991: 80).

However, the issue is complex. There is no complete congruence or agreement between a social class and its ideology (Eagleton, 1991: 100–106); social classes are not homogenous. Furthermore, following Gramsci, the hegemony, or overall dominance, of a particular ideology is strongly contested. There are clashes of opinion, 'culture wars' between different ideologies. In the struggle between ideologies, 'meanings and values are stolen, transformed, appropriated across the frontiers of different classes and groups, surrendered, repossessed, reinflected' (Eagleton, 1991: 101). Nonetheless, the complexity of the nature of ideology should not mask the link between social class (complex through that notion is too) and class consciousness – in other words, the material basis of ideology.

## Left, Right and Centre

This chapter places ideologies along a Left–Right continuum, so it is useful, initially, to explain what this continuum is. The Left–Right ideological continuum is in common use (see, for example, Jones *et al*, 1991: 109–75) and relates principally to economic and social policy (Jones *et al*, 1998: 72–73). Social policy, of course, includes education policy.

Some basic definitions are useful here:

- Politics is the allocation, distribution and control of scarce resources in society, such as wealth, income, education, status, and power. This includes the power to influence ideas and policy, for example through control of the media and of schooling and education, and through control of the law and law enforcement.

- Socialism is a Left-wing ideology founded on the use of the state (local or national), or of other collective means (such as through workers' control/ownership) to limit or change the power of the ruling capitalist class. Socialists believe in the collective good and social justice, in contrast to an emphasis on selfish individualism. The Left's major objectives are social/collective control of the economy, the egalitarian redistribution of wealth, income and power in favour of working people and their families. Crucially, the goal of equality for socialists and Marxists to achieve not only the equality of opportunity but far more equality of outcome too. Ultimately, radical or Marxist socialists wish to transform and replace capitalism with socialism – collective and non-exploitative control of the economy.

- Liberal-progressivism is a view of society and education centred on the individual. It is often associated with the 'permissive' society of the 1960s, when legislative tolerance replaced the punitive repression of divorce, prostitution, abortion and homosexuality. During the 'swinging sixties' liberal-progressivism was championed by the *Guardian*, facilitated by 'the pill' and 'the women's movement' (against exploitation of women) and a reaction against the Victorian authoritarianism still evident in the first half of the 20th century. In schools, this authoritarianism was underpinned by teacher-centred and whole-class-based pedagogy, and corporal punishment. In contrast, liberal-progressivism focuses on the interests and responses of each child, to whom schooling is accountable (along with the teacher).

- The main principles of the Centre (whether liberal progressive or social democratic) in British and West European politics lie in between those of the Left and of the Right. Social democrats and liberal progressives both wish for a fairer economy and society with more equal opportunities and, to an extent, more equal outcomes, while, however, accepting the mixed (private/public sector) economy in which capitalism and private enterprise play the major part.

The Centre (especially the Liberal Party in its various manifestations) has often been associated with liberal-progressivism in education. However, the Left in particular, and many other positions in general, adopted liberal progressivism in the 1960s and 1970s, in reaction against old-fashioned, restrictive, traditionalist and repressive conservatism.

Conservatism is a Right-wing ideology that promotes the belief that there is, in general, too much emphasis on equality – certainly on equality of outcome. Instead, Conservatives claim that private enterprise, competition, choice, inequality and the capitalist system and an emphasis on individualism and profit work for the good of society as a whole. A corollary of the emphasis on private enterprise is hostility to an expensive welfare state. The major principles of the Right are freedom from state interference (except where the state is promoting and defending private enterprise), the promotion of individualism, free enterprise, inequality and hierarchy. In this vision, schools and education are businesses, reproducing the workforce and ideology for capital, and accountable to consumers and to the economy as such.

This range of ideologies is pragmatic rather than all-embracing. The main exclusions are fascist, insurrectionist/revolutionary anarchist, green, regionalist/ separatist/nationalist or religious fundamentalist ideologies.

As the chapter progresses, the outline given will be developed with more detail. For the meantime it establishes the significant feature of the 'ideological continuum' – namely, the association of different 'world views' with the political parties that exemplify and represent them.

The translation of ideology into action is by no means assured or straightforward. Much policy is short term, or responds to electoral considerations, or to international economic events. Yet long-term and overall policy is fundamentally related to ideology (Hill, 2001a). Whenever the ideas and values defined by a particular ideology do result in a certain form of action, then the power of ideology is fully realized. This is particularly apparent when political parties gain election to office and develop policy, such as education policy for legal ratification and enforcement.

Claims that we are in a 'post-ideological' or post-modernist 'New Times', that ideology (and class conflict) is dead, and that 'the government is non-ideological, and instead interested in "effectiveness", in "what works"' are themselves ideological. Such claims serve to uphold the status quo by denigrating and seeking to invalidate radical alternatives to the status quo (Cole, 1998; Cole, McLaren and Rikowski, 2001, Hill *et al*, 1999, 2001). (See the discussion of post-modernism in Chapter 7.)

## A brief history of ideology, education policy and equality in England and Wales

This is a very brief outline to show the dominant ideology behind education policies with specific impact on equality, since the late 19th century:

- *1880–1944.* During this period, schooling and education were dominated by conservatism, by an openly acknowledged class- and gender-based (see Kelly, 2000) elitism. For most of the period, only elementary schooling was provided for working-class children in general. Most middle-class children attended grammar schools (which were fee paying, although there were some scholarships). 'Public schools' (fee-paying private schools) catered for virtually all upper-class children. With few exceptions boys and girls studied different curricula. The style of teaching was mostly traditional and teacher centred. The curricula and the hidden curricula of these different types of schools related to – indeed were geared to – producing citizens and workers for different positions within the existing hierarchies of income, gender, wealth and power. There was no official government concern in either discourse or policy with equal opportunities, let alone greater equality of outcome. Schooling was obviously based on social class (and gender), with different types of school, different types of curriculum, and different anticipated occupational outcomes for the different social classes and genders.

- *The 1944 Education Act* introduced free secondary schooling for all. Initially, and until the mid-1960s, it established the tripartite system and the 'eleven-plus' selection exam (selecting pupils for grammar, secondary technical or secondary modern schools). Private fee-paying schools remained the schooling for virtually all children of the upper classes. Schooling was left very much to the autonomy of professionals, the teachers and the local education authorities (LEAs). In this period, despite considerable debate, there was a broad social democratic consensus on education. The purpose of education was generally seen as to create a better society, whereas the broad (though contested) consensus held that the tripartite system was 'fair' and merito-cratic, and enabled bright working-class children to go to grammar school, university, and a middle-class future. Thus, both the tripartite system itself and, subsequently (when this was shown to be class-based and class-divisive), the comprehensive model of secondary schooling were deliberately intro-duced to ensure more equality of opportunity, regardless of social-class background. Indeed, for some proponents of comprehensive schools (called 'multilateral schools' in the 1940s) (see accounts by Simon, 1991; Barber, 1994) the aim of comprehensive schools was to achieve more equality of outcome, not simply more equality of opportunity.

- *The 1950s–1970s* were a period of gradual comprehensivization of secondary schooling. During Harold Wilson's Labour government, Circular 10/65 redefined not the aims of education, but how to achieve them. In the light of considerable evidence during the 1950s and 1960s that the selective system was not meritocratic, that working-class children were heavily underrepresented in grammar schools, and heavily overrepresented in secondary modern schools, the Labour governments of the 1960s and 1970s promoted comprehensive schooling. The Wilson governments of 1964–66 and 1966–70 also expanded university education, building new universities such as Sussex and Warwick and inaugurating the Open University. These social democratic policies – using state action to promote more equality of opportunity – occurred side-by-side with the spread of liberal-democratic, child-centred, progressive education for the development of the individual.

- *1976–79*. The 1976 Ruskin College speech by Labour Prime Minister James Callaghan came after the international economic crisis of 1973, and the decline in profitability of British (and indeed, Western) capital and capitalism. Western governments, including Callaghan's, redefined the purposes of education for much more utilitarian purposes. Henceforth, education was to serve the economy rather than being aimed at promoting either the (liberal-progressive) full flowering of each child's individuality and potential, or the (social democratic) creation of a more socially just society. The Ruskin speech was also a reaction against 'the William Tyndale Affair', involving the condemnation of an ultra-progressive school by parents and the Inspectorate (see Simon, 1991: 446–61 for a discussion). The Ruskin speech is commonly seen as the end of officially sanctioned social democracy in education, and the beginning of more conservative policies. In the 1970s, for the first time since 1944, Her Majesty's Inspectorate of Education began to issue strong guidance on the school curriculum. The first signs of reducing teacher and professional autonomy appeared.

- *1979–97*. Radical right-wing Conservative governments instituted the 1988 Education Reform Act. This introduced the market and competition into schools and other sectors of education, at the same time as the national curricula and compulsory publicized assessments and league tables for both schooling and (in effect) for initial teacher education. This is analysed in detail below.

- *Since 1997*. The education policies of the New Labour government can be seen in some respects as continuing social democratic education policies committed to extending equal opportunities. At the same time, in New Labour's period in office between 1997 and 2001, it has also sustained and extended the radical Right amalgam of neo-conservative 'back to basics' traditionalism with neo-liberal policies of competition, increased privatization, diversity and hierarchy in schooling.

The tension between the social democratic and radical Right impulses within the education policy of the New Labour government is returned to at the end of this chapter. To approach this issue it is useful to identify, first, the key principles involved.

## Ideology, political principles and education policy

### Principles of social democracy

The ideological orientation of Labour in government 1945–51, 1964–70 and 1974–76 is considered to be broadly social democratic (Benn and Chitty, 1996;

Hillcole Group, 1997) in education as in its wider policy. (Labour was actually in power until 1979, but during 1976–79, after Callaghan's Ruskin College speech, it changed its education policies.)

The main principles of social democracy, according to Heffernan (1997) are:

- full employment;
- the welfare state;
- redistributive taxation as a positive social good;
- a mixed pseudo-Keynesian economy (an economic mix of public sector and private sector control and provision, together with government reflation during recessions).

**Table 1.1** *Social democracy and education*

In education, social democratic principles require:

---

1.  Comprehensive schooling.
2.  Expansion of educational opportunities and provision (for example, expansion of higher education, the Open University).
3.  Local community involvement in schooling, further and higher education.
4.  Local community control over schooling, further and higher education (through democratically elected and accountable LEAs).
5.  A commitment to policies of equal opportunities.
6.  A degree of positive discrimination and redistribution of resources within and between schools.
7.  A curriculum and education system that recognizes issues of social justice and that aims at producing a technically efficient, but fairer, capitalist society.
8.  The teacher as authoritative but relatively democratic and anti-authoritarian.
9.  A desire to develop a contextual (or situational) type of teacher reflection, an awareness of the impact of the societal context of education and its impact on inequalities in achievement.
10. The aims of education to include the flourishing of the economy and society as well as the flourishing of the individual.

---

(Adapted from Hill, 1999: 15)

## Principles of liberal progressivism

Prior to the ascendancy of the radical Right in the late 1970s, the dominant paradigm in primary schooling and in primary teacher education in England

and Wales was the liberal progressive one. This was encapsulated by the philosophy of the Plowden Report (CACE, 1967) championed by Labour governments and accepted as mainstream thinking in other parliamentary parties. It claimed to be child centred and thereby to educate the whole child. This involved addressing children's emotional/affective development as well as cognitive development. Liberal-progressivism stressed the worth of all children and their right to be active in the learning process, rather than passively absorbing facts. The process of learning, teaching children how to learn and how to find out were priorities, as opposed to a rigid curriculum with subjects restricted to timetabled slots. A flexible curriculum was based on the assumption that children would integrate knowledge in their own minds through a project, or thematic approach (owing much to Piagetian and Brunerian psychology). Although not universal, and while contested within schools, colleges and LEAs, this paradigm was widely viewed as the norm. The key educational principles are given in Table 1.2.

**Table 1.2** *Liberal progressivism and education*

1. Child centredness, in terms of the individualistic and individualized nature of the curriculum.
2. 'Readiness' (eg reading readiness).
3. A curriculum emphasis on interdisciplinary topic work.
4. The curriculum organized in an 'integrated day'.
5. A curriculum emphasis on 'relevance' (eg of the curriculum to working-class children in general and to Asian, black and other minority ethnic group children in general).
6. The teacher as a guide to educational experiences rather than a distributor of knowledge.
7. The non-authoritarian teacher as friend and guide.
8. 'Discovery learning.'
9. Little competitive testing.
10. An emphasis on both individual work and also on group cooperation and group work rather than competitiveness.
11. Some desire to develop a contextual (or situational) type of teacher reflection, an awareness of the influence of contextual factors on educational achievement.
12. A schooling system the aim of which is the flourishing of the individual.

(Adapted from Hill, 1999: 16. See also Bennett, 1976; Silcock, 1999)

### The radical Left principles

Egalitarian socialist and Marxist groups and educationalists develop radical Left principles and policies based on achieving far more equality *of outcome* through comprehensive provision, democratic community control over education, and use of the local and national state to achieve a socially just (defined as egalitarian) anti-discriminatory society. The main principles for a radical Left /socialist education policy are developed at the end of this chapter and are referred to in the conclusion.

## Radical Right education policy and ideology

### Principles of the radical Right

The principles of the radical Right are evident in classically 'Thatcherite' Conservative policy on education (and state policy overall).[1] Thatcherism was the populist amalgam of neo-liberal and neo-conservative ideology developed when Margaret Thatcher replaced Edward Heath as leader of the Conservative Party in 1974. It is typified by a 'strong state' defending 'the free market'. It marked a distinct change from the more moderate, consensus education policies of the Conservative Party in the 1940s through to 1960s.

Despite the term 'Thatcherite', the Conservative government continued to apply radical Right policies on teacher education and schooling after Margaret Thatcher left Prime Ministerial office in 1990. Indeed, the most dramatic attempts at restructuring teacher education occurred during the John Major governments of 1990–92 and 1992–97. In addition a prominent pledge in John Major's 1997 Conservative general election campaign was to bring back selection at age eleven by setting up a (selective) 'grammar school in every town' (where there was parental demand).

In regard to education, radical Right principles are evident in the amalgam of neo-liberal and neo-conservative principles as shown in Table 1.3.

### The radical Right in power

While in government 1979–1997, the Conservatives established *a competitive market* for consumers (children and their parents) by setting up new types of schools such as city technology colleges and grant-maintained opted-out (of local authority control) schools and by extending the 'parental choice' of schools. Conservative governments also attempted to ideologically *recompose the consumers* (children/school students) through changes in the formal curriculum and the hidden curriculum in schools.

Similarly, with respect to teacher education, Circulars 9/92 (DFE, 1992) and 14/93 (DFE, 1993) created a new and *prescriptive* Conservative National Curriculum for 'teacher training'. In keeping with the National Curriculum for

**Table 1.3** *The radical Right and education*

## Six neo-liberal (or 'free marketeer') principles

- individualism
- privatization/private enterprise
- market competition/consumer choice
- surveillance of/strict control over and measurement of standards and performance in public services
- cost reduction of public services
- anti-producer power/distrust of the vested interests and 'inefficiency' of professionals and workers in the public sector (such as education)

## Six neo-conservative (or 'traditionalist'/authoritarian) principles: support for

- tradition (eg the monarchy) and the traditional family (ie marriage, anti-homosexuality)
- 'back to basics', eg in sexual and social morality, in focusing on 'the three Rs', and in pupil–teacher relationships
- nation and nationalism (as opposed to being pro-Europe or internationalist)
- monoculturalism regarding 'race'
- authority, order and social control
- elitism and hierarchicalism

## Four principles in common: neo-liberal and neo-conservative derision, distrust and disrespect for:

- public services
- socialist/Marxist egalitarianism
- liberal-progressivism
- the theory purporting to underlie what the radical Right sees as essentially practical activities, such as teaching and initial teacher education

schools, this prescribes not only the outcomes required but also circumscribes those same outcomes, in ideological terms, by strategies to marginalize discussion of alternative and oppositional beliefs.

Crucially, these prescriptive curricula were (and remain) surveyed, regulated and monitored, with funding advantages for those who adhere to and work the system and its requirements effectively and penalties for those who do not. Funding for schools by decision of the LEA was replaced with the system of per capita funding. This rises or falls according to intake numbers of pupils/ students, itself affected by 'league table' performance. This 'equality of treatment' contrasts dramatically with the attempts, prior to the 1988 Education Reform Act, of many LEAs to secure more 'equality of opportunity' by spending more on those schools and areas with greatest needs. The Conservative governments also cut the cost of schooling with the effect that class sizes in state primary schools increased.[2]

Jones (1989) takes the view, typical of many (such as Simon, 1992; Davies, Holland and Minhas, 1992) that the 1988 Act constitutes 'a fundamental attack on the policies of equal opportunity which developed in the thirty five years following the Education Act of 1944' (Jones, 1989: 185).

The Conservative assault on equality also removed LEA powers to pressure their schools into adopting anti-racist, anti-sexist and other – indeed any – egalitarian policies. Moreover, it is increasingly evident to education analysts and professionals that policies of 'diversity in schooling', including 'parental choice', have increased the hierarchical nature of schooling (Gewirtz, Ball and Bowe, 1995; Hill, 1997a; Whitty, Power and Halpin, 1998; Thrupp, 1999, 2000; Davies, 2000; Gillborn and Youdell, 2000; Cole, McLaren and Rikowski, 2001). Inequalities between schools have increased because in many cases the 'parental choice' of schools has become the 'school's choice' of the most desirable parents and children – and rejection of others. 'Sink schools' have become more 'sink like' as more favoured schools have picked the children they think are likely to be 'the cream of the crop'. 'Where you have selection, the sink schools just sink further and the privileged schools just become more privileged' (Hill, 2000b).

## Neo-liberalism

A number of Conservative government policies were classic manifestations of neo-liberal, free market ideology, including the transference of a substantial percentage of funding and of powers away from local education authorities to 'consumers' (in this case schools). 'Ostensibly, at least, these represent a "rolling back" of central and local government's influence on what goes on in schools' (Troyna, 1995: 141). Neo-liberalism also involves the privatization of education services. (This is discussed in Chapter 2.)

Under William Hague, radical Right thinking within the Conservative Party continued as part of the 'common sense revolution', which requires the effective abolition of LEAs. In a mid-2000 speech to the Politieia think tank, Hague announced that all schools should be 'Free Schools':

Head teachers and governors would be then free to manage their own budgets, free to employ their own staff, free to set their teachers' pay, free to determine their own admissions policy, free to manage their own opening hours and term times, and free to set and enforce their own standards and discipline. (Woodward, 2000)

With freedom to select, 'Free Schools will be free to determine their own admissions policies. . . some will wish to select 20 or 30 or 40 per cent of their intake, others will wish to be wholly selective' (Hague, quoted in *New Statesman*, in 2000). 'That means new grammar schools will appear' (Hague, quoted in Halpin, 2001). Thus, head teachers and governors would decide which pupils to admit and which to expel. Under Hague's plans, 'independent foundations, including companies, charities, churches, voluntary organisations and parents' groups would be allowed to run existing state schools and to set up new ones' (Halpin, 2001). (See also the Conservative Party General Election Manifesto for the 2001 election, Conservative Party, 2001.)

Conservative policy remains fundamentally hostile to two agencies or apparatuses thought to be involved in promoting equality and equal opportunities – local education authorities and initial teacher education. Hague's 'Free Schools' policy is an example of continuing radical Right discourse, and policy concepts based on its 'equiphobia' – fear of equality (Myers in Troyna, 1995; cf Hill, 1997a).

## Neo-conservatism

This second strand within the radical Right embraces social and moral authoritarianism, with an agenda to return to some Victorian values and a 'back to basics' philosophy. Apple refers to neo-conservatives as 'cultural restorationists' (Apple, 1989a, b, 2001). Radical Right luminaries such as Roger Scruton, Caroline (Baroness) Cox, Rhodes Boyson and Peter Hitchens (2000) stress traditional values such as respect for authority and 'the nation', 'Britishness', the values of a social elite, and the importance of a common culture (that of the elite). Neo-conservatives seek a disciplined society, a strong government, a Britain that veers selectively between Victoriana and John Major's childhood recollections of warm beer, cricket matches on the village green, and golden sunsets. Consequently, they support the return of 'traditional Britain' and, in regard to education, the Hillgate Group (1986; 1987; 1989) called in its various pamphlets of the 1980s for a reassertion of tradition, for both teaching methods and content.

Scruton, a co-author of Hillgate Group booklets, attacked anti-racism and accepted xenophobia as natural. At the *media level of discourse*, this particular type of anti-egalitarianism or equiphobia was so strident as to constitute *anti-anti-racism*. Honeyford and Palmer established a nationalist monoculturalist position from which to attack both multiculturalism and anti-racism. The neo-conservative strain of the radical Right is actively monoculturalist and supremacist, exploiting negative and traditional discriminations against the social classes, gender and cultures it defines as non-elite (Lawton, 1994). For Scruton, 'nations depend on the creation of new elites [and the] only way to save our education system is to spend less public money on it. Schools need to be taken out of the public sector once and for all' (Scruton, 1990).

## The questionable unity of the radical Right

In policy, as in ideology, the unity of the radical Right is by no means assured. At the micro-policy level of policy towards schools, both neo-liberals and neo-conservatives have common views on some policies, but disagree on others. For example, a number of free marketeers oppose the National Curriculum, or any state legislation for and control over the school curriculum, as being inconsistent with the rolling back of the state and with the full free play of market forces (cf Flew, 1991; Tooley, 1996, 1999, 2000). Yet in one significant area, neo-liberals and neo-conservatives are in agreement. As Jones (1989) observes, a strong alliance is forged in joint opposition to egalitarian practice:

> Jointly they have popularised the most powerful theme of right-wing educational discourse: that the decades long quest for equality has resulted only in the lowering of standards. Cultural analysis of what Scruton has called 'the impractical utopian values that will destroy all that is most valuable in our culture', and free market assertion about the evils of state monopoly, combine in an anti-egalitarian crusade (Jones K, 1989: 38; cf Lawton, 1994).

The educational writings of the radical Right and speeches by government ministers are very clear. They loathe what they describe as the permissive society, 'trendy teachers', 'loony left' staffrooms, 'the false cult of egalitarianism' (O'Hear, 1988), 'antiracism' (Hillgate Group, 1986; 1987; Thatcher, 1993; Major, 1993), mixed ability teaching (O'Keeffe, 1986, 1990), collaborative learning, democratic classrooms and democratic management of schools. Terms such as 'trendy', 'permissive' and 'caring' are applied as terms of abuse, and applied indiscriminately, to both liberal progressive and to social egalitarian schooling.[3]

The approach of the Conservative government under Thatcher to teacher education is one example of radical Right opposition to anti-racism. Certain 'teacher training colleges' were considered simply too successful in developing, disseminating and reproducing liberal progressive values, or socialist egalitarian values.

Thatcher wrote in her memoirs:

> there was the need to radically improve teacher training. Unusually, I had sent a personal minute to Ken Baker in November 1988 expressing my concerns. I said we must go much further in this area and asked him to bring forward proposals. . . There was still too little emphasis on factual knowledge of the subjects teachers needed to teach, too little practical classroom experience acquired and too much stress on the sociological and psychological aspects.
>
> (Thatcher, 1993: 598)

Much anger was expressed, from the Conservative Prime Minister downwards, against 'teacher training colleges'. Conservative ministerial rhetoric on teacher education reached a public climax at the 1992 Conservative Party Conference. Prime Minister John Major declared:

When it comes to education, my critics say I'm 'old fashioned'. Old fashioned? Reading and writing? Old fashioned? Spelling and sums? Great literature – and standard English grammar? Old fashioned? Tests and tables? British history? A proper grounding in science? Discipline and self respect? Old fashioned? I also want reform of teacher training. Let us return to basic subject teaching, not course in the theory of education. Primary teachers should learn to teach children how to read, not waste their time on the politics of race, gender and class.

(Major, 1993: 144)

It is interesting to consider now the degree to which New Labour education policy modifies and extends radical Right principles and anti-egalitarianism.

## New Labour, education policy and equality

In 1997, the six 'promises' in the New Labour general election manifesto were to cut class sizes to 30 or under for five, six and seven-year-olds; provide nursery places for all four-year-olds; attack low standards in schools; provide access to computer technology; provide lifelong learning through a new University for Industry; and to spend more on education as the cost of unemployment falls (Labour Party, 1997. See also Barber 1996, 2000; DfEE 1997. For the 'Third Way' ideology, see Mandelson and Liddle, 1996; Blair, 1998; Giddens, 1998, 2000; DfEE, 2001a, b).

New Labour's promises for its second term, contained in its 2001 election manifesto (Labour Party, 2001) were based directly on its March 2001 Education Green Paper, *Schools Building on Success* (DfEEs 2001a). The list below selects key areas of education policy referring to New Labour's plans for education until 2006 and its claims regarding its achievements between 1997 and 2001. Each point is offset by analysis of the principles and effects of New Labour policy on equality and inequality (for further detail and discussion, see Hill, 1999, 2000a, b; Muschamp, Jamieson and Lander, 1999; Power and Whitty, 1999; Docking, 2000).

### New Labour's principles in education and its 2001 Green Paper Schools: Building on Success

#### Improving standards
The government claims that this has been achieved through: a combination of support and pressure; regular inspections of schools and of LEAs; performance targets; published tables of achievement; delegating more resources to schools; the Beacon Schools initiative of rewarding selected schools financially so they could share their expertise; and 'getting tough', (partly through 'naming and shaming') with 'failing' schools and LEAs.

The 2001 Green (Consultative) Paper (DfEE, 2001a) catalogues New Labour's achievements in terms of 'more investment' and 'improved outcomes'. Thus:

- More children leave primary school able to read and write well. Seventy-five per cent of children achieved the standards for their age in 2000 compared to 54 per cent in 1996.
- More children leave primary school numerate. Seventy-two per cent achieved Level 4 and above in 2000 compared to 54 per cent in 1996.
- Progress in primary school English and mathematics is fastest in the most disadvantaged areas of the country.
- More young people now achieve five or more higher grades as GCSE – 49.2 per cent compared to 46.3 per cent in 1998.
- The percentage of children of parents whose occupation is 'unskilled or semi-skilled manual' achieving five higher grades at GCSE also rose faster than the national average (DfEE, 2001b: 4–5).

The document also notes fewer schools going into 'special measures' and fewer unsatisfactory lessons. It also promises to focus on improving secondary school standards in a New Labour second term, in contrast to the primary school focus of the first term in office.

### Analysis

With improvement through *standards and control*, the emphasis is on 'standards not structures'. Governmental and managerial control over education has been increased, and reinforced by punitive measures – for example through increasing use of compulsory testing, setting measurable targets, centralized control of the school and ITE curriculum, surveillance and monitoring of pupils, teachers and those involved in 'initial teacher training'; punishment of 'failing' teachers, schools, LEAs, teacher training departments, and 16–18 year olds who do not participate in the 'New Deal' (of education, training, voluntary work or work). The Green Paper promises a reduction in central control, with 'light touch' inspections, for example, in the future.

The focus for improvement is *managerialism*. This is secured through the focus of policy on 'improving schools' (and LEAs) and by school effectiveness strategies to raise standards; also by stratifying the teaching workforce, for example by performance-related pay (PRP) and 'superteachers' (see Allen, 1999 for a discussion).

The standards to be maintained and improved are, for the most part, traditional ones. *Traditionalism* is sustained through the continuation (despite the 1999 Review of the National Curriculum) of the eurocentric and traditionalist Conservative National Curriculum of 1995; the assault on liberal-progressive education (for example, attacks on mixed ability teaching and concentration on 'back to basics' in the curriculum with the literacy hour and numeracy hour in primary schools).

### *'Modernizing' comprehensive education/encouraging selection and diversity*

New Labour attacks 'bog standard' comprehensives and is steadily reintroducing selection into secondary schooling.[4] It claims that it is encouraging 'diversity' in types of schools to meet the needs and aspirations of all children. For example it claims that local parents can decide on the future of their grammar schools and insists that schools should 'abandon a dogmatic attachment to mixed ability teaching'. The number of 'specialist' schools (in technology, languages, sports and arts, with new specialisms in business, science, engineering and enterprise) should reach nearly a half of all secondary schools by 2006 (DfEE, 2001b: 7). These schools are allowed to select up to 10 per cent of their pupils 'by aptitude' and receive extra funding of £123 per pupil per year. The Green Pepper also proposes a more flexible National Curriculum 'to allow pupils to develop their special talents'.

### *Analysis*

New Labour's policy and plans for more *competitiveness and selection* are a continuation – indeed, an extension – of most of the structural aspects of the 1988 Conservative Education Reform Act, in terms of the macro-structure and organization of schooling. The radical Right principle of competition between schools (which results in an increasing inequality between schools) and the principle of devolving more and more financial control to schools through local management of schools are all in keeping with preceding Conservative opposition to comprehensive education and to the powers of LEAs.

The news media were in no doubt about the meaning of the Green Paper. The major focus of New Labour's February 2001 plan for education for 2001–2006 was greeted by a *Daily Mail* front-page article 'Death of the Comprehensive' (Halpin, 2001).

### *Inclusion*

New Labour promises to 'benefit the many not the few'. This includes targeted expenditure for areas of social exclusion, setting targets for schools to reduce truancy and exclusion rates by one third by 2002, and the 'New Deal' for 18–24-year-olds to ensure that young people without qualifications are in work, education or training.

New Labour's policies on social inclusion through targeted expenditure involve some increases in spending targeted at areas of social exclusion. These policies include: increased resourcing for inner city and other areas of social exclusion, Education Action Zones, education maintenance allowances for poor 16–18-year-olds, and increased funding for schools and LEAs capital and revenue budgets (for example to reduce primary class sizes and to repair and improve schools buildings). There is also a whole raft of (interventionist) measures such as summer schools, mentoring projects and school–post-school links, together with the 'Excellence in Cities' programme, which 'will include one third of all secondary age pupils by September 2001' (DfEE, 2001b: 7).

New Labour's 2001 Green Paper comments that 'universal nursery education for all 4-year-olds is now in place. There has been a significant expansion for 3-year-olds. In total there are 120,000 more free nursery places than in 1997' (DfEE, 2001b: 9). It also promises to 'ensure that every school with fewer than 25 per cent achieving 5 or more A★–C at GCSE or more than 35 per cent on free school meals receives extra targeted assistance' (p 9), and to expand Sure Start (a programme aimed at helping pre-school children in poorer areas) 'to include 500 programmes, to support 400,000 under-4s, one-third of under-4s living in poverty, by 2004' (DfEE, 2001b: 6).

*Analysis*
These classically social democratic equal opportunities measures of targeted expenditure occur within the overall context of New Labour privatization and low public expenditure strategies in their first term of office (see below). As the conclusion to this chapter suggests, this policy of social inclusion is contradicted, and, to an extent, interdicted, by the widening social and educational gaps consequent upon selection and hierarchy in schooling.

### Creating new partnerships/private sector involvement
The 2001 Green Paper promises to change the law 'to allow external sponsors to take responsibility for underperforming schools against fixed-term contracts of five to seven years with renewal subject to performance' (DfEE, 2001b: 3) and to expand the City Academy programme 'to enable sponsors from the private and voluntary sectors to establish new schools in areas of historic underperformance' (p 7). A major feature of the New Labour's 2001 general election campaign was, in the words of a *Guardian* front-page headline, 'Private roles for best schools', with 'successful schools and local education authorities being given new powers to contract out key services to the private sector in one of the first reforms of a Labour second term' (Woodward and Wintour, 2001).

*Analysis*
New Labour is strengthening the role of privatization and business involvement into the management/control of schools and LEAs. Indeed, this is a major feature of New Labour's 2001 General Election Manifesto 2001 (Labour Party, 2001) (see Chapter 2). Business has been courted to take the leading role in Education Action Zones and the Further Education Funding Council (FEFC) and Training and Enterprise Councils (TECs) have been replaced by a Skills Council. The Private Finance Initiative (PFI) enabling private funding for and ultimate control over new schools and colleges has been expanded and New Labour's introduction of student fees for higher education is beginning to show signs of reinforcing elitism and excluding poorer groups from study.

Furthermore, the first term of New Labour in office has been a regime of low public expenditure, which has strictly controlled and limited overall spending on education. Despite the increases announced in July 2000 by Chancellor Gordon Brown for extra spending (including an extra £12 billion for education over three years), it was then projected that by 2005 public spending would have risen to only 40.5 per cent of GDP – still less than in John Major's last year (*Guardian,* 1999b), a 'smaller share than in most other developed countries' (Coyle 2000) and less than the 49.9 per cent in 1976 (Toynbee, 2000). Toynbee also points out that the increase in funding on education under New Labour will be 3.8 per cent over the Parliament until 2002, compared to John Major's 1.6 per cent. But she adds that Gordon Brown's first two years as Chancellor 'saw the lowest public spending in 35 years'.

The government response is that in its first term of office its major concern was to reassure voters that it was economically competent and not spendthrift. Thus, for education, the 2001 Green Paper promises major increases in spending, for example that 'by 2003-04 we will be spending on average £700 more per pupil in real terms than in 1997–98' (DfEE, 2001b: 14).

## Teacher training and education

Prior to the 1997 general election, the message from Blair and Blunkett was that

> the Labour Party intends to launch a back to basics drive in the classroom. . . More emphasis on basic skills, classroom discipline and whole class teaching will become part of a drastic overhaul of teacher training. The plan has been sparked by the party's dissatisfaction with the quality of newly qualified teachers.
>
> (*Times Educational Supplement,* 1996)

New Labour is continuing the neo-liberal and neo-conservative policies of the previous government in the field of teacher education. Yet it is also modifying some of them slightly, in classically social democratic fashion and with a degree of positive effect. Critical pedagogy and critical reflection, for example, have been facilitated through the study of 'citizenship' in the National Curriculum (see Hill and Cole, 1999) and through modified requirements for student teachers (see Cole 1999a, b, 2000b). To some slight extent, education theory and equal opportunities work has therefore been relegitimated. They had been drastically restricted by the 1992/93 criteria from the (Conservative) Council for the Accreditation of Teacher Education (CATE) (Hill, 20001a).

However, when compared to the (Conservative) CATE Criteria of 1984 and 1989 (DES 1984, 1989), and when set in the context of what could have been done to promote critical reflection and a more egalitarian curriculum for teacher education, the New Labour changes here are modest indeed.

## A radical Left framework for education and equality

By way of a summary, the following highlights the key points making up a radical Left theoretical framework for education and equality. It is based on five overarching principles and 15 more detailed principles (developed from Hill,

1999) (see also Foot, 2001 for a wider framework and also Chapter 2 and the Conclusion to this volume, as well as the journal *Education and Social Justice*, Hillcole Group, 1991, 1997; and the manifesto of the Socialist Alliance for the 2001 General Election (Socialist Alliance, 2001)):

- vastly increased equality (of outcome);
- fully comprehensive provision at all levels of the education system;
- democratic community control of education;
- use of the local and national state to achieve a socially just (defined as egalitarian) anti-discriminatory society;
- the creation of educational institutions as centres of critical debate.

### Radical Left principles for education[5]

1. More resources and funding for education (for example through a higher rate of tax on profits and on the rich and less spending on defence). This could open the possibility for smaller class sizes.
2. An end to selection in schooling, whether by assessment or 'aptitude' and the development of a fully comprehensive schooling and further and higher education system – a change in the structure of schooling; an education system open to the whole community.
3. An end to the competitive market in schooling.
4. Egalitarian redistribution of resources within and between educational institutions, including affirmative action for underachieving individuals and groups.
5. A curriculum that includes critical discussion of both present capitalist society, state socialist societies and democratic socialist ones.
6. Opposition to some key aspects of liberal-progressive education, such as its aspects of non-structured learning and little assessment of pupils/school students and its reliance on the Piagetian concept of 'readiness'.
7. An egalitarian and anti-elitist common curriculum for all pupils/students.
8. An egalitarian and anti-elitist informal (hidden) curriculum for all pupils/ students.
9. The teacher as authoritative, democratic, anti-authoritarian, engaging in critical pedagogy, with a commitment to developing critical reflection, a commitment to social justice and equality inside and outside the classroom.
10. Increasing local community democratic accountability in schooling and further and higher education (for example, LEA powers) and eliminating those of 'business' and private enterprise.
11. Local community involvement in the schools and colleges.
12. Increasing the powers of democratically elected and accountable local government (education authorities) with powers of redistribution of resources, quality control engaging, inter alia, in the development and dissemination of policies for equality of outcome (for example, anti-racist, anti-sexist, anti-homophobic policies and policies seeking to promote equality for the working class and the disabled).

13. An education system, the aim of which is the flourishing of the collective society, the community, as well as the flourishing of the individual.
14. Fostering cultures within the classroom and within school and further education and higher education workplaces that are democratic, egalitarian, collaborative and collegiate – to replace what is sometimes a brutal managerialist culture with a more open and democratic one.[6]
15. Dialogic empowering education.

## Conclusion

New Labour has relegitimated the role of the state in promoting technical efficiency, in targeting spending and in promoting a greater degree of social inclusion. Giddens (1998), along with Driver and Martell (1998), suggests these changes apply to New Labour policies in general. It has also opened some minor space for the development of egalitarian and critical teaching.

However, alongside these traditional ideologically social democratic policies, the radical Right policies of the former Conservative government have been adopted almost *in toto*. Greater equality of outcome does not appear on the agenda, whereas greater equality of opportunity (via targeted spending) appears to be in considerable tension with, and subordinated to, the extension of the (neo-conservative and neo-liberal) selective hierarchical market in education and increased private business control of education.

## Notes

1. There have been many books and articles describing, analysing, and critiquing the effect of Thatcherism and the radical Right on schooling, the wider education system, and teacher education. On the broader societal analysis see Gamble (1983, 1988); Hall and Jacques (1983, 1989). For specifically educational analysis see, for example, Chitty (1989,1999); Chapter 2 in Hessari and Hill (1989); Hill, (1989, 1997a); Jones (1989); Ball (1990); Lawton (1994); Ainley (1999, 2000); Beckett (2000); Whitty and Menter (1989). Knights (1990) analyses radical Right influences on education policy from a radical Right perspective.
2. The number of primary age children in England taught by a single teacher in classes of more than 40 went up from 14,057 in January 1994 to 18,223 in January 1995. In January 1995 the number in classes of 36 or more taught by a single teacher rose by 11 per cent over the year to 107,985 whereas 1,155,726 primary children were in classes of 31 or more (Carvel and Wintour, 1995).
3. These frequently conflated attacks on liberal progressivism on the one hand, and socialist ideas and policies in education on the other, have a history

stretching from the 'Black Papers' of the 1960s and 1970s (see, for example, Cox and Dyson, 1969; Cox and Boyson, 1977) through to the Hillgate Group publications of 1986, 1987 and 1989.

4. The 1997 White Paper thus claims that 'the search for equality of opportunity in some cases became a tendency to uniformity [DfEE, 1997b: 11]' (1999: 540).

5. As an example of a Radical Left education programme in opposition to Conservative and New Labour policy and principles in education, the Socialist Alliance education policy contained in its manifesto for the 2001 British general election is as follows (Socialist Alliance, 2001: 9):

- Improve pay and conditions for teachers and other education workers.
- Stop and reverse Private Finance Initiative and Public-Private Partnership schemes in education.
- Abolish Education Action Zones.
- There should be a comprehensive review of the National Curriculum, to involve (among others) teaching unions and experts chosen by them.
- Abolish league tables and the current testing system.
- End charitable status and tax privileges for Eton, Harrow and other private schools. Abolish private education.
- Since the Tories destroyed the school meals service a million children living in poverty do not have access to a free school meal - for many the main meal of the day. We say all children should have free nutritional breakfast and lunch at school.
- For free after-school clubs and play centres for all who need them.
- Ensure provision of a full range of arts, sports and sex education in all schools.

Of course, education is not just about children. Young people and adults at colleges and universities – and the staff who work in them – have also suffered under both the Tories and Labour, which imposed tuition fees and ended free higher education. We say:

- Abolish tuition fees and student loans. We call for free education and a living grant for all further and higher education students, funded from taxation on the high paid and on big business, which wants skilled workers but is getting them on the cheap.
- People of all ages should be entitled to free education and training facilities.
- For the return to local democratic control of education at all levels, to include representatives of education workers, students and the wider community.

6. See the discussion of 'new public managerialism' in Chapters 1 and 2 of this volume and in Hill, 2001 and in Mahoney and Hextall, 2000.

# References

Ainley, P (1999) Left in a right state: towards a new alternative, *Education and Social Justice,* **2** (1), pp 74–78

Ainley, P (2000) *From Earning to Learning: What is happening to education and the welfare state?* Tufnell Press, London

Allen, M (1999) Labour's business plan for teachers in *Business, Business, Business: New Labour and Education,* eds M Allen *et al,* Tufnell Press, London

Althusser, L (1971) Ideology and State Apparatuses, in *Lenin and Philosophy and Other Essays,* New Left Books, London

Apple, M (1989a) How equality has been redefined in the Conservative Restoration in *Equity in Education,* ed W Secada, Falmer Press, London

Apple, M (1989a, b) Critical introduction: Ideology and the state in educational policy, in *The State and Education Policy,* ed R Dale, Open University Press, Milton Keynes

Apple, M (2001) *Educating the 'Right' Way: Markets, standards, God and inequality,* RoutledgeFalmer, London

Ball, S (1990) *Politics and Policy Making in Education,* Routledge, London

Barber, M (1994) *The Making of the 1944 Education Act,* Cassell, London

Barber, M (1996) *The Learning Game: Arguments for an education revolution,* Victor Gollancz, London

Barber, M (2000) High expectations and standards – no matter what, *Times Educational Supplement,* 7 July

Beckett, F (2000) Education, education, profit, *New Statesman,* 10 July

Benn, C and Chitty, C (1996) *Thirty Years On,* David Fulton, London

Bennett, N (1976) *Teaching Styles and Pupil Progress,* Open Books, Milton Keynes

Blair, M and Cole, M (2000) Racism and education; the imperial legacy, in *Education, Equality and Human Rights: issues of gender, 'race', sexuality, special needs and social class,* ed M Cole, RoutledgeFalmer, London

Blair, T (1998) *The Third Way: New politics for the new century,* Fabian Society, London

Carvel, J and Wintour, P (1995) Huge rise in primary classes of 40 plus, *Guardian,* 25 October

Central Advisory Council for Education (CACE) (1967) *Children and Their Primary Schools (The Plowden Report),* Department of Education and Science, London

Chitty, C (1989) *Towards a New Education System: The victory of the new Right,* Falmer Press, London

Chitty, C (1999) *The Education System Transformed,* 2nd edn, Baseline Books, Tisbury, Wilts

Cole, M (1998) Globalisation, Modernisation and Competitiveness: a critique of the New Labour project in education, *International Studies in the Sociology of Education,* **8** (3), pp 315–32

Cole, M (1999a) Time to liberate the mind: primary schools in the new century, *Education and Social Justice,* **1** (4), pp 63–66

Cole, M (ed) (1999b) *Professional Issues For Teachers And Student Teachers*, David Fulton, London

Cole, M (ed) (2000a) *Education, Equality and Human Rights: Issues of gender, 'race', sexuality, special needs and social class,* Routledge Falmer, London

Cole, M (2000b) Introduction, in *Education, Equality and Human Rights: issues of gender, 'race', sexuality, special needs and social class,* ed M Cole, RoutledgeFalmer, London

Cole, M, Hill, D, McLaren, P and Rikowski, G (2001) *Red Chalk: On schooling, capitalism and politics,* Institute for Education Policy Studies, Brighton

Conservative Party (2001) *Time for Commonsense – the Conservative Manifesto (for the 2001 General Election),*The Conservative Party, London, www.conservatives.com/manifesto.cfm

Cox, C and Boyson, R (eds) (1977) *Black Paper 1977,* Maurice Temple Smith, London

Cox, C and Dyson, A (eds) (1969) *Black Paper Two: The crisis in education,* Critical Quarterly Society, London

Coyle, D (2000) Prudence is still the word, say economists, *The Independent,* 19 July

Davies, A, Holland, J and Minhas, R (1992) *Equal Opportunities in the New Era,* 2nd edn, Tufnell Press, London

Davies, N (2000) *The School Report: Why Britain's schools are failing,* Vintage, London

Department of Education and Science (DES) (1984*) Initial Teacher Training – Approval of Courses: Circular 3/84,* HMSO, London

DES (1989) *Initial Teacher Training – Approval of Courses: Circular 224/89,* DES, London

Department for Education (DFE) (1992) *Circular 9/92: The Initial Training of Secondary School Teachers,* DFE, London

DFE (1993) *Circular 14/93: The Initial Training of Primary School Teachers,* DFE, London

Department for Education and Employment (DfEE) (1997*) Excellence in Schools,* DfEE, London

DfEE (1999) *Excellence in Cities,* DfEE, London

DfEE (2001a) *Green Paper: Schools: Building on success,* DfEE, London

DfEE (2001b) http://www.dfee.gov.uk/buildingonsuccess/summary/index.shtml, DfEE, London

Docking, J (2000) What is the solution? An overview of national policies for schools, 1979–1999, in *New Labour's Policies for Schools: Raising the standard?* ed J Docking, David Fulton, London

Driver, S and Martell, L (1998) *New Labour: Politics After Thatcherism,* Polity Press, London

Eagleton, T (1991) *Ideology,*Verso, London

Flew, A (1991) Educational Services: independent competition or maintained monopoly, in *Empowering the Parents: How to break the schools monopoly,* ed D Green, Institute of Economic Institute of Economic Affairs, London

Foot, P (2001) *Why You Should Vote Socialist,* Bookmarks, London

Gamble, A (1983) Thatcherism and Conservative Politics, in *The Politics of Thatcherism*, eds S Hall and M. Jacques, Lawrence & Wishart, London

Gamble, A (1988) *The Free Economy and the Strong State: The politics of Thatcherism*, Macmillan, London

Gewirtz, S, Ball, S and Bowe, R (1995) *Markets, Choice and Equity in Education*, Open University Press, Buckingham

Giddens, A (1998) *The Third Way: The renewal of social democracy*, Polity Press, Cambridge

Giddens, A (2000) *The Third Way and its Critics*, Polity Press, Cambridge

Gillborn, D and Youdell, D (2000) *Rationing Education: Policy, practice, reform and equity*, Open University Press, Buckingham

Gray, J (1996) *After Social Democracy*, Demos, London

*Guardian* (1999a) Kings of squeeze: Thatcher was more lavish than Labour, *Guardian*, 25 August

*Guardian* (1999b) Brown's beneficence, *The Guardian*, 17 July

Hall, S and Jacques, M (eds) (1983) *The Politics of Thatcherism*, Lawrence & Wishart, London

Hall, S and Jacques, M (1989) *New Times: The changing face of politics in the 1990s*, Lawrence & Wishart, London

Halpin, T (2001) Death of the Comprehensive, *The Daily Mail*, 13 February

Hattersley, R (1996) Bubble 'n' Squeak, in *Guardian*, 27 February

Hay, C (1996) *Restating Social and Political Change*, Open University Press, Buckingham

Heffernan, R (1997) Exploring the Power of Political Ideas: The rise of neo-liberalism and the re-orientation of political attitude in the UK 1976-1996, Paper to the Political Studies Association Annual Conference, University of Ulster (reported as New Labour, new paradigm, *The Times Higher Educational Supplement*, 11 April)

Hessari, R and Hill, D (1989) *Practical Ideas for Multicultural Learning and Teaching in the Primary Classroom*, Routledge, London

Hill, D (1989) *Charge of the Right Brigade: The radical Right's assault on teacher education*, Institute for Education Policy Studies, Brighton

Hill, D (1992) What the radical Right is doing to teacher education: a radical Left critique, in *Multi-cultural Teaching*, **10** (3), pp 31–34

Hill, D (1994) Cultural diversity and initial teacher education, in *Cultural Diversity and the Curriculum, Vol 4: Cross-curricular contexts, themes and dimensions in primary schools*, eds G Verma and P Pumfrey, Falmer Press, London

Hill, D (1997a) Equality and Primary Schooling: The policy context intentions and effects of the conservative 'reforms', in *Equality and the National Curriculum in Primary Schools*, eds M Cole, D Hill and S Shan, Cassell, London

Hill, D (1997b) Reflection in initial teacher education, in *Educational Dilemmas: Debate and diversity, Vol. 1: Teacher education and training*, eds K Watson, S Modgil and C Modgil, Cassell, London

Hill, D (1999) *New Labour and Education: Policy, ideology and the third way*, Tufnell Press, London

Hill, D (2000a) New Labour's neo-liberal education policy, in *Forum for promoting 3–19 comprehensive education*, **42** (1), pp 4–7

Hill, D (2000b) The Third Way ideology of New Labour's educational policy in England and Wales, in *Combating Social Exclusion Through Education: Laissez-faire, authoritarianism or third way?* eds G Walraven *et al*, Garant, Leuven-Apeldoon

Hill, D (2001a) State theory and the neo-liberal reconstruction of schooling and teacher education: a structuralist neo-Marxist critique of postmodernist, quasi-postmodernist, and culturalist neo-Marxist theory, in *The British Journal of Sociology of Education*, **22**, (1) pp 137–157

Hill, D (2001b) Interview, in R Haymer, How 11+ divided twin brothers with the same IQ, *Sunday Mirror*, 18 February

Hill, D and Cole, M (1999) Introduction, in *Promoting Equality in Secondary Schools*, eds D Hill and M Cole *Promoting Equality in Secondary Schools*, Cassell, London

Hillcole Group (1997) *Rethinking Education And Democracy: Education for the twenty-first century*, Tufnell Press, London

Hill, D, McLaren, P, Cole, M and Rikowski, G (eds) (1999) *Postmodernism in Educational Theory: Education and the politics of human resistance*, Tufnell Press: London

Hill D, McLaren, P, Cole, M and Rikowski, G (eds) (2001) *Marxism against Postmodernism in Educational Theory*, Lexington Press, Lanham, MD

Hillcole Group (1997) *Rethinking Education and Democracy: A Socialist alternative for the twenty-first century*, Tufnell Press, London

Hillcole Group/Chitty, C (ed) (1991) *Changing the Future: Redprint for education, Tufnell Press, London*

Hillgate Group (1986) *Whose Schools? A radical manifesto*, The Hillgate Group, London

Hillgate Group (1987) *The Reform of British Education – From Principles to Practice*, The Claridge Press, London

Hillgate Group (1989) *Learning to Teach*, The Claridge Press, London

Hitchens, P (2000) *The Abolition of Britain*, Quartet Books, London

Jones, B, Gray, A, Kavanagh, D, Moran, M, Norton, P and Seldon, A (1991) *Politics UK*, Philip Allan, London

Jones, B, Gray, A, Kavanagh, D, Moran, M, Norton, P and Seldon, A (1998) *Politics UK*, 3rd edn, Harvester Wheatsheaf, London

Jones, G (2001) Hague vows to restore grammars, *Daily Telegraph*, 14 February

Jones, K (1989) *Right Turn – The Conservative Revolution in Education?*, Hutchinson, London

Kelly, J (2000) Gender and Equality: one hand tied behind us, in *Education, Equality and Human Rights: Issues of gender, 'race', sexuality, special needs and social class*, ed M Cole, RoutledgeFalmer, London

Knights, C (1990) *The Making of Tory Education Policy in Post-War Britain 1950–1986*, Falmer Press, London

Labour Party (2001) *Ambitions for Britain (Labour Party General Election Manifesto)*, Labour Party, London

Larrain, J (1979) *The Concept of Ideology*, Hutchinson, London

Lawton, D (1994) *The Tory Mind On Education 1979–94*, Falmer Press, London

Mahoney, P and Hextall, I (2000) *Reconstructing Teaching: Standards, performance and accountability*, RoutledgeFalmer, London

Major, J (1993) Extract from speech to the 1992 Conservative Party Conference, in *Education Answers Back: Critical responses to government policy*, eds C Chitty and B Simon, Lawrence & Wishart, London

Mandelson, P and Liddle, R (1996) *The Blair Revolution*, Faber & Faber, London

Muschamp, Y, Jamieson, I and Lauder, H (1999) Education, education, education, in *New Labour, New State? The third way in British social policy*, ed M Powell, The Policy Press, Bristol

O'Hear, A (1988) *Who Teaches the Teachers? A contribution to public debate*, Social Affairs Unit, London

O'Keeffe, D (1986) *The Wayward Curriculum: A cause for parents' concern*, Social Affairs Unit, London

O'Keeffe, D (1990) *The Wayward Elite*, The Adam Smith Institute, London

Patten, J (1993) Extract from speech to the 1992 Conservative Party Conference, in *Education Answers Back: Critical responses to government policy*, eds C Chitty and B Simon, Lawrence & Wishart, London

Power, S and Whitty, G (1999) New Labour's education policy: first, second or third way? *Journal of Education Policy*, **14** (5), pp 535–46

Scruton, R (1990) Why state education is bad for children, *Sunday Telegraph*, 29 December.

Silcock, P (1999) *New Progressivism*, Falmer Press, London

Simon, B (1992) *What Future For Education?* Lawrence & Wishart, London

Simon, B (1991) *Education and the Social Order 1940–1990*, Lawrence & Wishart, London

Socialist Alliance (2001) *People Before Profit: The Socialist Alliance manifesto for the general election*, Socialist Alliance, www.socialistalliance.net

Thatcher, M (1993) *The Downing Street Years*, HarperCollins, London

Thrupp, M (1999) *Schools Making A Difference: Let's be realistic!* Open University Press, Buckingham

Thrupp, M (2000) Compensating for Class: Are school improvement researchers being realistic? *Education and Social Justice*, **2** (2), pp 2–11

*Times Educational Supplement* (1996) 31 May 1996

Tooley J (1996) *Education without the State*, Institute for Economic Affairs, London

Tooley, J (1999) *The Global Education Industry: Lessons from private education in developing countries*, The Institute for Economic Affairs in association with The International Finance Corporation, London

Tooley, J (2000) *Reclaiming Education*, Cassell, London

Toynbee, P (2000) Gordon Brown speaks. And, as they say, money talks, *Guardian*, 19 July

Troyna, B (1995) The local management of schools and racial equality, in *Ethnic Relations and Schooling*, eds S Tomlinson and M Craft, Athlone, London

Whitty, G (1998) New Labour, education and disadvantage, in *Education And Social Justice*, **1** (1), pp 2–8

Whitty, G and Menter, I (1989) Lessons of Thatcherism – Education policy in England and Wales 1979–1988, in A Gamble and C Wells, *Thatcher's Law*, Basil Blackwell, London

Whitty, G, Power, S and Halpin, D (1998) *Devolution And Choice In Education: The school, the state and the market*, Open University Press, Buckingham

Woodward, W (2000) New Plan to aid poorer pupils, *Guardian*, 4 October

Woodward, W and Wintour, P (2001) Private roles for best schools, *The Guardian*, 2 June

## Useful addresses

Institute for Education Policy Studies
www.ieps.org.uk

# 2

# Global capital, neo-liberalism, and privatization: the growth of educational inequality

*Dave Hill*

## Editors' introduction

*This chapter locates the facts, concepts and policies relating to equality and inequality in schools and in the wider education system within the wider policy context of neo-liberalism, which emphasizes privatization and competitive markets in education and in social and welfare policy more generally. Neo-liberalism is also a global phenomenon – similar restructuring of schooling and education has taken place across the world. The chapter examines the effects of neo-liberal policies in increasing inequalities and makes a number of theoretical criticisms of neo-liberalism. The chapter concludes by constructing a critique of neo-liberalism and looking forward to critical transformative education for equality.*

## The big picture: neo-liberalism, capitalism and educational change

### The contexts of educational change

In order to explain what is happening to schooling and education in England and Wales – the development of a system characterized by exclusion rather than inclusion – I want to place it within a theoretical and a global context. Hence, much of this chapter will examine the concepts (and activities) of capital/ capitalism, neo-liberalism, and privatization. A number of these concepts are referred to and extended in other chapters of this volume.[1]

The current anti-egalitarian education system needs to be contextualized in two ways. Firstly, the policy context – the restructuring of the schooling and education systems in England and Wales – needs to be placed within the ideological and policy context of the links between capital, neo-liberalism (with its combination of privatization, competitive markets in education characterized by selection and exclusion) and the rampant growth of the inequalities described in the various chapters in this book.

It is important to look at the big picture. Markets in education, so-called 'parental choice' of a diverse range of schools, privatization of schools, cutting state subsidy to education by abolishing (most) student grants and by charging tuition fees and by slashing spending on school meals, adult education and the youth service are only a part of the educational strategy of the capitalist class. The capitalist class wishes to, and has succeeded in cutting public expenditure (see below). It does this because public services are expensive. Cuts serve to reduce taxes on profits. In addition, the capitalist class has a business plan *for* education and a business plan *in* education. The former centres on socially producing labour power (people's capacity to labour) for capitalist enterprises; the latter focuses on setting business 'free' in education for profit-making. Thus, business wants to make profits from education and to make education fit for business – to make schooling and further and higher education subordinate to the personality, ideological and economic requirements of capital.

## The current project of global capitalism

The fundamental principle of capitalism is the sanctification of private (or corporate) profit based on the extraction of surplus labour (unpaid labour-time – see the discussion in Chapter 7) as surplus value from the labour-power of workers. This is a creed of competition, not cooperation, between humans. As Mike Cole and I explain in Chapter 7, it is a creed and practice of class exploitation, exploitation by the capitalist class of those who provide the profits through their labour, the working class.

John McMurtry's *The Cancer Stage of Capitalism* (1999) describes 'the pathologization of the market model'. He suggests that to argue for a 'free market' in anything these days is a delusion: the 'market model' that we have today is really the system that benefits the 'global corporate market' – a system where the rules are rigged to favour huge multinational and transnational corporations that take over, destroy or incorporate (hence the 'cancer' stage of capitalism) small businesses, innovators, etc, that are potential competitors. Thus, opening education to the market, in the long run, will open it to the corporate giants – who will run it in their own interests (Rikowski, 2001a) and others argue that the World Trade

Organization (WTO) and other global clubs for the mega-capitalists are setting this agenda up in education across the globe.

## Globalization inequality and economic and social justice

This neo-liberal context has a global dimension, a global context. What is happening to schooling and education in England and Wales needs to be located within the context of what is happening internationally. England and Wales are not alone in the restructuring of education and the growth of economic, social, political and educational inequalities. These are a feature of the application of 'market forces', of neo-liberal policies, worldwide.

Global inequalities have been well described with the IMF/World Trade Organization/World Bank-inspired cuts in health and welfare budgets throughout the Third World.

In Britain the increasing inequalities, the impoverishment and creation of a substantial underclass has also been well documented (for example, in Chapter 7 of this volume).[2] For example, in Britain the ratio of chief executives' pay to average workers' pay stands at 35:1. In the United States it has climbed to 450:1 (from around 35:1 in the mid-1980s) (Hutton, 2001). Inequalities both between states and within states have increased dramatically during the era of global neo-liberalism. In the United States, the economic apartheid nature of capitalism has been widely exposed in the work of Peter McLaren (for example, 2000) and in a depiction of growing inequalities in California in the speech to the NAACP by Ralph Nader in July 2000:[3]

> I just bring to you a little fact from California. For those of you who are skeptical of people who tell you that things are getting better but we got to make them even better, try child poverty in California. In 1980, it was 15.2 percent; today it is 25.1 percent. And if you take near poverty – the children who are near poverty, who I would consider in poverty because I think the official levels of poverty are absurd, how can anyone support a four-member family on $17,200 a year – before deductions, before the cost of getting to work, et cetera?
>
> If you add the near poverty, 46 percent of all the children in California are in the category. This is not just a badge of shame for our country, the richest country in the world, it's a reflection of our inability to focus on the signal phenomena that is blocking justice, and that is the concentration of power and wealth in too few hands... And to give you a further illustration, the top 1 percent of the richest people in our country have wealth – financial wealth equal to the bottom 95 percent.[4]

To take another example, Chile, hailed as a beacon of neo-liberal policies

> boasts one of the most unequal economies in the world... in which only 10 percent of the Chilean population earns almost half the wealth and in which the richest 100 people earn more than the state spends on social services. Real

salaries have declined 10 percent since 1986 and they are still 18 percent lower than when Allende[5] was in power.

(McLaren, 2000: 27)

## Neo-liberalism

### The effects of neo-liberal capitalism

In discussing the market, as a part of neo-liberal ideology and policy, it is important to see how this impacts on people's lives, life chances and deaths, to become aware of the effects of the current 'cancer stage' of capitalism (McMurtry, 1999), and of market ideology in fiscal, social and educational provision.

The difference between classic (laisser-faire) liberalism of the mid-nineteenth century, and the neo-liberalism of today, based on the views of Hayek (see Ball, 1990; Gamble, 1996) is that the former wanted to roll back the state, to let private enterprise make profits relatively unhindered by legislation (for example, safety at work, trade union rights, minimum wage) and unhindered by the tax costs of a welfare state (see McLaren, 2000: 22–23).

On the other hand, *neo*-liberalism demands a strong state to promote its interests, hence Gamble's (1988) depiction of the Thatcherite polity as *The Free Economy and the Strong State: The politics of Thatcherism* (for an analysis of the radical Right, see Chapter 1 of this volume, and Hill, 2001). The strong interventionist state is needed by capital particularly in the field of education and training – in the field of producing an ideologically compliant but technically skilled workforce. The social production of labour-power is crucial for capitalism. It needs to extract as much surplus value as it can from the labour power of workers (Rikowski, 2001a).[6]

Neo-liberalism requires that the state establishes and extends:

- Privatization/private ownership of the means of production, distribution and exchange.
- The provision of a market in goods and services – including private sector involvement in welfare, social, educational and other state services (such as air traffic control, prisons, policing).
- Within education the creation of 'opportunity' to acquire the means of education (though not necessarily education itself, see McMurtry, 1991 below) and additional cultural capital, through selection.
- Relatively untrammelled selling and buying of labour power, for a 'flexible', poorly regulated labour market.
- The restructuring of the management of the welfare state on the basis of a corporate managerialist model imported from the world of business. 'As well as the needs of the economy dictating the principal aims of school education, the world of business is also to supply a model of how it is to be provided and managed' (Hatcher, 2000, 2001; see also Bottery, 1999).
- Suppression of oppositional critical thought and of autonomous thought and education (see the summary of McMurtry, 1991, below).
- Within a regime of cuts in the post-war welfare state and low public expenditure.

### Reducing Public Expenditure in Britain

New Labour Prime Minister Tony Blair, following 18 years of public expenditure cuts under Conservative governments (1979–97), claimed that 'public expenditure has more or less reached the limits of its acceptability' (Blair and Schroeder, 1999). By this they mean not that the level is as low as is acceptable, but the opposite. For Blair, the level of public expenditure has reached the highest level acceptable; hence, other perhaps than in a pre-election period, he is disinclined to raise public spending. Yet tax takes and public spending vary tremendously between different advanced industrial states. Taking taxes and social security contributions together, as a percentage of gross domestic product, there are wide variations across the European Union. The 1997 figures (from Coates and Barratt Brown, 1999: 50) (1986 percentages in brackets) are Sweden 53.3 per cent (52.5 per cent), Finland 47.3 per cent (42.4 per cent), France 46.1 per cent (44.0 per cent), UK 35.3 per cent (37.8 per cent), US (1986 figures only) 25.8 per cent.

Larry Elliott notes that spending on the nation's infrastructure has been lower in each of New Labour's four years in its first term of office than in the final 12 months of John Major's Conservative government – and only one quarter of what is was at the end of (Old) Labour Jim Callaghan's government in 1979 (Elliott, 2001).

Cuts in state spending on education have been savage throughout both the developed and developing economies. According to the 1998 OECD report on spending per secondary pupil, the UK is bottom of the league table with £2,680, as against the EU average of £3,145 (Germany spends £3,946 per pupil) (*Times Educational Supplement* (TES) 14 April 2000. See Marginson, 1997 for details, for example, on Australia).

## Privatization, business and education

How, in more detail, do education markets fit into the grand plan for schooling and education? What is capitalism's 'business plan for education'? McMurtry (1991: 209) is one among many who note that 'education as a social institution has been... subordinated to international market goals including the language and self-conceptualisation of educators themselves.'

Hatcher (2000, 2001) shows how capital/business has two major aims for schools. The first aim is to make sure schools produce compliant, ideologically indoctrinated, pro-capitalist, effective workers. That is, to ensure that schooling and education engage in ideological and economic reproduction. Rikowski and Hatcher both note the increasing importance of national state education and training policies in the business agenda *for* education. In an era of global capital, this is one of the few remaining areas for national state intervention – it is *the* site, suggests Hatcher, where a state can make a difference (cf Hatcher and Hirtt, 1999; Rikowski, 2000).

The second aim is for private enterprise, private capitalists, to make money out of it, to make private profit out of it, to control it: this is the business agenda *in* schools.

## The business agenda for schools

Hatcher suggests that,

> The first agenda – what business wants schools to do – is a broad transnational consensus about the set of reforms needed for schools to meet employers' needs in terms of the efficiency with which they produce the future workforce.
> The business agenda *for* schools is increasingly transnational, generated and disseminated through key organizations of the international economic and political elite such as the Organization for Economic Cooperation and Development (OECD). In that global context there is a project for education at the European level, which represents the specific agenda of the dominant European economic and political interests. It is expressed in, for example, the various reports of the European Round Table, a pressure group of 45 leaders of major European companies from 16 countries, and it has become the motive force of the education policies of the European Commission and its subsidiary bodies. (Hatcher and Hirtt, 1999).

He points out that:

> one of the most recent statements of this business agenda for schools is a report published earlier this year called *In search of quality in schools: The employers' perspective* (Confederation of British Industries, 2000), produced by an international working group of employers' organisations from 7 EU countries (including the Confederation of British Industry – CBI – in the UK and the BDA in Germany).

The school reforms advocated in the employers' report can be summarized as in Table 2.1.

Hatcher comments that Britain under the Labour government has gone further than any other European country in adopting and implementing this programme (Hatcher, 2001: 45). At the end of the report is an audit of progress by seven EU countries in adopting the business agenda for schools. Far and away the leader is the UK. Judged against 10 performance indicators, the UK succeeds on 9. The missing one was performance-related pay for teachers (PRP – merit pay). This has now been introduced.

## The business agenda in schools

In the United States the work of Alex Molnar (for example, 1996, 1999, 2000) and the Centre for Analysis of Commercialism in Education at the University of Wisconsin-Milwaukee), and in the UK work by Richard Hatcher and the journal

**Table 2.1** *The CBI's business agenda for schools*

---

*'National standards of achievement and independent evaluation.'*

- National standards.
- Regular national tests.
- Targets for progress set by government and schools.
- International benchmarking.
- Assessment of personal and social skills as well as academic.
- Independent body to evaluate school performance.

*'Co-operation and competition.'*

- Parental choice of school.
- Competition between schools to raise standards.
- School funding based on student numbers and school performance.
- Resources linked to results.

*'A 21st century curriculum.'*

- Active, lifelong learning.
- Citizenship.
- Preparation for work.

*'Autonomy for schools.'*

- 'Schools need the freedom to manage themselves.'
- 'Schools must make more effective use of existing resources.'
- 'The priority must be to reform the management of staff, teaching methods and the organisation.'

*'A top quality teaching profession.'*

- Heads as leaders, evaluated by results.
- 'The terms and conditions of the profession must be updated to ensure that heads and teachers have the incentives to succeed, with differentiated rewards depending on their tasks and their performance.'
- 'The quality control of teaching and learning is not adequate. [. . .] Reliable systems of accountability are needed to help ensure that schools provide value for money, and to ensure that the main cost elements (of which teacher costs are the most significant) are put under rigorous control.'
- 'Schools must seek to draw lessons on best practice, innovation and guiding values from a wide range of environments, including the entrepreneurial world of business.'

---

Extract from Confederation of British Industries, 2000, cited in Hatcher, 2000: 47

*Education and Social Justice* exemplify and analyse the many ways in which private enterprise is making profits from and controlling aspects of education.

In an incisive analysis of New Labour's 2001 Green Paper, *Schools: Building on success,* Glenn Rikowski (2001b) notes how this document, in effect New Labour's manifesto for a second term in office, consolidates and extends the role of business in school life. Rikowski notes that 'It is the extent of proposed business involvement in school life that is truly startling.' The following features can be expected in New Labour's second term of government:

- Business takeover of 'failing' schools: external sponsors are to take responsibility for underperforming schools (Introduction, p 4).
- Learning from business: those in the education service will be encouraged to 'learn from others, including business' (para 1.29, p 17).
- Consolidation of the role of the private sector in nursery education (para 2.18, p 24).
- Public–private partnerships in nursery education: from September 2004, every three-year-old whose parents want one will have a free nursery place. This provision 'will be based on partnerships between the public, private and voluntary sectors' (para 2.21, p 25).
- New specialist 'business schools': 'In addition to technology, languages, sport and the arts, we will offer schools three new specialist options: engineering; science; and *business and enterprise*. Business and enterprise schools will be expected to develop strong curriculum–business links and develop teaching strengths in business studies, financial literacy and enterprise-related vocational programmes' (para 4.15, p 47).
- Extension of the Private Finance Initiative (PFI): 'Many schools are also benefiting from the Private Finance Initiative. Twenty-one deals have been signed so far, and funding for a further 33 has been agreed in principle, bringing benefits to around 640 schools. The scale of activity is increasing' (para 6.19, p 81).
- Business sponsorship and business mentoring: a significant extension of these (especially business mentoring for head teachers) (para 6.34, p 85).

Rikowski suggests that:

> These proposals are set to open school doors to corporate capital on an expanding scale. They seek to break down barriers to trade within England's schools on an agenda that is consonant with the World Trade Organisation's (WTO) mission to open them up to corporate capital. The Green Paper has purchased a neo-liberal ticket for schools.
>
> (2001b)

New Labour's manifesto for the 2001 general election, *Ambitions for Britain,* proposed giving private firms a far greater role in the provision of state-run services such as health and education, claiming 'the spirit of enterprise should apply as much to public services as to business'. Widespread media reaction was that 'Blair wants to take Thatcherism further than Thatcher ever dared' (Cohen, 2001), that 'Blair's "big idea" means more private sector involvement' (Grice, 2001), and, in the words of a two-page spread in the *Daily Mail*, 'Blair's private enterprise' (Hughes, 2001).

### Local education authorities as business agents

Local education authorities (LEAs) have a specific and significant role to play. They must become the 'business agents' of school life. The Green Paper argues that for the crucial role of school improvement LEAs are simply inadequate. For:

> The lack of professional standards for school improvement services and those who work within them is. . . a key weakness of the current arrangements, and one which could hold back the pace of reform.
>
> (para 6.57, p 89)

Under proposals set out in para 6.58 (p 90), LEAs will be charged with assisting the corporate invasion of schools. There will be progressive contracting out of school improvement work, though some regulation (for quality) is deemed necessary. There are hints that LEAs not embracing the new business culture or hamstringing business penetration of English schooling are liable to be taken over by private sector operators.

Rikowski concludes his analysis of new Labour's Green Paper by suggesting that:

> On the basis of the Green Paper's agenda, the spirit of business will haunt educators in schools. The key tasks are to struggle for a comprehensive education that has neither human capital development or profit generation as foundation of its functioning - but is recast for collective human need and self-development. At every turn, the Green Paper defers to business values and outlooks, and the democratic impulse is suppressed or downplayed.
>
> (Rikowski, 20001b)

## The effects of neo-liberalism in education and society

Neo-liberal policies both in the UK and globally have resulted in a loss of equity (more inequalities and less economic and social justice) and democracy (as business values and interests are increasingly substituted for democratic accountability and the collective voice).

### The growth of educational inequality

There is a considerable volume of data on how poor schools have, by and large, grown poorer (in terms of relative education results and in terms of total income) and how rich schools (in the same terms) have grown richer. Markets exacerbate existing inequalities (see Davies, 1999a, b, c; Gewirtz, Ball and Bowe, 1995; Whitty, Power and Halpin, 1998; Thrupp, 1999, 2000). Neo-liberals (such as Tooley, 1998, 1999, 2000) claim that these data are not relevant. Tooley claims that this inequality is not the result of a market in education. However, although there is not a 'true' market in schools it is the extremely well-documented case that where governments in Britain, the United States, Australia, New Zealand have proceeded to marketize their school systems then (racialized) social-class patterns of inequality have increased (Whitty, Power and Halpin, 1999; Sanders, Hill and Hawkin, 1999; Hill, Sanders and Hawkin, 2001). (This point is developed in Chapters 1 and 8.)

## A critique of neo-liberal theory

I now want to look at the theoretical and academic aspect of some neo-liberal arguments and suggest where they fall down. Neo-liberals – James Tooley (1994, 1998, 2000) for example – make a number of unwarranted implications or conclusions about the role of the state in education and about the role of the market in education. These relate firstly to their concept of the market, secondly to their concept of equality and equal opportunities, and thirdly to their assumption that the market/privatization is compatible with education.

### Neo-liberalism and the market
The first criticism of neo-liberals is that their notions of the 'free market' are out of date. Their notions of free-market competition might have had some credence in the early stages of capitalism. Today, they merely open the door to vast corporations who wish to squash competition and any vision of society other than a capitalist one. Neo-liberals miss the point. They replace dependency on the state with dependency on the market, which now means dependency on vast corporations and the law of money.

Neo-liberals also, in this connection, fail to acknowledge or understand how management works in contemporary society. To hand over education to capital means to hand it over to a group of people to manage it. To take, as an example, the 'internal market' in the National Health Service, the numbers of administrators and accountants increased and the numbers of nurses fell. Similar results are happening with the quasi-market in education. Almost every school now has a bursar. Administration is being duplicated rather than centralized, as in the old LEAs. Tooley assumes that 'setting state institutions free' has no consequences for the generation of new forms of control, hierarchy and privilege if capitalist society remains the framework in which the new 'freedom' is expressed. The mythical hidden hand (of the market) cannot (and never did) work by itself. Neo-liberal analysis is locked into Adam Smith and the 18th century. According to one of the most successful exponent of neo-liberal economics, Margaret Thatcher, 'there is no such thing as society' anyway! Basically, neo-liberals have no substantial theory of society; thus they misread and misunderstand actually existing markets.

### Neo-liberalism and its concepts of equal opportunities and equality
Neo-liberals argue that the free market, in addition to raising standards through competition, are quite capable of advancing equal opportunities. James Tooley

puts forward an unduly minimalist argument on equal opportunities. He suggests that there is a respectable tradition in moral philosophy that points to an interpretation of equality, or equity, as meaning adequate opportunities for all. He claims, moreover, that even when this is not the intention, supposedly egalitarian philosophers can be seen as, in fact, arguing for this (1998: 278).

Again, in 1999, he suggests that:

> What emerges from an analysis of the arguments of several significant social philosophers is that, when they speak for 'equality' or 'equity', it is at least consistent with their views that they are actually demanding a level of 'adequacy' for all, or a 'priority' principle which entails that only the needs of the under-privileged are met by the state.
>
> (1999:13)

The range of philosophers that he has analysed is not valid or 'respectable'. Marxist analysis and policy is concerned not simply with 'those families or communities (which) are not responsible or resourceful' (Tooley, 1999: 12) (in any case, the so-called 'underclass' and the poor are solely comprised of these). Marxist analysis – indeed, traditionally much of social democratic analysis (such as Crosland's *The Future of Socialism,* of 1956*)* is concerned with the working class(es) as a whole, with securing or enabling *more equality of outcome* – a very different story and project from 'adequacy'. Tooley (1998, 1999) needs to look at Marxist as well as liberal Left definitions of equal opportunities. He ignores these.

The funding for education for the poor would, for Tooley, be *charity.* In arguing for the market, and recognizing the existence of the above benighted 'irresponsible' and 'unresourceful' who might not be able, or choose to avail themselves of the advantages of private schooling, he suggests that 'philanthropy may be all that is required to help that small minority'(1999: 14).

This is akin to a policy of Charity Schools for the poor and feckless. The status and standards of such schools would be unlikely to match those of fee-paying private schools (cf Winch, 1998: 435 for a similar rebuttal of this neo-liberal position). Such a policy would betoken an end to what Grace (1994) argues for: education as public good, free at the point of entry, and as a right. Instead, there would be a residual safety net provision. A parallel is in the changing nature of council housing in Britain since the 1950s. For decades it provided non-stigmatized housing for a range of working-class families. With the wholesale selling off/privatization of that moderately comprehensive housing service (at one time housing 27 per cent of the British population), the council housing that has remained has slumped in status – and, as Chapter 6 shows, has led to considerable social and educational problems.

Neo-liberals, furthermore, fail to provide examples of the market delivering equal opportunities and equity. Despite the preponderance of neo-liberal state policies and of quasi-markets in education, despite the global penetration of markets in society, and of quasi-markets in education, with all the thousands of examples there are, neo-liberals singularly fail to show that the market may deliver equal opportunities better than state intervention. He repeatedly implies that this could be the case yet does not show it.

In view of the above three criticisms, it seems unlikely that having 'examined what is meant by equity and equality' (Tooley, 1999: 16) (a definition unrecognizable and anathema to many Marxists) 'it seemed that a plausible position was that markets in education (with an appropriate safety net)', which many would not regard as appropriate at all, could potentially satisfy this demand for social justice in education.

### Neo-liberalism and education

My point here is that education is not a commodity, to be bought and sold. One can buy *the means* to an education, but not the hard graft of autonomous learning itself. This question has been often debated (for example by Rikowski, 1996; Winch 1996; the interchange between Tooley and Winch, 1998). John McMurtry's (1991) work is useful at this juncture. He sets out the oppositions in principle between education and the capitalist market in terms of their opposing *goals*, opposing *motivations*, opposing *methods*, and opposing *standards of excellence*. His key arguments (pp 211–14) can be summarized as follows.

Firstly, *the goals of education*:

> Private profit is acquired by a structure of appropriation, which excludes others from its possession. The greater its accumulation by any private corporation, the more wealth others are excluded from in this kind of possession. This is what makes such ownership 'private'. Education, in contrast, is acquired by a structure of appropriation that does not exclude others from its possession. On the contrary, education is furthered the more it is shared, and the more there is free and open access to its circulation. That is why learning which is not conveyed to others is deemed 'lost', 'wasted' or 'dead'. In direct opposition to market exchanges, educational changes flourish most with the unpaid gifts of others and develop the more they are *not* mediated by private possession or profit.

Secondly, *opposing motivations*, McMurtry notes that

> the determining motivation of the market is to satisfy the wants of whoever has the money to purchase the goods that are provided. The determining motivation of education is to develop sound understanding *whether it is wanted or not* [my italics]. The market by definition can only satisfy the motivations of those who have the money to buy the product it sells. The place of education, on the other hand, remains a place of education insofar as it educates those whose motivation is to learn, independent of the money-demand they exercise in their learning.

In addition, 'development of understanding is necessarily growth of cognitive capacity; wherein satisfaction of consumer wants involves neither, and typically impedes both'.

Thirdly, *opposing methods*:

> The method of the market is to buy or sell the goods it has to offer to anyone
> for whatever price one can get. . . The method of education is never to buy or
> sell the item it has to offer, but to require of all who would have it that they
> fulfil its requirements autonomously. . .

Everything that is to be had on the market is acquired by the money paid for it.
Nothing that is learnt in education is acquired by the money paid for it.

Fourthly, *opposing standards of excellence*:

> The measures of excellence in the market are (i) how well the product is made
> to sell; and (ii) how problem-free the product is and remains for its buyers. The
> measures of excellence in education are (i) how disinterested and impartial its
> representations are; and (ii) how deep and broad the problems it poses are to
> one who has it. . .

The first works through 'one sided sales pitches...which work precisely because
they are *not* understood', the second 'must rule out one-sided presentation
appetitive compulsion and manipulative conditioning'.

In analysing the relationship between neo-liberalism and education, the last
critical theoretical point I wish to make here is that the market suppresses critical
thought and education itself.

McMurtry concludes, powerfully:

> this fundamental contradiction in standards of excellence leads, in turn, to
> *opposite standards of freedom*. Freedom in the market is the enjoyment of whatever
> one is able to buy from others with no questions asked, and profit from whatever
> one is able to sell to others with no requirement to answer to anyone else.
> Freedom in the place of education, on the other hand, is precisely the freedom
> to question, and to seek answers, whether it offends people's self-gratification
> or not.

McMurtry succinctly relates his arguments above to the 'systematic reduction of
the historically hard won social institution of education to a commodity for
private purchase and sale' (p 216). 'The commodification of education rules out
the very critical freedom and academic rigour which education requires to be
more than indoctrination' (p 215).

## Restraints on neo-liberal policy

There are three restraining forces on the activities of neo-liberalism: infra-
structural, consumer-related regulation, and legitimation. The first is the need
for an educational, social, transport, welfare and housing infrastructure to enable

workers to get to work, to be trained for different levels of the workforce, to be relatively fit and healthy. This restraint, though, is fairly minimal. It is a basic needs provision that says nothing about and has no implications at all for equality in society or in education.

The second restraint on capitalism is consumer dissatisfaction and consumer protection in the form of regulations. These, and inspectors of various sorts, are criticized as 'red tape' and as bureaucrats. Yet without regulation and enforcement in Britain, BSE and foot and mouth disease have flourished and been exported to continental Europe. State regulation operates against the freedom of capitalism to do as it pleases. Hence Conservative Party policy on schools and universities is to deregulate them, to 'set them free', to allow them to charge what they want and run their own affairs. This 'regulatory' model, of the state regulating standards (for example, through Oftot, Ofsted, Oftel, the Rail Regulatory Body) can be weak or strong. It can demand only basic standards, perhaps failing to inspect regularly, or it can demand strong controls, including controls over profits. (It is interesting that some of the most vigorously enforced standards are those in education – testimony perhaps to the crucial nature of the state apparatus of schooling.)

The third restraint is that (as set out in Chapter 5) capital (and the political parties Capitalists fund and influence) needs to persuade the people that neo-liberalism – competition, privatization, poorer standards of public services, greater inequalities between rich and poor – are legitimate. If not, there is a delegitimation crisis, government and the existing system are seen through as grossly unfair and inhumane. This can lead to mass protest such as the anti-poll tax protests/riots of the early 1990s, inner-city rebellions, general or widespread strike action, the Seattle and London protests against neo-liberal globalization and other forms of large-scale direct action. To stop this delegitimation happening, to ensure that the majority of the population consider the government and the economic system of private monopoly ownership is legitimate, the state uses the ideological state apparatuses such as schools and colleges (see Chapter 5) to 'naturalize' capitalism – to make the existing status quo seem 'only natural'. Books such as this are written to contest the legitimacy of government policy and its subordination to/ participation in the neo-liberal project of global capital. Clearly for the eco-warriors of 'the Battle of Seattle' (see Rikowski, 2001a) and for various groups of socialists and greens, the current system is not legitimate! As Glenn Rikowski indicates, post-Seattle, it is obvious that the New Labour administration is

> for incorporating all spheres of social life within the orbit of global capital. Educators are implicated in this process, like everyone else. The school or university is no hiding place. The key point is what we do about it. The Battle in Seattle and its subsequent incarnations are reminders that educators are never off the hook until the need for further Seattle has been eradicated.

> (Rikowski, 2001a: 4)

Post-Seattle, and increasingly, educational debate is turning from 'standards' and 'school effectiveness' to wider questions such as 'what is education for?' and 'what should the purposes of education be?' Increasingly, many parents and students are questioning the legitimacy of a test-driven, anxiety-laden, sanitized, uncritical 'schooling for unquestioning conformity'. In the next 11 chapters, various contributors analyse and discuss facts, concepts and policies regarding equality and inequality in education, critically questioning what is happening to schooling and education.

## Notes

1.  For example the concepts and practices of capital/capitalism are developed in Chapters 5, 7, and 13. The concept of neo-liberalism is examined in Chapters 1 and 3. The concept and practice of privatization is also examined in Chapter 2. Throughout the book a number of chapters focus on exclusion, notably Chapters 4 and 12. In addition, each of the chapters examining specific areas of inequality and exclusion (Chapters 7 to 11) focuses on current policies for exclusion and inequality, and then proceeds to develop alternative policy suggestions on policy for inclusion and equality. See also Cole (ed) (2000), which addresses the issues of gender, 'race', sexuality, special educational needs and social class both per se and with respect to education, through history up to the present day.

2.  See Chapter 7 for data on social class inequalities in income, wealth and educational attainment – and how much inequality has increased since 1979.

3.  Ralph Nader was the Green candidate standing against Al Gore and George W Bush in the United States' presidential election of November 2000. He received around 3 million votes.

4.  www.washingtonpost.com/wp-srv/onpolitics/elections/nader071100.htm Ralph Nader's speech to the NAACP, 11 July 2000.

5.  Salvador Allende was the democratically elected Marxist President of Chile. He was overthrown and murdered in a military coup led by General Pinochet. The coup was supported by much of the Chilean and international capitalist class and by the Unites States' Central Intelligence Agency (CIA).

6.  Glenn Rikowski (1996, 1998, 1999 and 2001b) develops a Marxist analysis based on an analysis of 'labour power'. With respect to education, he suggests that teachers are the most dangerous of workers because they have a special role in shaping, developing and forcing *the single commodity on which the whole capitalist system rests: labour power*. In the capitalist labour process, labour power is transformed into value-creating *labour* and, at a certain point, *surplus value* – value over and above that represented in the worker's wage – is created. *Surplus value* is the first form of the existence of capital. It is the *lifeblood of capital*. Without it, capital could not be transformed into money, on sale of

the commodities that incorporate value, and hence the capitalist could not purchase the necessary raw materials, means of production and labour power to set the whole cycle in motion once more. But most important for the capitalist is that part of the surplus value forms his or her *profit* – and it is this that drives the capitalist on a personal basis. It is this that defines the personal *agency of the capitalist!* Teachers are dangerous because *they are intimately connected with the social production of labour power*, equipping students with skills, competences, abilities, knowledge and the attitudes and personal qualities that *can be expressed and expended in the capitalist labour process*. Teachers are guardians of the quality of labour power! This potential, latent power of teachers is why representatives of the state might have sleepless nights worrying about their role in ensuring that the labourers of the future are delivered to workplaces throughout the national capital *of the highest possible quality*.

The state needs to control the process for two reasons. Firstly, to try to ensure that this occurs. Secondly, to try to ensure that modes of pedagogy that are antithetical to labour-power production *do not and cannot exist*. In particular, it becomes clear, on this analysis, that the capitalist state will seek to destroy any forms of pedagogy *that attempt to educate students regarding their real predicament – to create an awareness of themselves as future labour powers and to underpin this awareness with critical insight that seeks to undermine the smooth running of the social production of labour power*. This fear entails strict control of ITE, of the curriculum, of educational research.

# References

Ball, S (1990) *Politics and Policy Making in Education: Explorations in Policy Sociology*, Routledge, London

Barratt Brown, M and Coates, K (1996) *The Blair Revolution: Deliverance for Whom?* Spokesman, Nottingham

Blair, T and Schroeder, G (1999) *Europe: The Third Way/Die Neue Mitte*, The Labour Party, London

Bottery, M (1999) After the Market – have we ever really been in one? in *Education as a Commodity*, eds N Alexadiou and C Brock, John Catt Educational, Saxmundham, Suffolk

Coates, K and Barratt Brown, M (1999) The third way to the servile state, in *The Third Way to the Servile State, (Spokesman 66)*, ed K Coates, Bertrand Russell Peace Foundation, Nottingham

Cohen, N (2001) Comment, *The Observer*, 20 May 2001

Cole, M (1998) Globalisation, modernisation and competitiveness: a critique of the New Labour project in education, *International Studies in Sociology of Education*, **8** (3), pp 315–32

Cole, M (ed) (2000) *Education, Equality and Human Rights; Issues of gender, 'race', sexuality, special needs and social class,* RoutledgeFalmer, London

Cole, M, Hill, D and Shan, S (eds) (1997) *Promoting Equality in Primary Schools,* Cassell, London

Davies, N (1999a) Crisis, crisis, crisis: the state of our schools: the fatal flaw at the heart of our education system, *Guardian,* 14 September

Davies, N (1999b) Bias that killed the dream of equality, *Guardian,* 15 September

Davies, N (1999c) Political coup bred educational disaster: Nick Davies talks to Lord Baker, *Guardian,* 16 September

Department for Education and Employment (DfEE) (2001) *Schools: Building on success – raising standards, promoting diversity, achieving results* (Green Paper), HMSO, London

Elliott, L (2001) It's about time Blair had a big idea, *Guardian,* 2 April

Gamble, A (1988) *The Free Economy and the Strong State: The Politics of Thatcherism,* Macmillan, London

Gamble, A (1996) *Hayek,* Westview Press, Boulder, CO

Gewirtz, S, Ball, S and Bowe, R (1995) *Markets, Choice and Equity in Education,* Open University Press, Buckingham

Grace, G (1994) Education is a public good: on the need to reist the domination of economic science, in *Education and the Market Place,* eds D Bridges and T McLaughlin, Falmer Press, London

Grice, A (2001) Like it or loathe it, Blair's 'big idea' means more private sector involvement, *The Independent,* 17 May 201

Hatcher, R (2000) *Schools Under New Labour – Getting Down to Business,* Paper presented at the Conference on Privatisierung des Bildungsbereichs Eigentum und Wertschopfung in der Wissengellschaft, 15–17 June, University of Hamburg

Hatcher, R (2001) Getting down to the business: schooling in the globalised economy, *Education and Social Justice,* **3** (2), pp 45–59

Hatcher, R and Hirtt, N (1999) The business agenda behind Labour's education policy, in *Business, Business, Business: New Labour's Education Policy,* eds M Allen *et al,* Tufnell Press, London

Hill, D (1991a) *What's Left in Teacher Education: Teacher education, the radical Left and policy proposals,* Tufnell Press, London

Hill, D (1994a) Cultural diversity and initial teacher education, in *Cultural Diversity and the Curriculum, Vol 4, Cross-Curricular Contexts, Themes and Dimensions in Primary Schools,* eds G Verma and P Pumfrey, Falmer Press, London

Hill, D (1994b) A radical Left policy for teacher education, *Socialist Teacher,* **56,** pp 23–24

Hill, D (1997a) Reflection in Teacher Education, in *Educational Dilemmas: Debate and Diversity, Vol 1: Teacher Education and Training,* eds K Watson, S Modgil and C Modgil, Cassell, London

Hill, D (1997b) Equality and primary schooling: the policy context intentions and effects of the Conservative 'reforms', in *Promoting Equality in Primary Schools* eds M Cole, D Hill and S Shan, Cassell, London

Hill, D (1997c) Brief autobiography of a Bolshie dismissed, *General Educator*, **44**, pp 15–17

Hill, D (1997d) Critical research and the death of dissent, *Research Intelligence*, **59**, pp 25–26

Hill, D (1999) *New Labour and Education: Policy, ideology and the third way*, Tufnell Press, London

Hill, D (2000a) The third way ideology of New Labour's educational policy in England and Wales, in *Combating Social Exclusion through Education: Laissez faire, authoritarianism or third way?*, eds G Walraven, C Day, C Parsons and D Van Deen, Garant, Leuven-Apeldoon

Hill, D (2000b) *Radical Left Principles for Social and Economic Justice in Education Policy*, Paper given to the BERA Conference, Social Justice in Education: Theoretical Frameworks for Practical Purposes, Nottingham Trent University, 10 April

Hill, D (2001) State Theory and the neo-Liberal Reconstruction of Schooling and Teacher Education: a structuralist neo-Marxist critique of postmodernist, quasi-postmodernist, and culturalist neo-Marxist theory, *The British Journal of Sociology of Education*, **22** (1), pp137-57

Hill, D and M Cole (eds) (1995) Marxist Theory and State Autonomy Theory: the case of 'race' education in initial teacher education, *Journal of Education Policy*, **10**, (2) pp 221–32

Hill, D and Cole, M (eds) (1999b) *Promoting Equality in Secondary Schools*, Cassell, London

Hill, D, Sanders, M and Hankin, T (2001) Marxism, class analysis and post-modernism, in *Marxism Against Postmodernism in Educational Theory*, eds D Hill, P McLaren, M Cole and G Rikowski, Lexington Books, Lanham, MD

Hillcole Group/Chitty, C (ed) (1991) *Changing the Future: Redprint for education*, Tufnell Press, London

Hillcole Group (1997) *Rethinking Education and Democracy: A socialist alternative for the twenty-first century*, Tufnell Press, London

Hughes, D (2001) Blair's private enterprise, *Daily Mail*, 17 May 2001

Hutton, W (2001) The rich aren't cleverer, just richer, *The Observer*, 1 April

Labour Party (2001) *Ambitions for Britain (Labour Party General Election Manifesto)*, The Labour Party, London

Marginson, S (1997) *Markets in Education*, Allen & Unwin, London

McLaren, P (2000) *Che Guevara, Paolo Freire and the Pedagogy of Revolution*, Rowman & Littlefield, Oxford

McMurtry, J (1991) Education and the Market Model, *Journal of the Philosophy of Education*, **25** (2), pp 209–17

McMurtry, J (1999) *The Cancer Stage of Capitalism*, Pluto Press, London

Molnar, A (1996) *Giving Kids the Business: The commercialisation of America's schools*, HarperCollins, Westview

Molnar, A (1999) *Cashing in on Kid: The second annual report on trends in schoolhouse commercialism, 1997–98 – 1998–99*, Centre for Analysis of Commercialism in Education, School of Education, University of Wisconsin-Milwaukee, Wisconson www.uwm.edu/Dept/CACE/documents/cashinginonkids.html

Molnar, A (2000) *The Commercial Transformation America's Schools,* John Dewey Memorial Lecture to the Association for Supervision and Curriculum Development Conference, New Orleans, Louisiana, 26 March, Centre for Analysis of Commercialism in Education, School of Education, University of Wisconsin-Milwaukee, Wisconson, www.uwm.edu/Dept/documents/cace-00-01.htm

Rikowski, G (1996) *Education Markets and Missing Products,* University of Birmingham School of Education Research Paper, developing and extending a paper first presented to the 1995 Annual Conference of the Conference of Socialist Economists, July, University of Northumbria at Newcastle.

Rikowski, G (1998) Nietzsche, Marx and mastery: the learning unto death, in *Apprenticeship: A new paradigm for learning,* eds P Ainley and H Rainbird, Kogan Page, London

Rikowski, G (1999) Education, capital and the transhuman, in *Postmodernism in Educational Theory: Education and the politics of human resistance,* eds D Hill, P McLaren, M Cole and G Rikowski, Tufnell Press, London

Rikowski, G (2000/2001) *New Labour's Knowledge Economy versus Critical Pedagogy: The significance of the Battle of Seattle for education,* Paper presented at the Annual Conference of Socialist Economists 2000, 'Global Capital and Global Struggles: Strategies, Alliances, Alternatives', University of London Union, London, 1 July

Rikowski, G (2001a) *The Battle in Seattle: Its significance for education,* Tufnell Press, London

Rikowski, G (2001b) Schools: building for business, *Post-16 Educator,* **3**, pp 14–15

Sanders, M, Hill, D and Hankin, T (1999) Education theory and the return to class analysis, in *Postmodernism in Educational Theory: Education and the politics of human resistance,* eds D Hill, P McLaren, M Cole and G Rikowski, Tufnell Press, London

TFPL (1999) *Skills for Knowledge Management: A briefing paper,* presented at 'Skills for the Knowledge Economy: A One-day Seminar', RSA, 5 July, TFPL Ltd, at http://www.tfpl.com

Thrupp, M (1999) *Schools Making a Difference: Let's Be Realistic!* Open University Press, Buckingham

Thrupp, M (2000) Compensating for class: are school improvement researchers being realistic? *Education and Social Justice,* **2** (2), pp 2–11

Tooley, J (1994) In defence of markets in education, in *Education and the Market Place,* eds D Bridges and T McLaughlin, Falmer Press, London

Tooley, J (1998) The neo-liberal critique of state intervention in education: a reply to Winch, *Journal of Philosophy of Education,* **32** (2), pp 267–81

Tooley, J (1999) Asking different questions: towards justifying markets in education, in *Education as a Commodity,* eds N Alexiadou and C Brock, John Catt Educational, Saxmundham, Suffolk

Tooley, J (2000) *Reclaiming Education,* Cassell, London

Whitty, G, Power, S and Halpin, D (1998) *Devolution and Choice in Education: The school, the state and the market,* Open University Press, Buckingham

Winch, C (1996) *Quality and Education,* Blackwell, London

Winch, C (1998) Markets, educational opportunities and education: reply to Tooley, *Journal of Philosophy of Education,* **32** (3), pp 429–36

3

# Policy, equality and educational research

## *Kenneth Dunkwu*

## Editors' introduction

*The fact of multi-ethnic diversity in English society has long been recognized within education. There is a history of ideas about how to shape education accordingly, and with it a history of gaps between provision and needs. Kenneth Dunkwu addresses the conceptual and practical difficulties of achieving integration without deprivation, in schools as in society. Drawing on significant post-war examples – such as the assimilationist approaches to the children of immigrant communities during the 1950s and 1960s, the Education Reform Act 1988, aspects of the contemporary National Curriculum and the reorganization of research – the discussion illustrates the limits imposed on egalitarianism (however conceived) by legislation for education that carries with it social and economic forms of discrimination. Turning this interplay to positive effect, the chapter develops an assessment of research principles and approaches and considers a political role for educational research, research in the achievement of social justice and diversity without disempowerment.*

This chapter begins by exploring the attempts of the British education system to cater for the specific needs of children through the introduction of pluralist approaches to education. The subsequent discussion of the second and third sections focuses on the impact of major policy developments on equality on education and educational research.

# Equality in education: concept and policy

## *Pluralism and equality*

Pluralism within the political state implies a dialogue: certain ethnic groups (defined by combination of religion, ethnicity of values) are both relatively endogamous and strive to retain their distinctive cultural identity through some degree of institutional separation. Berry (1979) stresses that the majority of individuals in all ethnic groups in the political state must value such a state before a society can be truly pluralist.

The overuse in Western societies of the plural society concept – originally developed to describe colonial societies in Burma, Indonesia and later used in a description of Dutch society (Bagley, 1972; Lijphart, 1977) – came to be seen as a crude political attempt to rationalize cultural domination. The most flagrant example of the division of cultures for domination occurred in South Africa, under apartheid. Pluralism involves the balance of power in a society and the power attributed to minority groups.

Verma (1989) assesses pluralism within the confines of 'race' and education, and argues that existing education processes and practices should respond to, respect and foster the cultural identity of particular racial groups in contemporary society, as well as acknowledging the particular needs and aspirations of other cultural groups. Crucially, the cultures of distinct groups should be maintained and preserved within society, so that their respective identities and cultural heritage remain an integral part of their very being.

Proposals to recognize *cultural pluralism* in education involved devising school curricula more closely related to local and social conditions, as well as the experience of pluralism within education. The nationwide, tripartite secondary education system, for example, was based on the distinctive needs of the three broad 'types' of adolescent identified by educational psychologists. However, as a form of education for diversity it was eventually found unacceptable due to the limits it imposed on the life chances of too many children and the way it sustained impermeable social class subcultures.

The post-war pendulum thus swung towards the common secondary school. Comprehensive reorganization was ideologically and structurally more in tune with social needs, and offered greater promise of social cohesion. But the antithesis of diversity and cohesion remained and the common secondary school in turn generated elaborate internal provision for the varied needs of its pupils – through banding, streaming, grouping and extensive programmes of options. These developments were accompanied during the 1970s by the proposal of Bantock and Midwinter for distinctive styles of education for working-class children (Lawton, 1975).

The controversy over what, in the 1960s and 1970s, was seen as *cultural deprivation* is a useful illustration of how the persistent working-class under-achievement in primary and secondary schools was explained. Many theorists argued that these children were suffering from 'cultural clash'. The language, the life experiences of schools and teachers were said to be so different from those of the working-class pupils as to put them at a considerable disadvantage. They were 'culturally deprived' and needed compensatory education to make up for their deficiencies (Bernstein, 1970; Milner, 1975; Tyler, 1977). Others argued that such children were different not deficient (Seitz, 1977; Stone, 1981; Pumfrey, 1983).

The argument typifies the wider antithesis of diversity and conformity. On the one hand, all cultures – working class/middle class, urban/rural, Roman Catholic/Protestant – have *intrinsic validity* and embody an intricate and often distinctive network of norms values and traditions. A social democracy committed to liberty and equality is committed to diversity and our schools have a prime responsibility to recognize and further it. On the other hand, in the interests of social cohesion and the survival of society, it is argued that children possessing varying home cultures must also be helped to acquire linguistic, cognitive and social skills of broader social value. Without such skills, Craft (1984) asserts, such children will experience a considerable 'handicap' within education and in other opportunities linked to educational achievement. 'Different' or 'deficient', they must not be disadvantaged. In this sense, education for conformity in a social democracy is the means to the fullest exploration of diversity.

Cultural pluralism sets the most challenging tests for political ideals, presenting a tension between education for diversity and education for consensus. Few societies are culturally homogenous and social class is a predominant source of pluralism. Moreover, there are vertical social divisions to the pluralism of ethnicity: a sense of peoplehood, of cohesive traditions, usually with distinctive religious and linguistic characteristics and sometimes with a regional basis but always cutting across the horizontal stratification of age and social class.

The debate about class differences in education concerns the question of which culture working-class children should be required to assimilate into in society. This is precisely paralleled in terms of 'ethnic minority' children, although the issues are more sharply defined and the dilemmas more conflictual, given the concerns associated with the educational attainment of African-Caribbean children (Mabey, 1981; Parekh, 1989; Gillborn, 2000).

One pluralist response is that the cultures of ethnic minorities should be maintained and fostered irrespective of their content and specific customs. The notion that these cultures should be exempt from critical comment, official disapproval or legislative interference may have arisen from the desire to compensate for the depredations of ethnocentrism, which ethnic minorities have all too often been forced to contend with, as relatively powerless communities. The dilemma relates to the theoretical basis of pluralism on philosophical and moral relativism.

## Relativism

Relativism is distinguished by the two related tenets that all cultures are equally valued and can only be properly understood and appreciated from within their own framework of 'rationality'. Therefore, the attempt to divest oneself of cultural presuppositions and to see matters from another culture's point of view is a prerequisite for moral judgement in interethnic contexts (Jeffcoate, 1984). This specifically rejects any belief in what Paul Zec (1980), in a valuable article on multicultural education and relativism, has called 'transcultural criteria of rationality' and 'right conduct' (in other words, an agreed core of minimal values) against which all cultures can be described, interpreted and judged. Pluralist strategies based on relativist concepts therefore seem particularly inappropriate for a public system of education. State schools could never be value free even if they wished to be; their curricula and other institutional arrangements are bound to be predicated on certain values, and those values are held to be so vital that they cannot be left to develop by chance.

The London School Board, for example, responded to the increased numbers of Jewish children in the school-age population at the end of the 19th century by handing over their elementary schooling to the Jewish community, so that it could be run on Jewish lines. The Board may not necessarily have subscribed to pluralist philosophy, and its policy may have been dictated by practical exigencies or simply part of the early confusion about what the new elementary schools were for; nonetheless the effect was the same. Jeffcoate (1984) notes, as if it had organized the emergence of a separate educational provision. A dual system had been inaugurated by pluralist education legislation of the 1870s, which enabled religious minorities to further the presentation of their faiths at the public expense.

In contrast, central and local government responses to the children of European and New Commonwealth immigrants, who began appearing in schools in the 1950s and 1960s, were patently not pluralist. There was never any suggestion of following the example set for Jewish children by the London Board over half a century earlier. Precisely what government policy was and how it was best characterized remained a matter of disagreement, but most of the local education authorities affected confirmed their arrangements for the teaching of English as a second language and for the introduction of the immigrant children to British life. (Central government attempted to assist them, after almost a decade of laissez faire, by making available the extra funding and resources for immigrant children known as Section 11 funding, albeit an anachronistic form of provision when compared with other trends and developments in multiracial education and race relations policy – Dorn and Hibbert, 1987.)

Indeed, in the early years of European and New Commonwealth immigration, it was not separatism but assimilation (in the sense of attempted cultural anglicization) that dominated the approaches of head teachers and teachers in staffrooms around the country. Evidence of this was provided by several local studies undertaken at the time. 'You can't tell which is which' a head teacher told Elspeth Huxley during her visit to Bedford schools in 1964, 'we're turning them all British' (Huxley, 1964: 224).

## Cultural 'assimilation'

Between 1965 and 1969, the Labour government developed funding initiatives for immigrant children. This occurred either exclusively as in the case of Section 11 or partially as in the case of Urban Aid. Yet as one ingredient in the bipartisan race relations philosophy that had been developed in a curious and ad hoc way by the Labour and Conservative parties throughout the 1960s.

The very definition of a Commonwealth immigrant was criticized for its 'assimilationist' assumptions, which effectively excluded Liverpool's black community. Critics who supported the 'assimilationist' charge seized on a key passage in the 1964 report by the Commonwealth Immigration Advisory Council (CIAC), which stated that 'a national system cannot be expected to perpetuate the different values of immigrant groups'. This was widely interpreted as pressure on schools to try to anglicize immigrant children. In fact, it meant exactly what it said – that 'a national system cannot be expected' to teach Muslims to be good Muslims, Hindus to be good Hindus, or Sikhs to be good Sikhs. Nowhere did central government mention assimilation as a desirable goal (except in Circular 7/65 where it referred to social integration, not cultural conversion). It was even cautious about forms of cultural affiliation that could conflict with the wishes of the immigrant parents and about schools imposing 'the kind of conformity that a too narrow interpretation of "integration" would involve' (Ministry of Education, 1963: 5–6). Arguably, this controversy is an epigraph for assimilationism, because it succinctly expresses the limits of pluralism.

In the 1970s, the teaching profession was turning against the assimilationists, although isolated acts of ethnocentric arrogance or insensitivity were still evident (Jeffcoate, 1984). The Townsend and Brittan investigation into teachers' opinions in the early 1970s recorded how one head teacher declared: 'I believe our duty is to prepare children for citizenship in a free, Christian, democratic society according to British standards and customs' (Townsend and Brittan 1972: 13). Such expressions of opinion were often accompanied by gratuitous acts of ethnocentrism, such as banning traditional dress and minority languages from school premises, ignoring parental wishes and flouting religious sensibilities.

Significantly, however, Jennifer Williams had completed research by the late 1960s in Sparkbrook, Birmingham, and found that assimilation was not only an aspect of immigration – it was also endemic. She summarized the role of the school (except in the Catholic voluntary sector) as that of a 'socialising, anglicising integrating agency', with teachers identifying their task to instil 'a certain set of values (Christian), a code of behaviour (middle class) and a set of academic and job aspirations in which white collar jobs had a higher prestige than manual, clean jobs than dirty... and interesting jobs than just "good money" jobs' (Williams, 1967: 237).

The debate on equality issues in education shows a history of the continuing attempt to cater for cultural pluralism, particularly by striking an acceptable balance between educating for difference and educating for similarity but also by acknowledging the policy structures, practices and beliefs beyond the education system, in the wider context of society as a whole. In the same way, the impact of post-war education policy for equality needs now be considered in relation to the social policy of which it is an aspect.

## Social discrimination and education policy

### Market forces and education

The impact of political and economic developments during the 1970s and 1980s, along with wider structural changes in society, radically altered the parameters in which education – as a commodity – could operate. A 'market' philosophy was introduced into education with the underlying intention that competition between schools would have the knock-on effect of raising standards and improving educational performance. Competition was fuelled by the publication of 'league tables' covering Standard Assessment Tests (SATS), examination results and truancy figures (Pyke, 1991; ACE, 1992, 1993; Lloyd-Bennett, 1993; Cohen *et al*, 1994).

Funding became more closely tied to roll numbers, forcing some schools to compete for pupils in order to maintain adequate funds. The combination of these market forces left schools with the dilemma of having to present an attractive, successful image to parents, and therefore resulted in competition for pupil standards and academic achievement. In contrast, difficult pupils or low academic achievers became 'unsaleable goods' (Lloyd-Bennett, 1993). The 2 per cent whose assessment resulted in statements of Special Educational Needs (SEN) were given a legal right to specified additional support. However, it was suggested that longer-term costs involved mainstream schools giving too high a profile to SEN, whereas market image, national testing, performance and staying-on rates in the sixth form would conspire to produce new kinds of exclusions or marginalization for SEN students (Bowe, Gintis and Gold, 1992).

## Quasi-markets and discrimination

Quasi-markets were introduced to the education system in England and Wales by the Education Reform Act 1988, although legislation passed earlier in the 1980s had set the scene for many of the changes implemented in 1988. The themes of education policy throughout the 1980s were also identified in other policies at the time, such as the promotion of 'choice' through a consumerist approach to public services; the strengthening of management and reduction in the power of professionals and unions; the increased power of intermediate bodies (governing bodies in the case of schools) to curb the power of professionals and local authorities. However, as McVicar (1991: 137) observed, earlier education legislation was to 'pale into insignificance' by comparison. The Education Reform Act 1988 (ERA) was credited with literally introducing a new 'ERA' into the education system (Le Grand and Bartlett, 1993).

The Education Reform Act 1988 introduced the National Curriculum, which was at the centre of the Conservative 'Right turn' for education. Learning programmes from the early years onwards would be laid out in clearly defined 'subject orders', which would specify what should be learnt and when. Teachers would be stripped of their influence over the general curriculum content and their freedom to use 'professional judgement' over its application was also to be severely curtailed. Student progress would be measured by a system of Standard Attainment Tests (SATs), soon to be renamed Standard Assessment Tests. Results would then be used to construct school 'league tables'. 'Cross-curricular' dimensions such as personal and social education were to be included, although they came to occupy a largely subordinate role and in some schools, cross-curricular work ceased to exist at all (Allen, 1999).

Maud Blair (1994) suggests that, despite responses within the education system, extensive discussions with African-Caribbean, Asian and other minority ethnic teachers and parents revealed that the 'black community' became fundamentally discontented because the Education Reform Act (1988) lacked receptiveness to the needs of black and minority ethnic children. Regulations governing the teaching of religious education required school assemblies to be 'mainly and broadly' Christian acts of worship. In addition, many schools attempting to implement anti-racist initiatives faced suspicion from white parents, with little support from education officials in most Local Education Authorities (LEAs). The few LEAs that had attempted to represent black communities and control service delivery towards anti-racist ends were the object of frequent vilification and political attack.

The Act also reinforced the notion of 'parental choice', thereby emphasizing the threat of detrimental exposure to market forces for the less 'popular', usually less 'successful' schools. The power of LEAs was further weakened with increased delegation of budgets from them to schools. From April 1990 onwards, heads and governing bodies of all schools with more than 200 pupils were responsible for all expenditure except capital and certain collective services. The Inner London Education Authority (ILEA) was abolished at the same time, despite parental opposition, thereby confirming how subordinate local authorities had become to central government (McVicar, 1991).

Anxiety was expressed that the multicultural nature of British society would not be incorporated into the design of particular subjects, especially because there did not appear to be any black representation on the subject working groups (Arnot, 1989; Burton and Weiner, 1990; Davies, Holland and Minhas, 1990). Indeed, the report from the mathematics subject working group was openly hostile to the concept of multicultural education. Blair (1994) argues that black teachers are professionally compromised when charged with the 'delivery' of this kind of National Curriculum. Within Britain, the voices of black groups were being silenced and the history of Britain divested of its imperialist and colonialist connections. This is illustrated by the lack of recognition given to languages spoken by black pupils, which consequently are not on a par with modern foreign (European) languages, whereas the multilingual diversity within schools and the needs of bilingual pupils have not been adequately recognized. Hostility to multiculturalism is also evident in the content imbalance of various curriculum subjects (in particular geography, history, and English literature) and the orders for religious education to emphasize Christianity and Christian worship. Schools are therefore placed in a contradictory position of having to ensure the equal treatment of all pupils while, as institutions, they are themselves structured by gender, class and 'race' discriminations.

### Reshaping the National Curriculum

In journals such as *Teaching London Kids*, efforts to reshape the curriculum by moving away from a hierarchically organized subject curriculum, 'delivered' by teachers and absorbed by students, appeared at their most challenging. They were also reflected, however, in a variety of 'best practice' documents from the Schools Council and Her Majesty's Inspectorate (HMI). Secondary schools generally accepted new curriculum areas such as 'social studies' (Lawton and Dufour, 1973), which encouraged students to ask such questions about the nature of society as we can safely assume will remain out of bounds for New Labour's model citizen (Allen, 1999).

In recognition of some of the curriculum weaknesses, and also the urgent need to respond to the increasing influence of New Right ideas, a Left alternative began to emerge. Alongside attempts to construct popular socialist agendas for education generally, a critique was produced by the National Union of Teachers (NUT, 1990) defining the wider assumptions behind the National Curriculum, and reaching beyond a narrow 'professionalist' stance to set out blueprints for the development of an 'alternative' curriculum. This was to 'actively oppose racism, sexism and disadvantage due to disability' and to 'not impose hierarchies amongst cultures or in relation to class, gender and ethnic origin' (1990: 20).

However, the overall effect of the introduction of market objectives to education by the Education Reform Act of 1988 was to create a new value context, as in other public services. As Ball (1993) observes:

> The introduction of market forces into the relations between schools means that teachers are now working within a new value context in which image and impression management are more important than the educational process, elements of control have been shifted from the producer (teachers) the consumers (parents) via open enrolments, parental choice and per-capita funding. In relations with parents, the use of performance indicators and tests places the achievements of students and the work of teachers in a new light.
>
> (1993: 108)

This new value context is particularly apparent in the redefinition of parents as consumers of education on behalf of their children, encouraged to exercise the power of 'choice' in relation to the school their children attend. In theory, this enables them to let professionals know what they want and do not want for their children, and effectively move funds around the system. Schools can no longer predict the number of children they will be educating via a headcount of the last year in nearby primary schools or population figures for their 'catchment areas' (which have in effect been abolished). Yet the notion of 'choice', although a real threat to the budget of schools, does not always amount to much of a choice for some parents in some areas. Furthermore 'choice' is also a misleading concept compared with what is legally offered – namely, the right to express a 'preference' (Hayden, 1997).

There is potential for conflict, between the changes brought about by a focus on value for money and the drive to raise educational standards, although the evidence here is inconclusive. There is evidence of some improvement, for example from certain measurable outcomes indicating that GCSE examination results have improved throughout the period of the Conservative reform, from the early 1980s onwards (DfEE, 1995). Many of the think tanks clearly aligned with New Labour emphasize the importance of raising levels of educational performance in ensuring national economic survival, although the argument that the changes from Fordist to 'post-Fordist' methods of production have created a potentially different type of education, is increasingly common (Bayliss, 1999; Wilkinson, 1999).

Critics such as Robinson (1999) question the direct relationship between increased educational performance (as measured by examination success) and national economic performance. If Robinson's arguments are controversial, they seem less contentious to maintain, and pertinent to the way Labour has used its version of the new education–economy correspondence as a stick to beat off the types of curriculum aimed at promoting social justice through challenging issues of class, 'race' and gender. Thus, reducing the discussion about the curriculum to issues about delivery and teacher 'competence' is also necessary, if Labour introduced the new management styles outlined in the Green Paper *Teachers Facing the Challenge of Change* (Allen, 1999: 29).

It is possible, however, to see the impact of social policy context of the 1970s and 1980s in shaping a particular form of change within the education service – a form in which the imperatives of change are not driven primarily by broader educational motives or by the needs of the children. Instead, changes are being driven by the desire to reorganize the system in a way that creates pressure to increase measurable academic output. This is a social policy context in conflict, also, with other policies, such as policy to increase the integration of children with Special Educational Needs (SEN) and to reduce residential care and 'out-of-county' placements (1997).

In a competitive system, it is argued, somebody loses out, and some individuals are in a better position to take part in the competition than others. Markets derive their efficiency from the fact that there are 'winners and losers risk takers and bankruptcies, entrepreneurs and "uncertainty"' (Veljanovoski, 1990: 6). Velajanov-oski's analogy applies to schools put under pressure to achieve better examination results, or to younger children's improvement in their attainments in the National

Curriculum levels. If they are successful, they are the winners, rewarded by increased popularity and increasing school rolls and therefore better able to plan financially for the future than the less popular schools. The losers risk 'bankruptcy' if they do not improve results sufficiently and compete successfully for children.

Thus, the introduction of published league tables of examination results and other indicators of performance in schools has created a climate less likely to be sympathetic to (SEN) children. Yet schools are not all responding the same way to the pressures of operating in a competitive market.

It was predicted by commentators throughout the 1980s, such as the Department for Cultural Studies (DCS) (1981, 1991), that the proposed reforms in the Education Reform Act 1988 were likely to marginalize further the most disadvantaged children. Exclusion may be seen as part of the formal representation of this process of marginalization. Stirling (1991) started research in 1989 on the effect of the 1988 Act upon children with emotional and behavioural difficulties. In doing so, Stirling, like Peagram (1991), was identifying the specific group of children expected to be most vulnerable to the changes in the education system.

Blyth and Milner (1996) speculate upon the possibilities for pupils with a potential spending power of approximately £2,000 a head at secondary school level. They point to the alternative programmes already developing to cater for pupils not attending school, for various reasons as well as exclusion. Blyth and Milner go so far as to suggest that it could be even in the interests of some children to be excluded from school so that they can gain entrance to alternative (and perhaps more appropriate) forms of preferred education. This may apply to pupils in school who have spent a considerable amount of their schooling in mainstream education, but younger pupils who have spent little time in the education system face concerns that could lead to long-term alienation, isolation and the risk of exclusion.

At this point, it is useful to consider the distinctive role of research in the assessment of changes to the provision of education introduced by legislation.

## Research for equality

This section focuses primarily on the concept and appraisal of research, followed by the discussion of educational research within the framework of policy-making and equality.

### What is research?

An essential characteristic of research is that enquiry should aim to increase knowledge. It should make a claim to knowledge, to tell something not known before. More commonly however, the knowledge expectation requires the researcher to publish findings to as wide an audience as possible – in the words of 19th-century scientist Michael Faraday, to 'work, finish, publish'.

A more recent perspective of research is that it purposely seeks to generate knowledge that informs both policy-makers and practices, evaluating its successes in terms of its stated aims and objectives (Walford, 1991). Some theorists refer to research as 'systematic enquiry' (Bell, 1993; Verma and Mallick, 1999) and fail to see research as part of a professional task. This definition can be unhelpful, because whenever decisions are made, they are based on assumptions and values that are sometimes clearly stated but more often than not are implicit in attitudes and actions.

For others, the term 'research' refers to a more rigorous and technically more complicated form of investigation. Howard and Sharp (1983) discuss this in *The Management of a Student Project*, stating:

> Most people associate the word 'research' with activities which are substantially removed from day-to-day life and which are pursued by outstandingly gifted persons with an unusual level of commitment. There is of course a good deal of truth in this viewpoint but we argue that the pursuit is not restricted to this type of person and indeed can prove to be a stimulating and satisfying experience for many people with a trained and enquiring mind.
>
> (1983: 6)

Research is often criticized negatively for being insufficiently relevant to the work of people it is intended to inform. Behind this conception of the role of research and the complaints about its failure to fulfil its role effectively, there often lies the assumption that the influence of research on practice will necessarily be beneficial, so that it is in everyone's interest to maximize that influence. Few would go as far as Macdonald in 'rejecting the concept of information misuse completely' (Macdonald, 1974: 18) but it must be acknowledged that relatively little attention has been paid to the ways in which research findings can be misused (Hammersley and Scarth, 1993). Cole (1999) shows the necessity of integrated enquiry, arguing that assessments of equality in education must recognize the importance of social class, 'race' and racism, sexuality and gender both per se and with respect to their relationship to education (1999: 63); also that such issues must be considered both conceptually and empirically (for example, Hill and Cole, 1999a) and addressed both historically and in a contemporary context (for example, Cole, 2000). Moreover, as an aspect of education provision, the issue of equality needs to be considered with respect to individual subjects of the National Curriculum of both the primary and secondary schools (Cole, Hill and Shan, 1997; Hill and Cole, 1999).

Whether valued within its own technical terms or by the relevance of its application, research is not immune from the impact of legislative changes. As the Teacher Training Agency (TTA) has taken more control of the teacher education curriculum, equality issues have been marginalized or neglected. Cole (1999) argues vehemently that it is high time to resurrect them, in a manifestly unequal society (for example, Hutton, 1995; Cole and Hill, 1999) which asserts itself in schools as much as in areas of research (Cole, Hill and Shan, 1997).

### Educational research and misuse

The function of educational research, it is widely agreed, is to inform policy-makers and practitioners and thereby to improve education. There has long been concern, however, about the impact of research on policy and practice (Hammersley and Scarth, 1993; Bassey, 1995). For too long there has been something rather uncertain about educational research, which leaves it wide open to ill-informed criticism and academic snideness (Bassey, 1995), whether it is perceived as focusing on educational process (Butcher, 1968; Nisbet and Entwistle, 1972; Simon, 1978; Ransom, 1992), on improving educational practice (Williams, 1969; Stenhouse, 1978) or as an activity conducted solely in educational settings (ESRC, 1991; Tripp, 1993).

The misuse of educational research findings was poignantly typified in February 1992. The Department for Education and Science (DES) published what was widely dubbed the report of the *Three Wise Men* (DES, 1992), partly because it was due to appear soon after Christmas. The men involved were Robin Alexander (a professor of education), Jim Rose (the Chief Primary Inspector) and Chris Woodhead (then Chief Executive of the National Curriculum Council). Instructed by Kenneth Clarke, then Secretary of State for Education, they were to review evidence about the current state of primary education and to make recommendations about school organizations and teaching for the successful implementation of the National Curriculum.

Yet there was relatively little sustained critical assessment of this report, in public at least (Hammersley and Scarth, 1993). The *Three Wise Women* report concentrated on the prospects for a fruitful debate about the educational issues raised, emphasizing the value of educational theory, and showed how the research evidence could be marshalled to very different conclusions from those of Alexander, Rose and Woodhead. While both of these critiques are very useful, neither focuses in a very specific way on the report itself (Hammersley and Scarth, 1993).

Despite the general lack of sustained research, however, the reports can be perceived as a watershed in the history of British educational policy. There were clear signs of change in the direction of policy. This was particularly evident in the development of 'Plowdenism' in key educational reports (after the Plowden Report of 1967), which were seen as representing not only the influence but the official endorsement of progressivism in primary school practice (Hammersley and Scarth, 1993). By the late 1970s, the advocates of radical Right policy were describing Plowdenism as a threat, a form of 'decline' that must be challenged, if the standards of education and society were to be protected (Cox and Dyson, 1971; Wright, 1977).

### The political role of educational research

Social research has a vital role to play in support of democracy – finding out what is happening in society, reflecting on it, evaluating it, thinking creatively about it and communicating the findings to as wide an audience as possible in order that the future can be determined by the democratic will of people, not by the autocratic will of an elite. Insofar as learning is the central activity of human beings, educational research should be at the centre of social research (Bassey, 1995).

Yet education today in the UK bears the impact of a maelstrom of change – a National Curriculum on educational policy development for ages 5 to 16 has been introduced, couched mainly in terms of a transmission theory of learning; teacher training is changing from a predominately higher education-based experience to more school-based; local education authorities are losing most of their powers – and few of these changes are based on research evidence (Bassey, 1995).

Arguably, research is reactive, in the sense that changes happen and there is a need for researchers to react, to monitor the change, analyse, evaluate, reflect and report on it. But research extends beyond this, to areas where educational researchers can be proactive. Stewart Ransom (1992), for example, argues that educational researchers should broaden their typical preoccupation with schools, teachers, children and classrooms, and embrace all members of society. At the same time we need to create a political situation where research evidence and expert opinion are wanted, welcomed and debated, so that when decisions about the future of our society are made, reason and not rhetoric is triumphant (Bassey, 1995).

## Social justice in education

There is a growing body of literature around the issue of what to understand by 'social justice' in education, now that 'equal opportunities' is no longer the kind of political and intellectual rallying cry it once was (Denzin, 1997; Griffiths, 1998; Lister, 1999; Gerwirtz, 2000). The issue itself is complex: 'social justice' may have become an accepted term but it is not well understood or agreed; 'social inclusion' is a term widely used, but ambiguous. Some of the literature on this issue focuses directly on the question of meaning (Rath, 2000), drawing on conceptual, political and historical sources. Some of it is more enigmatic, helping itself to assumptions about meanings of the term 'social justice' in order to further separate arguments about race, gender, special needs, social class, disability or sexuality (Griffiths, 1998).

Rikowski (2000) alters the focus. In this social universe, he argues, all phenomena assume particular *social forms*. Therefore the key question is not what 'social justice' means but what form it assumes in a capitalist society (Rikowski, 2000). This is a perspective that marks the limits imposed on education, yet also the prospects for creating social justice within it.

As this chapter has shown, legislation from the 1970s to 1990s accentuated the principles and objectives of the competitive market within education provision, reshaping the organization of significant aspects of education to meet the demands of capital, not children. Capital requires the social production of labour power and, in contemporary capitalist society, education and training are crucial elements (among other institutions) of this production.

Significantly, capital defines only the *formal* equality of labour powers (and labourers), so that insofar as (or wherever) education and training are concentrated on the production or enhancement of labour power, then each individual involved in the process is entitled to receive an equal share of labour time and quality of input from teachers, trainers and others involved in the process of labour production (Rikowski, 1990; 1999b). Consequently, where the education process is subordinated to the principles of the capitalist market it is subject to the formal and reductive limitations imposed by capital upon the recognition, realization and development of social equality.

Therefore the struggle for social justice in capitalist society, Rikowski argues, is one aspect of struggle for a form of life where social justice is possible. In this, struggles for equality and for labour market equality are necessarily linked to the struggle against the social force that oppresses us all: capital. There are not two separate struggles, one against inequalities within capitalism and one against capitalism itself, as a social force flowing through social relations (Rikowski, 1999a). Social justice remains 'a latent social form within capitalist society that cannot attain real existence' (Rikowski, 2000: 5). The struggle for social justice in capitalist society, therefore, is part of the attempt to ground principles of social life on a rational basis, to make the virtuality of social justice *real*. In doing so, 'we start to put the social universe of capital at risk, its fragility is exposed' (Holloway, 1995: 3).

The overview of educational research in the second part of this chapter identified the main areas of research and principles of application. Contemporary education professionals are identifying significant and discriminatory changes in education provision. If research that investigates issues of social justice in education is conducted on a merely reactive basis, then it will at least contribute to scrutiny of the processes of these changes.

If researchers are ready to be flexible and committed to improvement – to adopt the research methods appropriate to a given situation (see Adelman, Jenkins and Kemmis, 1980; Bell, 1993) and concentrate on the relation of capitalism to social equality – then the impact of research will be significant indeed, for developing equality in educational policy and practice and in contemporary society.

## References

Adelman, C, Jenkins, D and Kemmis, S (1980) Rethinking case study: notes from the second Cambridge Conference, in *Towards a Science of the Singular*, ed H Simons, University of East Anglia, Norwich

Advisory Centre for Education (ACE) (1992) *Exclusions*, ACE, London

ACE (1993) Chickens coming home, *Bulletin* **51** (January–February), ACE, London

Allen, A (1999) A curriculum for 2000, *Education And Social Justice*, **2** (1), pp 28–31

Arnot, M (1989) Consultation or legitimisation? Race and gender, the making of the national curriculum, *Critical Social Policy*, **27** (3), pp 40–52

Bagley, C (1972) Racialism and pluralism: a dimensional analysis of 48 countries, *Race*, **13** (2), pp 38–50

Ball, S (1993) Education policy, power relations and teachers' work, *British Journal of Educational Studies*, **41** (2), pp 2–6

Bassey, M (1981) Pedagogic research: on the relative merits of search for generalisation and study of single events, *Oxford Review of Education*, **7** (1), pp 73–94

Bassey, M (1995) *Creating Education Through Research: A global perspective of educational research for the 21st century*, Kirklington Newark, Newark

Bayliss, V (1999) *Opening Minds*, Royal Society of Arts, London

Bell, J (1993) Doing your research project: a guide for first-time researchers in education and social science, in *Education And Social Science*, 1st edn, Open University Press, Buckingham

Bernstein, B (1971) *Class, Codes And Control*, 1, Routledge & Kegan Paul, London

Berry, J (1979) Research in multi-cultural societies: implications of cross-cultural methods, *Journal of Cross-Cultural Psychology*, **10** (3), pp 40–62

Blair, M (1994) Black teachers, black students and education markets, *Cambridge Journal of Education*, **24** (2), pp 20–32

Blair, M and Cole, M (2000) Racism and education: the imperial legacy, in *Human Rights, Education and Equality*, ed M Cole, Falmer Press, London

Blyth, E and Milner, J (1996) *Exclusions from School: Inter-professional issues for policy and practice*, Routledge, London

Bowes, S, Gintis, H and Gold, A (1992) *Reforming Education and Changing Schools*, Routledge, London

Bryman, A (1988) *Quantity And Quality In Social Research*, Unwin Hyman, London

Burton, L and Weiner, G (1990) Social justice and the National Curriculum, *Research Papers In Education* **5** (3), pp 12–15

Butcher, H J (1968) *Educational Research in Britain*, University of London Press, London

Cicourel, A (1964) *Methods And Measurement In Sociology*, The Free Press, New York

Cohen, L and Manum, L (1989) *Research Methods in Education*, 3rd edn, Routledge, London

Cohen, R *et al* (1994) *School's Out: The family perspective on school exclusion*, The Barnardos and Family Service Units, London

Cole, M (1999a) Professional issues and initial teacher education: what can be done and what should be done, *Educational Social Justice*, **2** (1), pp 63–66

Cole, M (1999b) *Time to Liberate the Mind: Primary schools in the new century*, Cassell, London

Cole, M and Hill, D (1999) Equality and secondary education: what are the conceptual issues, in *Promoting Equality in Secondary Schools*, eds D Hill and M Cole, Cassell, London

Cole, M, Hill, D and Shan, S (1997) *Promoting Equality in Primary Schools*, Cassell, London

Cope, E and Gray, J (1979) Teachers as researchers: some experiences of an alternative paradigm, *British Educational Research Journal*, **5** (2)

Cox, B and Dyson, A E (1971) *The Black Papers on Education*, revised edn, Davis-Poynter Ltd, London

Craft, M (1984) *Education and Cultural Pluralism*, Falmer Press, London

Davies, A, Holland, J and Minhas, R (1990) *Equal Opportunities in the New Era*, Hillcole Group, London

Denzin, N (1997) *Interpretive Ethnography: Ethnographic practices for the 21st century*, Sage, London

Department for Cultural Studies (DCS) University of Birmingham (1981) *Unpopular Education: Schooling and Social Democracy in England since 1944*, Hutchinson, London

DCS (1991) *Education, Limited Schooling and the New Right Since 1979*, Unwin Hyman, London

DES (1992) *Education in Social Services Establishments: a report by (HMI 4/92/NS)*, DES, London

DfEE (1995) Press release: *Discipline at the Heart of Schools* – Standard Drive, Shephard, DfEE, London

Dorn, A and Hibbert, P (1987) A comedy of errors: section 11 funding and education, in *Racial Inequality in Education*, ed B Troyna, Tavistock Publications, London

Economic and Social Research Council (ESRC) (1991) *Postgraduate Training Guidelines*, ESRC, Swindon

Filmer, P *et al* (1972) *New Directions In Sociological Theory*, Collier Macmillan, London

Gerwitz, S (2000) Social justice, New Labour and school reform, in *Rethinking Social Policy*, eds G Lewis, S Gerwitz and J Clarke, Cassell, London

Gilborn, D (2000) *Educational Inequalities in Mapping Race, Class and Gender*, Ofsted, London

Griffiths, M (1998) *Educational Research For Social Justice: Getting off the fence*, Open University Press, Buckingham

Hammersley, M and Scarth, J (1993) Beware of wise men bearing gifts: a case study in the misuse of educational research, in *Educational Research In Action*, eds W Gomm and P Woods, Open University Press, London

Hayden, C (1997) *Children Excluded From Primary School: Debates, evidence, responses*, Open University Press, Buckingham

Her Majesty's Inspectorate of Schools (HMI) (1978) *Behavioural Units*, Department of Education and Science, London

Hillcole Group (1991) *Changing the Future*, Tufnell Press, London

Hillcole Group (1997) *Rethinking Education and Democracy*, Tuffnell Press, London

Holloway, J (1995) From scream of refusal to cream of power: the centrality of work, in *Emancipating Marxism*, vol. 3, *Open Marxism*, ed G Bonefield *et al*, Pluto Press, London

Howard, K and Sharp, J (1983) *The Management Of A Student Research Project*, Gower Publishing, Aldershot

Hutton, W (1995) *The State We're In*, Johnathan Cape, London

Jeffcoate, R (1984) *Ethnic Minorities and Education*, Harper & Row, London

Lister, R (1999) Work for those who can, security for those who cannot: a third way in social security reform? Paper given at Social Policy Association Annual Conference, Roehampton Institute London, 20–22 July

Lawton, D (1975) *Class, Culture and the Curriculum*, Open University Press, Milton Keynes

Lawton, D and Dufour, B (1973) *The New Social Studies*, Heinemann, London

Le Grand, J and Bartlett, W (1993) *Quasi-Markets and Social Policy*, Macmillan, Basingstoke

Lijphart, A (1977) *Democracy In Plural Societies: A comparative exploration*, Yale University Press, New Haven, CT

Lloyd-Bennett, P (1993) Stockpiling the unsaleable goods, *Education*, **3** (2), pp 34–45

Mabey, C (1986) Black pupils achievements in inner London, *Educational Research*, **28** (3), pp 10–13

Macdonald, B (1974) Evaluation and the control of education, in *SAFARI Innovation, Evaluation, Research and the Problem of Control*, eds B Macdonald and R Walker, University of East Anglia, Norwich

McNeil, P (1990) *Research Methods*, 2nd edn, Routledge, London and New York

McVicar, M (1991) Education policy: education as a business? *Public Policy Under Thatcher*, eds S Savage and L Robins, Macmillian Education, Basingstoke

Milner, D (1975) *Children and Race*, Penguin Books, Harmondsworth

National Commission on Education (NCE) (1995) *Standards in Literacy and Numeracy, 1948–1994*, NCE Briefing at NCE, London

National Union of Teachers (1990) *A Strategy for the Curriculum*

Nisbet, J D and Entwistle, N (1972) *Educational Research Methods*, Hodder & Stoughton, London

Parekh, B (1989) The hermeneutics of the Swann Report, in *Education For All: A landmark in pluralism*, ed G Verma, The Falmer Press, London

Peagram, E (1991) Swings and roundabouts: aspects of statementing and provision for children with emotional and behavioural difficulties, *Maladjusted and Therapeutic Education*, **9** (3), pp 4–15

Peters, R and White, J (1969) The philosophers' contribution to educational research, in *Research Perspectives In Education*, ed W Taylor, Routledge & Kegan Paul, London

Pumfrey, P (1983) *Educational Attainments Issues and Outcomes in Multi-Cultural Education*, The Falmer Press, London

Pyke, N (1991) Excluded pupils who vanish, *Times Educational Supplement*, 26 June

Ransom, S (1992) *The Management and Organisation of Educational Research*, ESRC, Swindon

Rath, J (2000) Bounding social justice? Paper given at Approaching Social Justice in Education: Theoretical Frameworks For Practical Purposes Seminar, Nottingham Trent University

Rikowski, G (1990) *The Recruitment Process and Labour Power*, Epping Forest College, Essex, unpublished paper, Division of Humanities and Modern Languages, Epping Forest College, Loughton, Essex

Rikowski, H (1999a) Nietzsche, Marx and mastery: the learning unto death, in *Apprenticeship: Toward a new paradigm of learning*, eds P Ainley and H Rainbird, Kogan Page, London

Rikowski, G (1999b) Education, capital and the transhuman, in *Postmodernism In Educational Theory: Education and the politics of human resistance*, eds D Hill *et al*, Tufnell Press, London

Rikowski, G (2000) Education and social justice within the social universe of capital. Paper given at Approaching Social Justice in Education: Theoretical Frameworks For Practical Purposes Seminar, Nottingham Trent University

Robinson, P (1999) Presentation to NUT national education conference, July

Seitz, V (1977) *Social Class and Ethnic Group Differences in Learning to Read*, New Jersey International Reading Association, Newark, NJ

Simon, H ed (1980) *Towards A Science Of The Singular*, University of East Anglia, Norwich

Stenhouse, L (1978) Case study and case records: towards a contemporary history of education, in *British Educational Research Journal*, **4** (2), pp 21–39

Stirling, M (1991) The exclusion zone managing schools, *Today*, **1** (3), pp 23–30

Stone, M (1981) *The Education Of The Black Child In Britain: The myth of multicultural education*, Fontana, Glasgow

Townsend, H and Brittain, E M (1972) *Organisation in Multi-cultural Schools*, NFER, Slough

Tripp, D (1993) *Critical Incidents in Teaching*, Routledge, London

Tyler, W (1977) *The Sociology of Educational Inequality*, Methuen, London

Veljanovoski, C (1990) Foreword, in *A Market Socialism: A sanctuary of the 'Square Circle'*, ed A De Jaysay, Croom Helm, London

Verma, G K (1989) *Education For All: A landmark in pluralism*, Falmer Press, London

Verma, G K and Mallick, K (1999) *Researching Education Perspectives and Techniques*, Falmer Press, London

Walford, G (1991) *Doing Educational Research*, Routledge, London

Wilkinson, H (1999) The case of the eternal student, in *Times Educational Supplement*, 25 June

Williams, J (1967) The younger generation, in *Race, Community And Conflict*, eds J Rex and Moore, Institute of Race in Research and Theory, London

Williams, J (1969) Educational research, in *Blond's Encyclopaedia of Education*, Blond Educational, London

Wright (1976) How much interference? *Times Educational Supplement*, 14 May

Zec, P (1980) Multi-cultural education: what kind of relativism is possible? *Journal of Philosophy of Education*, **14** (1), pp 30–45

Zec, P (1993) Dealing with racist incidents in schools, in *Education for Cultural Diversity: The challenge for a new era*, eds A Fyfe and P Figueroa, Routledge, London

4

# Excluded voices: educational exclusion and inclusion

## Leena Helavaara Robertson and Rachel Hill

## Editors' introduction

*In this chapter, Leena Helevaara Robertson and Rachel Hill consider the inequalities suffered by 'the excluded' within the education system. The chapter refers to two small-scale research projects that listen to the voices of the excluded. These voices, white working-class teenagers in north-east England and from Pahari/Mirpuri-speaking early years children in Watford are located within their broader family, cultural and policy contexts. The chapter identifies different types of exclusion – from physical exclusion from school, to self-exclusion from school, to wider social exclusion, and the links between them. It draws distinctions between the more inclusive early years curriculum in England and Wales and the more exclusive 5–16 National Curriculum and comments critically on the literacy hour in schools. The chapter calls for inclusive education to be embedded in practice and pedagogy at all levels.*

## Introduction

This chapter explores exclusions from school. The term 'exclusion' is the official term used to refer to the expulsion (permanent) or suspension (fixed-term) of a child from school, but here we will also use it to discuss how some children's learning experiences, their prior knowledge and understanding contribute to their exclusion from school – from the hidden curriculum and the more formal curriculum itself. This is perhaps the most sinister of all types of exclusions. It starts early in young children's school lives, and it is highly likely that this type of invisible exclusion results in varying degrees of disinterest, disaffection, truancy and exclusion from school later on.

The effects of being excluded on children themselves, their families, schools and society at large, are serious and long-term. In this chapter we provide, first, an overview of main concepts and facts, the tip of the iceberg. We then use two very different qualitative research projects to look beneath the surface to highlight two important aspects.

Firstly, we want to emphasize that it is crucial to listen to the excluded children themselves to explore their perspectives of the exclusion process. Children's voices must be heard in attempts to identify those characteristics that make some children more 'at risk' of exclusion than others. And once back at school, the children's reflection on being excluded provides valuable insights. Overwhelmingly, the children in our study thought that exclusions do not work for everyone. Three major sets of feelings were identified: anger at being excluded ('I felt like hitting him again'); remorse ('I found out later it was a big mistake, I felt horrible, dead guilty, I'd gone too far'); and concern about telling parents ('me real dad was contacted and he wasn't very happy'). In fact parents were seen as playing a crucial role in the effectiveness of exclusions.

Secondly, there is a need to contrast exclusion with inclusion. We discuss how the new National Curriculum 2000 and new the Foundation Stage Curriculum promote inclusion. We also examine literacy legislation and use young bilingual children's experiences during their reception year and during their literacy hours to ask how exclusive/inclusive is a 'typical' literacy hour?

## Exclusion: concepts and facts

The term 'social exclusion' has generally been used to refer to long-term unemployment and 'modern poverty', which have resulted in groups of people being excluded from participating in institutional, social, cultural and political associations (Walraven, 2000: 13). Educational exclusion, on the other hand, is best understood as consisting of three distinctively different types:

- Formal exclusion from school – permanent or fixed-term.
- 'Self-exclusion' – truancy or school phobia.
- Subtle, 'invisible' ways in which some children and groups are excluded, for example through the formal and hidden curriculum.

## Formal and 'self-exclusion' from school

The first two (formal exclusion and 'self-exclusion') are clearly defined and it is relatively easy to obtain quantitative evidence for both school- and pupil-driven exclusion. Within both primary and secondary schools, these two types show increasing trends throughout the 1990s (NUT, 1992; Ofsted, 1993; SEU, 1998; Parsons, 1999). There is overwhelming evidence that more children are permanently excluded from schools in England; English schools are 10 times more likely to exclude a child than schools in Northern Ireland and four times more than schools in Scotland (Parsons, 1999; Wertheimer, 1999). In 1990/1 the total number of permanent exclusions from schools were 2,910 and by 1997/8 this number had risen to 13,041 (Parsons, 1999:22). In 1998/9 exclusions fell sharply, due to increased governmental emphasis, and the proportionally greatest fall was among children from minority ethnic groups (www.jrf.org.uk).

The Labour government's concern regarding exclusions takes into account the strong link between exclusions from school and subsequent criminal offending. For example the Audit Commission (1996) found that 42 per cent of young criminal offenders had been excluded from school. Consequently government targets aim to ensure that all excluded pupils receive alternative, full-time equivalent tuition by 2002. The Audit Commission (TES, 2001a) figures suggest, however, that in 1999/2000 only 9 per cent of excluded pupils received the target of more than 20 hours of education a week, and that the alternative provision was very patchy between different LEAs.

On a wider policy level there is a paradoxical contradiction between New Labour's inclusive 'one-nation rhetoric' and their moral authoritarian two-nation exclusive rhetoric. One-nation rhetoric includes the whole of society as deserving protection, encouragement and support in times of need. In contrast, two-nation rhetoric excludes rather than includes particular groups in society. Examples are the attacks on those who do not get jobs, on single-parent inner city teenage mothers, on asylum seekers, on 'squeegee merchants', on the homeless. Those who won't – or can't – climb out of their poverty are stigmatized as 'the undeserving poor', who have excluded themselves from 'the one (deserving) nation'. Hence this can be termed 'two-nation' rhetoric (see Hill, 2001:36).

There is also a second paradox here. While, on the one hand there is some socially inclusive, 'one-nation' rhetoric and policy (such as targeting extra funds at schools in deprived urban areas and instituting the national minimum wage), on the other hand, New Labour is pursuing various neo-liberal policies (see Chapters 1, 2 and 7 of this volume). These policies, such as deregulated labour markets (minimal protection for some groups of workers) and the competitive market in schools, serve to increase inequalities in society and between schools. This exacerbates the situation of the poorest sections of society, the 'socially excluded'. The poor are increasingly forced into poor schools and subsequently into the low wage, temporary contract and alternative economies.

The correlation between social and educational exclusion is well established. The more specific causes leading to exclusion, as with underachievement (see

Chapter 5) fall in three categories: socio-economic and cultural factors, institutional factors and individual factors (Parsons, 1999). This overall rise of exclusion, however, cannot be divorced from the 1988 Education Reform Act (ERA). It is not possible to discuss here whether or not exclusions are an 'innocent' by-product of increased marketization of education (but see Chapters 1, 2 and 3). League tables of school performance, however, do force schools to measure selected areas of the curriculum and concentrate on performance, which sits rather uncomfortably with underachieving pupils. The links with performance, league tables and assessment-driven education system as a whole, and exclusion of those pupils who disrupt lessons, demand a disproportionate amount of teacher time, perform badly in tests and examinations and who have very different needs, are clear (see Richard Rose's Chapter 12 in this volume, and Wright, Weeks and McGlanghlin, 2000). This increase in exclusion figures is a direct consequence of the ERA.

As with formal school-driven exclusions, the causes of disaffection, disruption and truancy are linked with socioeconomic and cultural factors, institutional factors and individual factors. The levels of 'self-exclusion' or truancy increase as children transfer from primary to secondary school peaking in Years 10 and 11 (Parsons, 1999; Hallam, 1997). Over one million children truant (SEU, 1998) but much more qualitative research is needed to establish the more specific causes leading to truancy and what schools can do about it. Many studies locate the problem with the children and their families or as part of youth culture (Parsons, 1999). Yet, the problem is clearly wider and the children's perceptions and experiences are crucial in beginning to find solutions.

That there is an increase in the number of exclusions is not in dispute. Many factors are identified in research literature that place a child or young person at a greater risk of exclusion (age, gender, 'race', ethnicity, 'in local authority care, poverty and having special educational needs (SEN)). The reasons behind the rise and more importantly what can be done are under debate. On a positive note, most research (Ofsted, 1996; Blyth and Milner, 1996; Lloyd-Smith and Dwyfor Davies, 1995) suggests that although certain children are predisposed (through no fault of their own) to being excluded, schools can and frequently do make a difference. School management style is often cited as a key factor (Wright, Weeks and McGlaughlin, 2000; Mitchell, 1996). The head teacher's philosophy is crucial in making difficult decisions regarding protecting the rights of the disaffected, often violent minority and of those of the well-behaved majority.

The consequence of exclusion, however, can often be to exacerbate an already fragile and vulnerable situation for the child and may, indeed, hasten the involvement of social services (Hayden, 1997). Problems may be compounded by destabilizing what may be the only predictable and stable components of a child's life. The long- and short-term economic, social, educational and psychological impact on families of having an excluded child at home all day cannot be ignored – aggravating financial problems, increasing family tension, having to catch up on missed work. . .

Schools have not found an effective way to deal with excluding children. Sometimes exclusion works as a deterrent or shock tactic, but more often than not it is used as a reprieve for the school, with little or no reintegration package. It is therefore important to establish when and how exclusions work well, and to question whether this is due to the quality of the reintegration packages as much as the act of exclusion. There have been frequent calls for greater inclusion of children's views in recent legislation and literature. Studies that have attempted to get into the world of excluded child are few and far between. Those that have, tend to focus on permanently excluded pupils, interviewing them about their differing experiences of schooling in pupil referral units (PRUs) compared with mainstream schools. The main themes to emerge from these studies (John, 1996) are the children's dissatisfaction with mainstream schools, in particular the respect with which teachers relate to them, and the low self-esteem the majority of these children have. Solutions need to begin by addressing these issues to make any impact on emotional, social and behavioural difficulties.

## Exclusion through formal and hidden curriculum

This third type of exclusion, the more 'subtle', invisible exclusion is more problematic, and quantitative evidence for this is more difficult to obtain. Much has been written about the hidden, discriminatory factors in school and education system as a whole. (See Chapter 5, which analyses how the subject and the hidden curriculum serve to exclude particular social types/groups of children and to reproduce and confirm inequalities in education and society.) Governments have, at various times, initiated large-scale projects and reports to establish facts and ways forward (for example DES, 1981; DES 1985; Ofsted, 1993, 1999.) Gillborn and Gipps (1996) and Gillborn and Mirza (2000) have shown that 'race', class and gender are still factors in educational achievement. Pupils who live in the most economically deprived areas do less well in public examinations and league tables. Multicultural and anti-racist education have been another attempt to address these issues (see for example Rattansi, 1992; Cole, 1997, 1999). In Chapter 8 of this volume the authors draw attention to and discuss The Swann report (DES; 1985), The Stephen Lawrence Inquiry report (Macpherson, 1999) and the Commission on the Future of Multi-Ethnic Britain (2000) (The Parekh report) (see also Parekh, 2000) and summarize their recommendations designed to combat the educational exclusion suffered by many minority groups.

# Excluded voices

This section is based on a small qualitative study (Hill, 1998) that explores the child's perspective of the exclusion process in an attempt to identify those characteristics that make some children more 'at risk' of exclusion than others. The focus is on the experiences of 12 secondary school pupils in an average-sized, mixed 11–16 comprehensive school in a town in the north of England. The town itself has suffered from the effects of economic decline, especially of the coal and steel industries. Job prospects are not promising and unemployment is high. These Year 8 and 9 pupils all experienced at least one fixed-term exclusion. Their views, experiences and perceptions were gathered through semi-structured interviews by a researcher who was well known to the children as an empathetic former teacher. Quantitative data were also gathered about all 23 children from Years 8 and 9 who had experienced a fixed-term exclusion.

## At-risk factors

Poverty was one of the key indicators in the findings and can be seen in the context of child poverty having tripled since 1979 (Brodie, 1998). The free school meals average for the excluded sample was more than double that of the whole school population. Having Special Educational Needs also emerged as an equally strong 'at risk' factor with 57 per cent of excluded children having SEN, compared with 20 per cent of the overall school population. The evidence supports previous findings that boys are likely to be excluded (Parsons, 1999). In a sample, 78 per cent were male, compared to 51 per cent of the total school population. Race did not emerge as an 'at-risk' factor, the total excluded sample being white. However, given that only 0.2 per cent of the school population was black, this is not surprising.

The average reading age on entry to secondary school for the excluded sample was two-and-a-half to three years behind their chronological age. While average CAT (Cognitive Ability Tests) scores for the school reveal that the school population in general is slightly lower than average, there is significant evidence that children with learning difficulties, especially with literacy, are more 'at risk' of exclusion'. Typical explanations for the difficulties included, 'It's hard to learn because I'm in all the bottom sets and everyone is naughty and I can't concentrate', and 'When teachers write on the board and I can't read it 'cause it's all scribbly 'n that [sic]'. Not surprisingly, then, the children's enjoyment of subjects at school was primarily determined by the amount of writing involved.

## The exclusion process

It was abundantly clear that many of the exclusions were triggered by external events that manifested themselves in school. A quarter of the children directly attributed their difficulties in school to home events: 'It was the time when I'd lost my sister. . . I hadn't got over it. . . I had it all bottled up inside. . . I felt cheated, like punching something.' The results showed that, out of the sample of 12 children, at least 11 had experienced a series of stressful life events ranging from parental separation (75 per cent), and bereavement (25 per cent) to domestic violence, substance abuse, parental prostitution, illness and rape. The impact of these events cannot be underestimated. An understanding to the background of these difficulties leads to serious questions about whether exclusion is a realistic solution to some of these problems.

By far the majority of the exclusions were for violence to other children (8/12). Other reasons included verbal abuse to staff; disruption; 'hoying' (local slang for throwing) a seat of the bus; 'setting a fire alarm off'; and 'bringing an empty cannabis pipe into school'. One child had been excluded for a variety of misdemeanours including 'pulling a moony at the golf club'; 'hiding a porno mag up my sleeve'; 'chucking bangers'; and 'hiding an egg in my pocket'.

Almost all of the children (10/12) were grounded for the duration of the exclusion, with a third using the time to do homework. Only one child mentioned being allowed out of the house: 'I went down the river fishing.'

Once back at school, 9 out of the 12 children believed that there had been an improvement since their return in terms of work and/or attitude. Two felt there had been no improvement due to a lack of monitoring by school staff. Post-exclusion monitoring cards were rated positively because they identified specific targets to work towards and gave permission for the children to behave. Comments such as 'the cards help you concentrate' were typical. Those children who were not put on a card felt the school wasn't taking the situation seriously enough and had subsequently asked to be 'put on a card'. Behaviour contracts conversely gained little respect, more often that not because of the lack of follow-up it received. One child saw this as something that did not really have a direct impact on his behaviour, saying 'I had to sign a contract to tell the governors that I'm back in school', and another said he had signed 'about seven'. Praise, not surprisingly, was an important factor in keeping the children on track. One particular boy commented that it is 'nice to be told by (deputy head) when I'm doing well'.

Children's perceptions of what had made a positive difference following an exclusion were variable. While the improvement was partly attributed to the monitoring by the head of year and deputy heads, 10 out of 12 mentioned the role of their friends in the exclusion process. At least half the children said their friends had been fully involved, mostly 'egging on' and 'winding up' situations. On child was fully aware of the impact of his classmates: 'They dare us and call us chicken, I hate being called chicken'. Others mentioned the support they received when they returned to school: 'Sometimes it's me friends that help us get on with me work more than teachers. . . when I talk, P (friend) just tells us to "pack it in", I don't realize it half the times 'cause he tells us'. But emphasis was also placed on how important trust, courtesy and respect were: 'Teachers talk to you in school and outside of school' and staff who, 'even if you've got a bad name, [recognize] that doesn't mean it was you'. The children categorized the type of person for whom exclusions would not work as, 'an idiot, he just reckons he's hard'.

## Children's interpretations and understanding

Questions related to the perceived justice of the exclusion raised some interesting and surprising issues. Children frequently felt uninformed about the exclusion process and the consequences for others involved, often mistakenly believing that others had got away without punishment. The majority (9/12) had expected to be excluded, but in many circumstances (5/12) the children felt wronged because they did not know what punishment the other child had received, many making comments such as 'it wasn't fair just me getting the blame'. It was clearly important for the children to know the fate of the other parties involved and this did not always happen. Had this been the case, it might have taken away some of the anger and confusion that some of the children felt and in some cases may have increased their confidence in the school system.

Many children gave intrinsic reasons for wanting to remain in school. These varied from, 'making you look bad when you come to get a job' and 'I wouldn't want to be excluded again, especially with it being twice, I'd get a bad reputation'. Others mentioned the effect on their families and the upset caused their parents: 'Me real dad was contacted and he wasn't very happy.' Some of the most effective turnarounds in behaviour were due to financial incentives. One child was promised £20 a week if she behaved. Another said, 'I play football now, and me mum said if I didn't get chucked out from now until the end of school, I'll think about getting you a season ticket'. However, two thought it was likely that they would be excluded again; one having a fairly fatalistic view about the situation commenting, 'definitely, at least four times', and the other a little more realistically saying, 'not for the next two months'.

Discussion of punishment as a form of reprisal revealed that, on the whole, children did not think that exclusion worked when it was purely used as a punishment. However, the children themselves saw parents' role in the exclusion process as crucial. Comments such as 'if their parents are more bothered, not for those people whose parents can't be bothered and don't deal with it' and 'it depends how sensible you are and what your parents did' were typical. Acceptance of responsibility for their actions was evident in many cases where there had been discussions with school staff and there was parental back-up of the school. Where they accepted no blame or responsibility, this tended to reflect their parents' views. For those whose parents condoned their actions, they were less likely to own the responsibility or accept any fault. It seems that parental values are the most important factor in attributing blame and accepting responsibility.

The values of parents were clearly sometimes working against the school ethos. In these situations we may be blaming the child for the values of their family. The most significant things that made reintegration effective was when the child felt important enough through effective monitoring and support from both school and parents. The power of parental input cannot be underestimated.

Children's understanding of the reasons behind being excluded supported the research by Kinder et al (1997) in which exclusions tend to be categorized as removal, reprisal or remedy:

- Two-thirds of the sample mentioned punishment, 'so that you can't do anything wrong again' and a quarter linked this to parental involvement, 'to make their mams hit them' or 'so you get wrong off your parents'.
- One-third mentioned work-related issues, 'so you get behind with your work, so you have to work harder to catch up and not get into trouble',

which contrasted with being given time to 'catch up with your work'.
- A further quarter thought that exclusion served as a warning to themselves and others, 'to let them know it's not allowed' and 'so no one else will get away with it'.
- Other comments included, 'to try and give other people a better education'; 'to try and make them [the school] look good'; 'to try and keep them away from the teacher or pupils that they had disagreements with'; and 'so they can think what to do when you come back'.

There was an overwhelming consensus that exclusions do not work for everyone and that the difference was whether parents were supportive or not. Parental involvement was seen as far more important that the school's role.

The study highlights the importance of having an effective reintegration process, which clearly monitors children following a fixed-term exclusion, listens to children and involves them in their own target setting within a supportive school ethos. Where efforts by staff were not seen as having a high priority, the effect was negligible and often damaging in that the child felt undervalued. Specific, realistic and frequent feedback about progress was valued. The importance of schools working in partnership with parents to both identify children who are 'at risk' of exclusion, and also to support them back into school is crucial. While senior school staff were aware of the vast majority of difficult situations the children faced, they were clearly not aware of them all and may have handled the situations differently with increased knowledge. The only way to ensure 'at risk' children are supported, is to create an ethos where parents recognize the importance of, want to, and do inform schools if circumstances have changed at home or of incidents or issues that might be affecting their child. Given the familiar repetitive cycles within families of negative associations, experiences and attitudes towards schools and schooling, this is no easy task.

## Inclusion and young bilingual children

In the light of the excluded children's experiences it is particularly important to focus on inclusion, partnerships with parents and on how schools attempt to meet children's needs. In recent years state schools and teachers have adapted to many government-driven changes. One of the major changes since ERA has been the centralization of control of school curriculum. As in the United States (Hoffman, 2000), in England and Wales the primary literacy instruction and curriculum for Years 1–6 (for 5–11-year-old children) have become increasingly prescriptive in nature (Dadds, 1999; Martin, 1999). The model of literacy instruction – soon to be replicated in Year 7 (12-year-olds) – seems to have had an impact on other curriculum areas in terms of structure and method of teaching. There are signs that as this tight control in literacy instruction gathers pace, other areas of learning (social and emotional, for example) and other learning styles are reduced in significance. The amount of writing involved in all subjects is increasing. This presents serious dilemmas for schools and teachers who deal with pupils with emotional and behavioural difficulties.

It is, therefore, important to consider how the current curriculum framework relates to children 'at risk'. One such group in danger of underachievement is that of Pakistani pupils. Their performance 'in the early years of schooling remains depressed' (Ofsted, 1999: 7), and although they often catch up later, their overall attainment at GCSE level remains problematic (see Chapter 8).

## National Curriculum and inclusion

The new National Curriculum 2000 (DfEE, 1999a) demonstrates a recognition and acceptance that, despite the earlier attempts (DFE, 1995) to provide and deliver a national, broad, balanced and relevant curriculum for all, this cannot be achieved without responding to diverse range of individual pupils and groups of pupils and their different learning needs, and without overcoming potential barriers to education. This new document, implemented since September 2000, has a specific section on inclusion, and its location before all the other subject programmes of study demonstrates an official, worthwhile concern for exclusion and inclusion:

> When planning teachers should set high expectations and provide opportunities for all pupils to achieve, including boys and girls, pupils with special educational needs, pupils with disabilities, pupils from all social and cultural backgrounds, pupils of different ethnic groups including travellers, refugees and asylum seekers, and those from diverse linguistic backgrounds. *Teachers need to be aware that pupils bring to school different experiences, interests and strengths which will influence the way in which they learn.*
>
> (DfEE 1999a: 31, our italics)

The National Curriculum sets out its three principles for inclusion:

- Setting suitable learning challenges.
- Responding to pupils' diverse learning needs.
- Overcoming potential barriers to learning and assessment for individual pupils and groups of pupils.

The document expands on each one of the principles and provides examples, and yet they remain problematic. The actual programmes of study for different subjects (from English to PE) map out the specific areas of knowledge, skills and understanding which are to be *taught*. The main focus throughout the programmes of study is on teaching rather than learning, which sits rather uncomfortably with the acceptance that 'pupils bring to school different experiences, interests and strengths which will influence the way in which they learn' as stated in the previous quotation. Furthermore the specific areas selected for knowledge, skills and understanding are presented as neutral – detailed but 'obvious', 'natural' 'common sense' – whereas any selection is ideologically located. In the English programme of study, for example, other languages or scripts do not receive a mention, not even a footnote, even though an example from the inclusion section recommends 'using home or first language, where appropriate' (DfEE 1999a: 37). The programmes of study and their different attainment targets remain exclusivist and separate from the main principles for inclusion.

When schools have a tight focus on performance and are attempting to meet school, LEA and national targets (those for literacy, for example, which will be discussed later) there are tensions between providing suitable learning challenges in terms of responding to pupils' diverse learning needs and raising academic standards in literacy and numeracy. Many learning needs are not measurable; there are no national targets for pupils gaining high self-esteem, and teachers and practitioners may not agree what constitutes 'diverse' learning needs. What does 'using a home language where appropriate' really mean? Does it mean that the incidental use of home languages is to be tolerated until some basic fluency in English is achieved or could home languages be used every day and in every lesson to develop an inclusive curriculum *and* raise standards in English further?

The research on American bilingual education demonstrates that pupils in two-way bilingual programmes (using two languages consistently) achieved higher standards in English (end of secondary schools) than the national average (Thomas and Collier, 1997). While in England there are no bilingual state pro-grammes, some brave schools seem to be achieving similar results: a Birmingham primary school, Regents Park, has raised its English Key Stage 2 results (percent-age of pupils achieving Level 4 in year 6) from 36 per cent in 1997 to 87 per cent in 2000 by having a clear whole-school policy on using home languages as much as possible in all lessons (TES, 2001b). Not everything should depend on test and examination results. But it is highly likely that this type of open inclusion – responding and attempting to recognize pupils' learning needs, building actively and consistently on their interests and strengths – not only raises academic standards but also reduces disaffection.

In the next section we will examine inclusion within the context of early years education and care. The provision of high-quality, inclusive early years education is generally accepted as crucially important for children's later educational success (it is also internationally accepted as a significant factor in raising standards in education), but above all, it is important for the young children themselves, for what they *are* – here and now, today, this year – and not just for what they will *become* in later life.

## Inclusion and early years

It is interesting to contrast the above National Curriculum principles with the Foundation Stage Curriculum (DfEE, 1999b, 2000), which provides the framework for education and care for children between three and five years of age. It is not divided into subjects but six broad areas of learning: personal, social and emotional; communication, language and literacy; mathematical; knowledge and understanding of the world; physical; and creative (DfEE, 1999b). It brings together a number of settings (reception classes, nursery schools, playgroups, childminders, after-school clubs) and the partnership between practitioners and parents, including carers and other people like grandparents who play a primary role in young children's care, which is one of the main principles of Foundation Stage.

Given the general need to work closely with all parents – and especially with parents whose children have been formally excluded from school or who are 'at risk' – it is surprising that this partnership does not permeate the principles of inclusion in the National Curriculum 2000 (DfEE, 1999a). The excluded children in our study were unequivocal regarding the role of parents in serious school matters. Furthermore, developing partnerships between parents and practitioners and teachers is potentially powerful in developing an inclusive curriculum. It is difficult to see how teachers might become aware of pupils' prior experiences, interests and strengths without the involvement of parents (see Kenner, 2000, for a case study on parental involvement and early literacy). Similarly, while the National Curriculum acknowledges per se that children's prior experiences influence the ways in which they learn, the Curriculum Guidance for the Foundation Stage states very explicitly that 'Early Years experience should build on what children know and can do' (DfEE, 2000:11). In essence its approach to inclusion can be viewed as more inclusive than that of the National Curriculum. It is highly likely that it is crucial to build on prior experiences when beginning to respond to pupils' learning needs.

Early years practitioners are, therefore, particularly well placed in leading other professionals to develop new ways of building on all children's prior learning and in developing an inclusive curriculum. The practitioners have the possibility to discover with parents and families the knowledge and understanding young children bring from their homes *and* communities. The term 'community' is currently missing from the National Curriculum (DfEE, 1999a) – its focus is on society at large and on citizenship, though this can be seen to include communities. In order to develop an inclusive curriculum it is important to locate parents and families within communities as these have established traditions, practices, values and beliefs, which in return influence the ways in which children's learn. This is particularly pertinent in terms of literacy.

## Literacy hour, inclusion and bilingual children

Learning difficulties, especially with literacy, are key signifiers of school success and there is a correlation between children with low levels of literacy and those likely to be 'at risk' of exclusion. This section seeks to explore how the National Literacy Strategy enables teachers to become aware of all pupils' different sets of experiences, interests and strengths (including those of five-year-old British Pakistani children) as recommended by the National Curriculum 2000 (DfEE 1999a) and to build on what young children know and can do as advocated by the Curriculum Guidance for the Foundation Stage (DfEE, 2000). In a nutshell, this section seeks to examine how inclusive/exclusive a 'typical' literacy hour is.

Continuing with the previous Conservative government's drive to raise standards in literacy, in 1998 the Labour government rushed through its National Literacy Strategy (DfEE, 1998a) without any evaluation or consultation. This strategy, based on a two-year pilot project (The National Literacy Project), aims to raise standards in literacy, which are to be measured by Key Stage 2 Standard Assessment Tests (SATs) in 2002. Its 'Framework for Teaching' provides an overview of the knowledge and skills that are required for reading and writing and it categorizes these in three different levels: word, sentence and text. These levels form the backbone of the termly and yearly learning objectives.

A central aspect of this strategy is the literacy hour, which all state primary schools (five- to 11-year-olds) in England and Wales have been expected to teach since September 1998.

It is expected that teachers will use 'big books' during the first 30 minutes, especially in Key Stage 1; the text in these books is often large to enable the whole class to read it together. The strategy also provides specific instructions regarding the order of learning objectives taught, timescale and vocabulary used.

The literacy hours presented here are part of an ongoing, longitudinal ethnographic research project that explores young bilingual children's early literacy. The data (participant observations and audiotapes) come from an urban infant school in Watford, Hertfordshire, and were collected in spring 2000. The focus here is on a reception class and on its five children who are of Pakistani background. The children were five years old and in the second term of their reception year. Their home language is Pahari, and they are familiar, in varying degrees, with Urdu, the national language of Pakistan, and with classical Arabic, which they know to be the language of the Qur'an. All these five children are Muslims and they often see and hear their parents and family members read the Qur'an out loud at home.

The class teacher, Ms L, qualified in 1998, soon after the government had introduced a national curriculum for teacher training students. Ms L had no difficulties in demonstrating that she had met all the required standards for achieving the Newly Qualified Teacher status as identified in the Circular 4/98 (TTA, 1998). In September 1998, when Ms L began to teach her first class, she also began to implement the National Literacy Strategy, together with the majority of state primary school teachers in England and Wales. Ms L has never taught English in any other way. The school in question is Ms L's first post and at the time of the study she is in her second year of teaching. The school's recent Ofsted report (February 2000) identified her teaching of her reception class as 'consistently high standard', the curriculum as 'very good' and activities as 'appropriately linked to the key areas of learning'. She has been teaching the Reception classes since leaving university.

The excerpt in Figure 4.1 shows how a typical literacy hour begins in Ms L's class. The majority of these lessons follow this same pattern. The initial focus is generally on book and text terminology; the children repeat (often with

7/6/2000

| Child's Name | Children's turns | Class teacher's turns |
|---|---|---|
| | | What's its title? What's it called? Title? Sharon? |
| Sharon | The hungry caterpillar | |
| | | The hungry caterpillar. There's also another word in there, the. . . Emma? |
| Emma | Very | |
| | | The very, very, he was very, the very hungry caterpillar. And it was by a man called Eric Carle. Does anybody know what, if, if you wrote the book, what you'd called? [sic] |

**Figure 4.1**

excitement) the definitions for 'title', 'cover page', 'author' and so on, as recommended by the text-level learning objectives. There are very few opportunities to discuss the whole context of the story or what 'hungry' or 'caterpillar' means – crucial for those not yet fluent in English. Moreover there are no culture-level learning objectives, in spite of all stories being inextricably interwoven with cultural practices and concepts. It is assumed that all children are familiar with the culture of the stories. There are virtually no opportunities for children to relate the technical terms, stories or concepts to their own experiences. Their prior learning experiences, or life experiences, are excluded. Ms L's intention is to meet the class, school and LEA-based targets to raise standards in literacy.

The selection of the technical vocabulary in the National Literacy Strategy seems an ad hoc, motley group of terms from linguistics and English literature studies, which has not been part of primary teachers' discourse before, consequently causing a feeling of inadequacy. For example, Ms L's reception children should know the difference between 'rime' (word-level objective) and 'rhyme' (text-level objective) (DfEE, 1998a: 69) – difficult with all young children and quite inappropriate when there are other immediately more satisfying words to talk about (see Figure 4.2).

Again reflection and discussion about the broader, wider aspects of the text (and specifically about more intriguing aspects of the book such as grunting men) are not included in this lesson. But at the same time it is important to remember that one of the key findings of the school's recent Ofsted report was that the teaching in the reception class was 'consistently high standard' and this included 'effective' pacing. This is supported by the strategy, together with the 4/98 standards for English (TTA, 1998), which both maintain that one of the key characteristics of successful teaching is 'well- paced [lessons] – there is a sense of urgency, driven by the need to make progress and succeed' (DfEE, 1998: 8). Ms L is simply following the key documents and teaching in the style that has been assessed as 'very good'.

3/4/2000

| Child's name | Children's turns | Class teacher's turns |
| --- | --- | --- |
| | | Guh. There it is, grunt, grunt? |
| Maria | What does grunting mean? | |
| | | It means like that sound that Jamie was just doing, you know like a grunting piggy sound. |
| | Why's there men down there doing it? | |
| | | Well, that's for you to think about, you have to use your imagination with that page. Next one. Hope? |

**Figure 4.2**

This whole notion of quantifiable literacy and the whole 'banking approach' (Freire, 1972) which requires predetermined sets of knowledge to be deposited in the learner, presents a very narrow concept of learning and literacy. First of all it fails to acknowledge that learning is not a linear process nor does it take place necessarily in a given timescale. Second, children develop in diverse social and cultural practices and subsequently it overlooks the variety of literacy practices in children' lives (Street, 1984). It assumes that literacy can be learnt separately from the social context in which it will be used, and that the transfer from school literacy to wider literacy practices is an automatic, natural process. Gregory's work (1998, 2000) on children of Bangladeshi origin in Tower Hamlets, London, and on their 'unofficial' literacies reveals the broader range of learning that children engage in at home with siblings, and in play, and in wider community practices, such as Qur'anic classes and other community language classes. In contrast to many bilingual children's literacy and learning experiences, the strategy reduces 'literacy' to a narrow set of terms and drilling of skills.

After the initial focus on terminology, Ms L moves on to phonics and the phoneme–grapheme relationship (see Figure 4.3).

7/6/2000

| Child's name | Children's turns | Class teacher's turns |
| --- | --- | --- |
| | | Who can come up to write the first sound. Amil. I bet you can write the first sound. |
| Amil | Cuh | |
| | | Caterpillar. Cuh-caterpillar. What sound? |

**Figure 4.3**

The children's turns tend to be short answers to direct questions. As before, this is possibly to ensure that the pace of the lesson remains fast. In its overview of phonics teaching, the strategy excludes accents and dialects and the challenges bilingual children face in learning a new set of sounds at the same time as they are learning the grapheme-phoneme relationship and the new vocabulary. The bilingual children are also learning a new script, which uses different conventions from home languages (both Urdu and Arabic writing move from right to left). The pilot study leading to this project revealed that young bilingual learners demonstrate many additional strengths and interest (Robertson, 2000). They have an excellent starting point in terms of learning to read as they demonstrate a heightened awareness of languages and scripts as systems – something that the native speakers do not yet have. They show heightened metalinguistic awareness and metacognitive strategies by asking questions about words ('What's a cupcake? I don't eat that at home') and focusing on their own learning.

However, the structure of the literacy hour is such that very few children have a chance to say more than few words. Table 4.1 summarizes the patterns of the turn taking in three literacy hours (within the whole class sections, approximately 30 minutes each) and reveals the number of turns given to the bilingual children.

**Table 4.1**

| | No of Teacher's Turns | No of all Pupils' Turns | 1 | 2 | 3 | 4 | 5 |
|---|---|---|---|---|---|---|---|
| Lesson 3.4.2000 | 92 | 38 | 0 | 0 | 1 | 4 | 1 |
| Lesson 24.5.2000 | 75 | 50 | 1 | 0 | 0 | 3 | 1 |
| Lesson 7.6.2000 | 81 | 78 | 2 | Absent | 4 | 3 | 1 |

1=Tasneem (female) 2=Saira (female) 3=Talib (male) 4=Amil (male) 5=Ikram (male)

That teacher talk should dominate is no surprise. Most children have a chance to answer at least one direct question during the lesson, and the majority of all children's turns are one- or two-word responses. Saira is often quiet and prefers to listen. Amil is the lowest-achieving child in the whole class and during these whole-class sessions Ms L tries very hard to include him. What is surprising, though, is how closely Ms L's teaching, her interaction with her reception class and her questioning match the type of teaching promoted by the National Literacy Strategy (for more detailed analysis see Robertson, 2002). Figure 4.4 gives an excerpt from the National Literacy Strategy (DfEE, 1998b) training video.

It is clear that Ms L's teaching is based on this type of interaction. Just as in Ms L's classrooms, the training video lessons begin with terminology and teacher's questions that demand basic recollection of 'correct' definition. These lessons do not acknowledge any child's interests or strengths or build on their previous learning experiences, except for the more specific school-based book and text

| Child's name | Children's turns (reception class) | Teacher's turns (Joan) |
|---|---|---|
| | | Now, Mitchell, what can you see at the top of the page on the front cover? |
| Mitchell | The title | |
| | | The title. Now I'm going to turn over. And we're going to look at this page. Who knows what this page is called here. Ah, let's have look. Stuart? |
| Stuart | The inside cover | |
| | | Yes, and it's got a special name, Jessica? |
| Jessica | Title page | |
| | | Title page. Well done. What can you see on the page, Josh? (DfEE,1998b) |

**Figure 4.4**

| Child's name | Children's turns (reception class) | Teacher's turns (Joan) |
|---|---|---|
| | | Jumping. He is jumping, isn't he? I wonder if Ravi, could you tell me what jumping begins with? What sound can you hear? |
| Ravi | Tuh, tuh, tuh, tuh | |
| | | Not quite right Ravi. (DfEE,1998b) |

**Figure 4.5**

terminology and phonic knowledge, which have been discussed in these lessons before. And as in Ms L's lessons the emphasis then moves on to phonics (Figure 4.5).

Virtually all of the teacher's questions are closed rather than open-ended questions and each short, often one-word answer is followed by evaluative comment. If we acknowledge and accept that children have very diverse experiences, interests and strengths, which have a strong impact on the ways in which they learn, arguably the National Literacy Strategy fails to build on these. Our observations seem to suggest that the principles of inclusion have no space within the literacy hour. As a result the National Literacy Strategy legitimizes practice and pedagogy that excludes many children's prior experiences and their knowledge and understanding.

## Conclusion

Tackling educational exclusion and inclusion needs holistic, long-term solutions (Hayden and Dunne, 2001). The following themes emerge strongly from our studies: the,

- strong link between poverty, cultural and linguistic difference and exclusion;
- importance of keeping children in school, especially in the case of disrupted home circumstances, and acknowledging and accepting the impact of such life events;
- importance of a credible and monitored school reintegration package for excluded children;
- necessity to use exclusions to identify potentially poor literacy levels;
- necessity to enhance levels of literacy in ways that match individual learning styles and cultural and linguistic experiences;
- recognition that assessment-driven curriculum and concentration on performance, SATs and league tables promote exclusion and legitimize hidden exclusion;
- need for more studies that focus on listening to children;
- crucial nature of involving parents/carers and children in decision-making at all levels;
- necessity for the development of increased awareness and further development and training in teacher education and training courses in connection with the above issues.

When one of the excluded children in our study was asked what would make the school a better place, he answered: 'It would be great to have a swimming pool and a jacuzzi.' While most children would probably agree, in the absence of these unrealistic changes we suggest other more immediate and more achievable solutions. There are tensions between different government documents and between different recommendations that must be resolved. The inclusive principles of the National Curriculum (DfEE, 1999a), however worthwhile, do not permeate the subject programmes of study. The initial teacher training 4/98 standards (TTA, 1998), Ofsted and the National Literacy Strategy (DfEE, 1998) have a very different kind of view of inclusion. There is clearly a need to make these more cohesive, and to build on inclusion.

The challenge of embedding inclusive education in practice and pedagogy at all levels, from initial training onwards and in all age phases, in foundation stage settings and in primary and secondary schools, is a necessary attempt.

# References

Audit Commission (1996) *Misspent Youth*, Audit Commission, London

Blyth, E and Milner, J (eds) (1996) *Exclusion from School*, Routledge, London

Brodie, I (1998) *Exclusion from school*, National Children's Bureau, London

Cohen, R *et al* (1994) *School's Out: The family perspective on school exclusion*, The Barnardo's and Family Service Units, London

Cole, M (1997) Equality and Primary Education: what are the conceptual issues? in *Promoting Equality in Primary Schools*, eds M Cole, D Hill and S Shan, Cassell, London

Cole, M (1998) Racism, reconstructed multiculturalism and antiracist education, *Cambridge Journal of Education*, **28** (1), pp 37–48

Cole, M (1999) Professional issues and initial teacher education: what can be done and what should be done, *Educational Social Justice*, **2** (1), pp 63-66

Cole, M, Hill, D and Shan, S (1997) *Promoting Equality In Primary Schools*, Cassell, London

Commission on the Future of Multi-Ethnic Britain (2000) *Report of the Commission on the Future of Multi-Ethnic Britain* (the Parekh report), Profile Books, London

Dadds, M (1999) Teachers' Values and the Literacy Hour, *Cambridge Journal of Education*, **29** (1), pp 7–19

Department of Education and Science (DES) (1981) *West Indian Children in Our School* (the Rampton report), HMSO, London

DES (1985) *Education for All* (the Swann report), HMSO, London

Department for Education (DFE) (1995) *Key Stages 1 and 2 of the National Curriculum*, HMSO, London

DfEE (1998a) *The National Literacy Strategy: Framework for teaching*, DfEE, London

DfEE (1998b) *The National Literacy Strategy – Video 2*, DfEE, London

Department for Education and Employment (DfEE) (1999a) *The National Curriculum*, DfEE, London

DfEE (1999b) *The Early Learning Goals*, DfEE, London

DfEE and Qualifications and Curriculum Authority (QCA) (2000) *Curriculum Guidance for the Foundation Stage*, QCA, London

Freire, P (1972) *The Pedagogy of the Oppressed*, Penguin, Harmondsworth

Gillborn, D and Gipps, C (1996) *Recent Research on the Achievement of Ethnic Minority Pupils*, HMSO, London

Gillborn, D and Mirza, H (2000) *Educational Inequality; Mapping race, class and gender – a synthesis of research evidence*, Ofsted, London

Gregory, E (1998) Siblings as mediators of literacy in linguistic minority communities, *Language and Education: An international journal* **12** (1), pp 33–55

Gregory, E (2000) Work or Play: 'Unofficial' literacies in the lives of two East London communities, in *Multilingual Literacies: Reading and writing in different worlds*, eds Martin-Jones, M and Jones, K, John Benjamins Publishing Company, Amsterdam

Hallam, S (1997) Truancy: Can schools improve attendance?', *Viewpoint, 6*

Hayden, C (1997) *Children Excluded From Primary School: Debates, evidence, responses*, Open University Press, Buckingham

Hayden, C and Dunne S (2001) *Outside, Looking In: Children's and families' experience of school exclusion*, Children's Society, London

Hill, D (2001) State theory and the neo-liberal reconstructing of schooling and the teacher education: a structuralist neo-Marxist critique of postmodernist, quasi-postmodernist, and culturalist neo-Marxist theory, *British Journal of Sociology of Education*, **22** (1), pp 135–55

Hill, D and Cole, M (1999) *Promoting Equality in Secondary Schools*, London, Cassell

Hill, R (1998) *Excluded Voices: the experiences and perceptions of excluded secondary school children*, University of Newcastle upon Tyne, MSc Dissertation

Hoffman, J V (2000) The de-democratization of schools and literacy in America, *The Reading Teacher* **53** (8), pp 616–23

John, P (1996) Damaged goods? An interpretation of excluded pupils' perceptions of schooling, in *Exclusion from School*, eds E Blyth and J Milner, Routledge, London

Kenner, C (2000) *Homepages: literacy links for bilingual children*, Trentham Books, Stoke-on-Trent

Kinder, K, Wilkin, A and Wakefield, A (1997) *Exclusion – Who needs it?* National Foundation for Educational Research, Slough

Lloyd-Smith, M and Dwyfor Davies, J (eds) (1995) *On the Margins: The educational experience of 'problem-pupils'*, Trentham Books, Chester

Macpherson, Sir W (1999) *The Stephen Lawrence Inquiry, Report of an inquiry*, The Stationery Office, London

Martin, D (1999) Bilingualism and literacies in primary school: implications for professional development, *Educational Review*, **51** (1), pp 67–79

Mitchell, L (1996) The effects of waiting time of excluded children, in *Exclusion from School*, eds E Blyth and J Milner, Routledge, London

National Union of Teachers (NUT) (1992) *Survey on Pupil Exclusion*, NUT, London

Parsons, C (1999) *Education, Exclusion and Citizenship*, Routledge, London

Office for Standards in Education (Ofsted) (1993) *Education for the Disaffected Pupils 1990–1992*, Department of Education, London

Ofsted (1999) *Raising the Attainment of Minority Ethnic Pupils, School and LEA Responses*, Ofsted Publications Centre, London

Parekh, B (2000) Introduction to the Report of the Commission on the Future of Multi-ethnic Britain, *Multicultural Teaching* **19** (1), p 7

Rattansi, A (ed) (1992) *Race, Culture and Difference*, Sage Publications in Association with Open University Press

Robertson, L H (2000) Early literacy and emergent bilingual pupils: the exclusive nature of the National Curriculum and the National Literacy Strategy, in *Combating Social Exclusion Through Education*, eds G Walraven *et al*, Garant Publishers, Leuven-Apeldoorn

Robertson, L H (2002 forthcoming) Title talk, idle talk? Learning to read in additional language English within the literacy hour, in *Language and Education: An International Journal*

Social Exclusion Unit (SEU) (1998) *Truancy and Social Exclusions*, HMSO, London

Street, B (1984) *Literacy in Theory and Practice*, Cambridge University Press, Cambridge

*Times Educational Supplement* (TES) (2001a) *Neglect of Excluded Teenagers*, 19 January

TES (2001b) *The brave new world of bilingual teaching*, 2 March

Thomas, W and Collier, V (1997) *School Effectiveness and Language Minority Students*, National Clearinghouse for Bilingual Education, Washington DC

Teacher Training Agency (TTA) (1998) *Initial Teacher Training National Curriculum for Primary English (Annex C of DfEE Circular 4.98)*, DfEE, London

Walraven, G (2000) General Introduction: discourses in politics and research on social exclusion, in *Combating Social Exclusions Through Education*, eds G Walraven *et al*, Garant Publishers, Leuven-Apeldoorn

Wertheimer, F (1999) Expulsion is not the answer, *The Times,* 17 September

Wright, C, Weekes, D and McGlaughlin, A (2000) *Race, Gender and Exclusion From School*, Falmer Press, London

# 5

# The National Curriculum, the hidden curriculum and equality

*Dave Hill*

## Editors' introduction

*In this chapter Dave Hill considers the formal curriculum and the hidden curriculum and their impact on equality in schooling. He discusses how the National Curriculum was developed, and identifies the mixture of gains and losses it has created in terms of educational equality regarding 'race', gender, special needs, sexual diversity and social class. Critical concepts from Bourdieu and Althusser are used to illustrate the crucial connection between social power and social worth, in terms both of curriculum knowledge that has been selected and in terms of the cultural behaviours privileged and rewarded through both the formal and the hidden curricula. These concepts provide insight to the reproduction of inequalities through these aspects of education, which serve to advantage or disadvantage teachers, students and pupils with different cultural characteristics.*

## Introduction

This chapter examines the political nature of the construction of the National Curriculum, and the impact it has on equality in schooling. One central issue addressed is whether the current curriculum can contribute to increased equal opportunities and lead to more equal outcomes between different social groups.

It is suggested that the National Curriculum has not in general (with the exception of gender equality) increased equal opportunities. The other central issue concerns the hidden curriculum, which includes the values, attitudes, and culturally loaded expectations expressed through school/institutional arrangements, through pedagogic relationships, and through rewards and punishments typical of the daily life in schools/colleges. It is suggested that, with exceptions, the hidden curriculum serves to reproduce educational, social and economic inequalities.

In order to illuminate the cultural issues involved reference is made to particular concepts defined by Althusser and Bourdieu. In the course of discussion the chapter relates issues about cultural dominance to Bourdieu's concepts of 'cultural capital', 'symbolic violence' and 'cultural arbitrary', then to Althusser's concepts of education as a form of 'ideological state apparatus' with some characteristics of a 'repressive state apparatus'. At the outset, it is necessary to establish that reference to these writers neither indicates an uncritical acceptance of their works, nor does it refer to the whole body of either writers' output (Althusser, in particular has been criticized for some aspects of his work – see note 8).

## The political nature of the National Curriculum

The National Curriculum is clearly a political creation. Any curriculum is, although some curricula are clearly more openly partisan than are others. The National Curriculum of 1988 created by the Conservative government attempted to create a Conservative hegemony in ideas and to remove liberal, progressive and socialist ideas from schools and from the minds of future citizens. In the process of development, the National Curriculum subject working parties were preselected and not representative of the education profession. Several of the programmes of study were manipulated by Prime Ministerial and ministerial diktat. Thus, for example, subject working party recommendations to include the social effects of science, to study the history of the last 20 years, and to have a considerable concern for creative writing were all rejected by Margaret Thatcher or her education ministers. This is clearly set out in Margaret Thatcher's autobiography (Thatcher, 1993) and in those of Minister of Education, Kenneth Baker, (1993, Chapter 9) and the first chair of the National Curriculum Council between 1988–91, appointed by Kenneth Baker, Duncan Graham (see Graham and Tytler, 1993). Graham accused ministers of 'a wilful distortion for political ends'.[1] The 1995 National Curriculum revision by Lord Dearing and New Labour's revised National Curriculum of 2000 have made little change here.

The inherent political nature of any curriculum becomes apparent when it is subjected to particular questions about the power relations it defines. For example, whose curriculum is it? Who selected the curriculum content? Does it represent and affirm the ideology, the values and attitudes, of a particular social group of people? Does it thereby invalidate and disempower the values and attitudes it does not represent? Does it give some children/students an easier time and others a harder time?

In terms of content, is it, for example, a National Curriculum that is culturally elitist, with emphasis on the history, music and literature of the ruling upper and upper middle classes? Or, conversely, and to what extent, is it an appropriately eclectic curriculum, in terms of its programmes of study? Does it draw from and represent a variety of cultures and perspectives? Does it do so to an adequate extent, or are its nods towards, for example, African-Caribbean, gay and lesbian or working-class culture, tokenistic?

The Conservative National Curriculum is widely criticized as overwhelmingly elitist (Davies, Holland and Minhas, 1992; Hill, 1997a; Hillcole Group, 1997; Searle, 1998; Hill and Cole, 1999b), returning to more formal, test-driven methods and incorporating specific *dis*advantages for particular groups, such as working-class and minority ethnic groups. Is a policy aimed at *cultural assimilation* (to English upper- and middle-class male, heterosexist white values) likely to contribute to increased equal opportunities and to a harmonious and more socially mobile society and workforce? Conversely, should students be 'ghettoized' into the curriculum of their particular subcultures?

There are different views on whether there should be culturally specific curricula for different social and ethnic groups. Should there be a curriculum common in many respects to children of all abilities and aptitudes? Or should there be an academic/vocational divide, even though such divisions have, historically, been primarily based on social class.[2]

Clearly a *National* Curriculum is, to a large extent, operationalizing the belief that the same body of formal curriculum content should be available to all (at least within the state sector – it is not compulsory for the private sector of schooling) within the primary and secondary state school systems. Yet the political principles informing the development and application of any specific curriculum are crucial to the effect it will have on equalities of opportunities and outcomes for diverse groups.

The political principles behind a curriculum for 'national' education, whether it is overtly egalitarian or anti-egalitarian, support the wider objectives of governmental policy and these are, of course, not only social but also economic. The National Curriculum has aims beyond the controlled reproduction and re-validation of particular cultural forms and elites. It is also 'a bureaucratic device for exercising control over what goes on in schools' (Lawton and Chitty, 1987: 5). Michael Barber has noted about the 1988 Act that it 'not only provided for a market, but also a standardized means of checking which schools appeared to be performing best within it' (Barber, 1996: 50).

## The National Curriculum and its effect on equality

The negative effect of education policy on equal opportunity is described by Tomlinson and Craft (1995) as the following shift of emphasis:

the last decade has seen some major changes in both the philosophy and implementation of an education appropriate for all children. . . the national policy
objectives of the early 1980s. . . embodied an idealistic preoccupation with social
justice. . . but by the beginning of the 1990s they had been by-passed by a broader
mainstream drive to raise educational productivity through a return to the market
place, and by a weakening of the advocacy of equal opportunities.

(Tomlinson and Craft, 1995: foreword)

Within the Left, broadly, a considerable sympathy developed since the 1970s in
England and Wales for a pronounced child-centred curriculum, and 'black' and
'working-class' studies – whether they were termed as such or not. This child-
centred curriculum was expressed both in terms of 'relevant' curriculum content
and in terms of more democratic pupil (student)/teacher (tutor) relationships.
Here, both the formal and the informal curriculum attempted to validate, to
welcome, a whole range of home cultures and experiences. As suggested in
Chapter 1, this was in reaction to the authoritarianism of schooling and pedagogic
relationships that characterized most state education of the pre-war and
immediate post-war era.[3]

In contrast, the post-1988 National Curriculum, in all three of its versions,
asserts the centrality of particular socio-economic/social class definitions of
national culture – against the increasing tendencies to both *ethnic and social class
pluralism* that were at work in many schools and local education authorities in
the 1970s and 1980s. The post-2000 National Curriculum is driven more by a
project of cultural homogeneity than by the rhetoric of equal opportunity. The
National Curriculum, despite the minimal changes made by New Labour and
implemented in September 2000, is the embodiment of a Conservative vision
of a national culture.

Hatcher suggests:

What was crucial about equal opportunities in the 70s/80s was that a 'vanguard' of
progressive teachers had been able to reach a much wider layer of teachers in the
'middle ground' – the role of *LEAs and school policies* was important here, and so
was the prevalence of *working groups* on equal opportunities. At school and LEA
levels these were the key organisational forms feeding equal opportunities into the
wider arena. ERA has drastically attenuated this link between 'vanguard' and masses
(sic) and one key way has been work overload. Once we had equal opportunities
working groups in schools, now we have National Curriculum or SATs working
groups, or none. This has been a major material factor - many equal opportunity
activists have become preoccupied with other issues now deemed more important
or are suffering from National Curriculum and Assessment overload.

(Hatcher, 1995, cf Turner, Riddell and Brown, 1995, specifically in respect of gender)

Examining the effects of the current National Curriculum and its associated
testing arrangements shows that there is an improvement in standards overall,
in relation to what is being assessed. Chapter 1, discussing New Labour's Green

Paper *Schools: Building on success* (DfEE, 2001) details some of the increases in meeting government attainment targets. But this is inevitable. If a curriculum concentrates on basketball skills, or macramé or numeracy or the ability to decipher words, then attainment in those skills will inevitably rise. However, literacy and numeracy are highly important skills. With respect to equality issues, the Green Paper points out that:

- The biggest jump in standards in the Excellence in Cities city schools is in the most deprived schools (DfEE, 2001: 13).
- The percentage of black pupils achieving five or more A★-Cs at GCSE rose faster than the national average between 1998 and 2000 (p 14).
- The percentage of children of parents whose occupation is 'unskilled or semi-skilled manual' achieving five or more A★-Cs at GCSE also rose faster than the national average (p 14).

In order to assess the developments it needs to be asked what has been lost as well as what has been gained. With the National (or Common) Curriculum and standardized testing now in place there is a greater degree of comparability attaching to student experience across the country in purely curriculum terms, and more information regarding school performance for parents. There is now considerably greater surveillance (by parents, media, Ofsted) of the standards of teachers and schools.

In assessing the effective gains and losses of the current curriculum, it can be said that alongside the potential to partially reduce some aspects of negative discrimination, a degree of breadth has been lost, as has a consideration of cross-curricular and social objectives in schooling. Whitty, Power and Halpin observe that:

> Within England and Wales, the specification and design of the original National Curriculum and its assessment in terms of separate academic subjects has, in many cases, led to a narrowing of the school curriculum. The emphasis on the 'core' subjects, together with the requirements that schools publish test results as the main indicator of educational success, is leading to pressure on non-core subjects, such as music and art (Pollard *et al*, 1994). Non-assessed learning appears particularly vulnerable to marginalization.
>
> (Whitty, Power and Halpin, 1998: 87–88)

## Which inequalities have increased and which have decreased?

Some effects of the National Curriculum and, more widely, of Conservative education and other social policy in relation to social class, are discussed in Chapter 7 of this volume (see also Whitty, Power and Halpin, 1998; Hill, 1999). The essential *intention* of Conservative government policy may have been to increase social class differentiation – that is, to increase differences between and within the social classes (see Hill, 1997a): the rich *did* get richer under Conservative governments, while the poor did get poorer (see Chapter 7; Sanders, Hill and Hankin, 1999; Hill, Sanders and Hankin, 2001; *Social Trends*, 2001: 103). This continued under New Labour (*Social Trends*, 2001: 103) – with the exception that most of the very poor have seen their relative incomes rise (Toynbee and Walker, 2001). In this enterprise of increasing differences in income and wealth, however, it is *not* necessarily an essential intention to demarcate and intensify gender and 'race' differentiation more rigidly.

However, it is necessary here to note the links between 'race' and class. A higher proportion of the African-Caribbean population than the national average has a working-class location, and some Indian descended groups (although not Bangladeshi or Pakistani) have a more middle-class profile than the national average.

In other words, the racialized nature of the class system needs to be recognized: since most members of Asian, black and other minority ethnic group communities are working class in socio-economic terms they are thereby disproportionately affected by increased social class differentiation, by the general increase in the inequalities between working-class and non-working-class income and wealth. They are, of course, also affected by personal and by structural racism, just as, for example, girls and women are affected by personal and structural sexism, and gays and lesbians by homophobia. (These issues and developments are addressed in detail in later chapters in this volume.)

To look at *intention* of any policy or series of policies is not the same as looking at actual or likely *effects*. The actual effects of the 1988 Education Reform Act and Conservative policy on schools since 1979 have indeed been to increase social class differentiation. In terms of test and exam results, in a competitive schools market privileged schools have become more privileged and 'sink' schools have sunk further. As set out in Chapter 1, there has been a degree of increasing polarization between schools.

Yet if the social class factor is removed and *de-classed gender* is considered, then the effect, not least of the legally enforceable National Curriculum (with mathematics, science and technology being compulsory, and assessed, for girls as well as for boys), is actually to reduce gender differentiation. In general, the effect on gender equality appears to be that girls/young women are benefiting from this curriculum, for example from the injunction of 'science for all' and the *apparent* attack on gender stereotyped subject choices. There is now greater gender equality in terms of the school curriculum, with improvements in girls' results in comparison to boys. There are, however, non-school factors at work here, such as the 'feminization' of lower and middle-income levels of the work force (see Weiner, Arnot and David, 1997; Kelly, 1999; and Chapter 9 in this volume, for a discussion of the bigger picture of societal trends in education and employment). However, it must be noted that these have not substantially affected post-16 career choices, which are still largely gender stereotypical.

On this same basis, if de-classed 'race' is considered, the National Curriculum may also serve to reduce 'race' differentiation by diminishing 'race'-based stereotyping of subject choices. However, there are other 'race' related aspects/ effects of government schools policy. As Chris Gaine (1995) has pointed out, along with Whitty, Power and Halpin (1998), schools choosing pupils not only operates against working-class children but also against other groups often stereotyped as 'difficult' (such as African-Caribbean boys) or 'expensive' (such as pupils for whom English is a second language, or who have special educational needs). This together with the 'white flight' from 'black' or 'Asian' schools, can exacerbate the racialized hierarchy of schools. In connection with this it is worth noting the cultural effects of the National Curriculum in offering success to middle-class Asian and black pupils in a white nationalist curriculum (Hill, 1997a; Searle, 1996, 1997).

Overall, the effects on 'race' and ethnicity again appear to be mixed: subject stereotyping is less permissible under the National Curriculum than before it, yet this same curriculum gives very considerably less space for and validation to minority ethnic group cultures and histories than many of the pre-1988 school curricula, particularly those in the big cities.

The effects on children with disabilities and special needs appear to be more seriously negative. Children with moderate disabilities are being penalized by the bureaucratic insistence on keeping up the same pace in their curriculum coverage as the rest of the class (see Richard Rose, Chapter 11 of this volume, also Jones and Docking, 1992). In addition, there is considerable negative impact from the National Curriculum and the educational and wider legislation on sexuality, and on teachers and school students who are gay, lesbian or bisexual (as Iain Williamson shows in Chapter 10).

## Bourdieu and the National Curriculum as cultural reproduction

The work of Pierre Bourdieu (1976; Bourdieu and Passeron, 1977; Lareau, 1997; Grenfell and James, 1998) analyses the relationship between education and cultural formation. Bourdieu criticizes the desirability of a curriculum which is culturally elitist, culturally restorationist. The concepts of *culture* and *cultural capital* are central to Bourdieu's analysis of how the mechanisms of cultural reproduction function within schools.[4] For Bourdieu, the education system is *not* meritocratic. Its major function is to maintain and legitimate a class divided society. In his view schools are middle-class institutions run by and for the middle class. In summary, Bourdieu suggests that this cultural reproduction works in three ways.

Firstly it works through the formal curriculum and its assessment. Exams serve to confirm the advantages of the middle class while having the appearance of being a free and fair competition. Examinations and the curriculum clearly privilege and validate particular types of 'cultural capital', the type of elite knowledge that appears the natural possession of middle- and, in particular, upper-class children, but which is not 'natural' or familiar to non-elite children and school students. (See Leena Helavaara Robertson and Rachel Hill's Chapter 4 for a discussion of how some minority ethnic groups are, in relative terms, excluded from the literacy hour.)

Secondly, cultural reproduction works through the hidden curriculum. This hidden curriculum categorizes some cultures, lifestyles, ways of being and behaving (for Bourdieu the *habitus*), attitudes and values as praiseworthy, as being 'nice', as being characteristic of the child of whom one can more likely expect and encourage academic aspiration and success.

In contrast, other ways of being and behaving, language, clothing, body language, and attitudes/values are not viewed quite as tolerantly or supportively. 'Loud-mouthed' (assertive) girls/young women, or large African-Caribbean young men or boys, or shell-suited cropped-headed working-class white young men/boys tend to be regarded as regrettable, 'nasty', alien and/or threatening – indeed, suitable subjects for exclusion, if not from school itself (see Gillborn and Gipps, 1996, and Chapters 4, 8 and 12 of this volume), then from academic expectation and success.

Thirdly, cultural reproduction works, in Britain, through the separate system of schooling for the upper- and upper-middle classes, nearly all of whom, in a form of educational apartheid, send their children to private (independent) schools.

## Cultural capital

Bourdieu argues that the culture transmitted by the school confirms, values and validates the culture of the ruling classes. At the same time, and as a consequence, it disconfirms, rejects, invalidates the cultures of other groups. Individuals in classrooms and school corridors bring with them and exhibit different sets of linguistic and cultural competencies. In Giroux's summation, they inherit these:

> by way of the class-located boundaries of their family. A child inherits from his or her family those sets of meanings, qualities of style, modes of thinking, and types of dispositions that are assigned a certain social value and status in accordance with what the dominant class(es) label as the most valued cultural capital. Schools play a particularly important part in legitimating and reproducing dominant cultural capital. They tend to legitimize certain forms of knowledge, ways of speaking, and ways of relating to the world that capitalize on the type of familiarity and skills that only certain students have received from their family backgrounds and class relations. Students whose families have only a tenuous connection to the dominant cultural capital are at a decided disadvantage.
>
> (Giroux, 1983: 268)

The significant aspect is that school pupils/students (and, indeed, individuals in the workforce, such as teachers in schools or lecturers in colleges seeking promotion, or a permanent instead of a temporary contract) stand to benefit if they possess or show the 'right sort' of cultural capital.

This dominant cultural form is expressed in two ways. Firstly, there is actual knowledge, of facts and concepts, acquaintance and familiarity with particular forms of, for example, historical, musical, artistic, literary, geographical culture. Knowledge of the current form of Premiership soccer clubs, of clothing style, or of contemporary *argot* tends to be viewed as less important, of lower status in the hierarchy of knowledge than the selection of knowledge represented in the formal curriculum. This type of cultural capital is 'knowing that' something is something – that a particular theatrical production of Shakespeare is about to take place rather than that a particular soap star is about to launch into something or other; that Milton wrote *Paradise Lost* rather than that a particular pop group is splitting up; or knowing about the significance of May Day marches or where to get cheap food or 'knock-off gear'. This type of knowledge, *knowledge that*, is presented, and rewarded (or rejected and penalized) for being part of, or not part of, the formal curriculum. In addition, lots of 'elite' knowledge and experiences not represented in the National Curriculum are rewarded through the hidden curriculum – the praise, estimation and expectations of teachers and of schooling. Some types of learning experiences or educational visits within the family, peer group or school – trips to the theatre, museums, exhibitions – are more highly validated and recognized than, say, a seaside holiday in Benidorm or Brighton.

A second type of cultural capital is *'knowing how'* – how to speak to teachers, not only knowing *about* books, but also knowing *how* to talk about them. It is knowing *how* to talk with the teacher, with what body language, accent, colloquialisms, register of voice, grammatical exactitude in terms of the 'elaborated code' of language and its associated *habitus*, or code of behaviour.

> In a number of social universes, one of the privileges of the dominant, who move in their world as a fish in water, resides in the fact that they need not engage in rational computation in order to reach the goals that best suit their interests. All they have to do is follow their dispositions which, being adjusted to their positions, 'naturally' generate practices adjusted to the situation.
>
> (Bourdieu, 1990: 109, quoted in Hatcher, 1998)

For pupils/students, this is knowledge of the system, of whether or not their practices adjust in conformity with teacher aspirations, practices that are part of how to get on with the teacher. Teachers' judgements take into account not only 'knowledge that' but also 'knowledge how' intangible nuances of manners and style – style of speaking, style of clothing, of eating – which are scarcely perceptible manifestations of an individual's relationship to, or behaviour with, knowledge.

Some topics and ways of talking about them have more value in the eyes of schools in general. The 'nice child' is one who appears to be middle class, or who appears to be able – and willing – to cease exhibiting working-class, or Islamic or Rasta characteristics, and to adopt those of the white or assimilated middle class. In other words, the 'nice child' is usually one who also meets stereotypes of gender, ethnicity and sexuality. For example, once a Moslem young woman takes the decision to wear the Moslem scarf (*hijab*), then she is liable to be regarded as 'less acceptable' by many teachers, to be regarded as 'not as sensible as I thought you were' (Khan, 1998).[5]

## The arbitrariness of the National Curriculum

Bourdieu's concept of the *cultural arbitrary* refers to school education being arbitrary in that the cultural values offered are not intrinsically *better* than any other but are the values of the dominant class. In this sense, the selection of knowledge represented in the National Curriculum can be seen as arbitrary, as one selection of knowledge among many possible selections. For example, standard English is one dialect among many but happens to have been adopted as the most prestigious form; also the National Curriculum programmes of study for art, English and music privilege 'high art' rather than popular culture. Giroux succinctly defines how:

> working-class knowledge and culture are often placed in competition with what the school legitimates as dominant culture and knowledge. In the end, working-class knowledge and culture are seen not as different and equal, but as different and inferior. It is important to note that high-status knowledge often corresponds to bodies of knowledge that provide a stepping stone to professional careers via higher education. Such knowledge embodies the cultural capital of the middle- and upper-classes and presupposes a certain familiarity with the linguistic and social practices it supports. Needless to say, such knowledge is not only more accessible to the upper classes, but also functions to confirm and legitimate their privileged positions in schools. Thus, the importance of the hegemonic curriculum lies in both what it includes – with its emphasis on western history, science, and so forth – and what it excludes – feminist history, black studies, labour history, in-depth courses in the arts, and other forms of knowledge important to the working-class and other subordinate groups.
>
> (Giroux, 1983: 268–9)

The arbitrariness of the National Curriculum is far from random. It is fundamentally and primarily the imposition of ruling-class knowledge over working-class (and other subaltern[6] cultural) knowledge. That is its stratifying and subordinating intention and function.

# Symbolic violence

The National Curriculum did not arrive by accident. Its content, as indeed virtually any national curriculum content, was keenly fought over. To use Ira Shor's expression and book title (Shor, 1986) it was and remains part of the 'culture wars'.

This imposition of one range of knowledge was not consensual, peaceful, or unquestioned. Although there were no pitched street battles over the National Curriculum English proposals, to take one example, there were culture wars, angry conferences and letters in the broadsheet and educational press, and the victors ended by enforcing – indeed enforcing through the law – their victory.

Thus the National Curriculum is an example of what Bourdieu termed *symbolic violence,* the legal enforcing of one set of cultural symbols over another or others.

By symbolic violence, Bourdieu is referring to the way in which symbolic forms of communication such as language and culture are used as weapons to maintain power relations. The success of symbolic violence depends on the way that it is commonly unrecognized. It is commonly accepted unquestioningly and exercises power through the complicity of those who, subjectively, do not wish to know they are subject to it. Most accept the loaded rules or the game. Most 'buy in', at least on a conscious level, to the elitist model by which they have a deficit. As a result, working-class children tend to become either submissive or to opt out, become alienated from and/or resistant to school culture. In contrast, middle-class children are familiar and at ease with 'desirable' symbolic forms. To legitimate what are in fact *imposed* meanings is a form of *symbolic violence.* In Bourdieu's view, and indeed, in the view of the new sociology of knowledge of the 1970s (see Whitty, 1985), official educational culture is arbitrary in both its content and its form (its way of being organized into subjects disciplines, topics, themes).

The National Curriculum is symbolic violence in a further sense: it shows 'what's what'. It shows and displays not only what is elite culture but also that this is high-status culture, whereas its challengers are not – they are not worthy of inclusion in the National Curriculum. The message displayed day after day in schools is that in order to get on in society (other than through winning the National Lottery, becoming a model or pop star or a Premier League footballer) then you have to adopt, ape, or approximate to the cultural, linguistic and dress codes of the ruling elite. The creators of the National Curriculum have either failed to recognize, or have deliberately created, the partiality of the National Curriculum. As Diane Reay has pointed out in unpublished comments on a draft of this chapter, it represents the creators' own very particular depictions of the social world. In doing so they have imposed a very distorted means for comprehending the social world and so committed symbolic violence.

While there might be a solidarity among millions over soap operas, or grieving over Princess Diana's death, or World Cup soccer, and while there is considerable cultural resistance and inverted snobbery and pride in subaltern culture,[6] and while there is widespread disavowing of the superiority of the habitus and codes of the ruling elite, the subaltern (majority of the) population are well aware of the way society works in terms of symbolic violence. They know that in the way schooling and society work, in the way academic and vocational success work, whether they like it or not, they 'are being done a mischief'. They are, in general, consistently downgraded, disregarded, underpromoted, undervalued – because of their culture, and not simply the individual culture they affirm or possess but because that culture is part of a group, or class culture.

# Althusser and schooling as ideological reproduction

There is a relationship between the pedagogic work[7] of schools and the capital advantages associated with particular cultural attributes. Importantly, the school in this relationship 'is not neutral: it embodies the "cultural arbitrary", the interests of the dominant class. Cultural capital is not conceived of as an individual attribute but as a relational concept to institutionalised class power' (Hatcher, 1998: 17). To appreciate the institutional role of education as part of this process it is useful to refer to specific concepts within Althusser's work.[8]

Althusser's analysis of schooling concerns a particular aspect of cultural reproduction, namely, ideological reproduction – the reproduction of what is considered 'only natural', or as common sense. Althusser (1971) defines and shows the means by which a small but economically, politically and culturally powerful (capitalist) ruling class perpetuates itself in power, and can reproduce the existing political and economic systems that work in its favour. He distinguishes the repressive state apparatuses (RSAs), such as the law, the police and the armed forces, from the ideological state apparatuses (ISAs) such as the family, schooling and education, religion and the media. The term 'state apparatus' does not refer solely to apparatuses such as government ministries and various levels of government. It applies to those societal apparatuses, institutions and agencies that operate on behalf of, and maintain the existing economic and social relations of production. In other words, the apparatuses that sustain capital, capitalism and capitalists.

The RSAs function by discipline and control. This can be by making illegal the forces and organizations and their tactics that threaten the capitalist status quo and rate of profit. Thus, for example, many restrictions have been placed on strike action and trade union activities; teachers' pay bargaining has ended, and within state schools it has been made illegal not to teach the National Curriculum (except for officially sanctioned disapplications). More extreme versions of using the RSAs are to engage in heavy intimidatory policing of demonstrations and in other forms of state-sanctioned political repression and violence by the police and armed forces.

Governments, and the ruling classes in whose interests they act, prefer to use the second form of state apparatuses – the ideological state apparatuses (ISAs). Changing the school and initial teacher education (ITE) curriculum is less messy than sending the troops on to the streets or visored baton-wielding police into strike-bound mining villages. And it is deemed more legitimate by the population in general. As Bourdieu (and Althusser) has also noted, schooling and the other sectors of education are generally regarded as politically neutral, not as agencies of cultural, ideological and economic reproduction. The school, like other institutions in society such as the legal system and the police, is always presented in official discourse as neutral, non-political, and non-ideological. (Of course those who have direct, negative experiences of any of these, such as being half-strangled in a police assault, or a community whose children are frequently excluded from school, and those who have a critical political consciousness, do not see it this way.)

The task of the ISAs is to battle for and to secure the widespread (hegemonic) acceptability of the ideas of the ruling capitalist class, of its ideology – the individualist, consumerist, pro-capitalist ideology that justifies the status quo. All ISAs play their part in reproducing 'the capitalist relations of production', that is, the capitalist/worker *economic relationship* based on the economic power of the former over the latter, and the *social relationships* (of, for example, dominance and subservience) that are produced by those economic relationships.

For Althusser the dominant, the most important ISA in developed capitalist societies/economies/social formations is the educational ideological state apparatus. In this are included all aspects of the education system, from schools to further and higher education, to (what is of particular importance in ideological and in cultural reproduction) the 'teacher training' and education system. For Althusser, school and family have replaced the Church and family ISAs that were the dominant structures in ideological reproduction in previous centuries. Schools are particularly important since no other ideological state apparatus requires compulsory attendance of all children for eight hours a day for five days a week.

How does the school function as an ISA? Althusser suggests that what children learn at school is 'know-how'. But besides techniques and knowledges, and in the course of learning them, children at school also learn the 'rules' of good behaviour, 'rules of respect for the socio-technical division of labour and ultimately the rules of the order established by class domination'. The school takes children from every class at infant-school age, and then for years in which they are most 'vulnerable', squeezed between the family state apparatus and the educational state apparatus, it drums into them, whether it uses new or old methods, a certain amount of 'know-how' wrapped in the ruling ideology in its pure state (Althusser, 1971: 147).

As Sarup summarizes, 'in this system each mass of children ejected en route is practically provided with the ideology which suits the role it has to fulfil in class society' (Sarup, 1983: 13).

## Ideological and repressive state apparatuses in schooling and initial teacher education

Althusser suggests that *every ideological state apparatus is also in part a repressive state apparatus*, punishing those who dissent:

> There is no such thing as a purely ideological apparatus. . . Schools and Churches use suitable methods of punishment, expulsion, selection etc, to 'discipline' not only their shepherds, but also their flocks.
>
> (Althusser, 1971: 138)

Ideological state apparatuses have internal 'coercive' practices (for example, forms of punishment, non-promotion, displacement, being 'out of favour'). The education ISAs engage in repressive activities. Thus they dismiss, or render likely to be dismissed, teachers and lecturers who teach subjects derided by the government. School and college/university subjects can be made invisible – sociology can be virtually exorcised from the ITE curriculum, for example, and its protagonists made redundant (see Hill, 1997b,c d). Resistant pupils/students who challenge the existing system are liable to be excluded, and resistant, counter-hegemonic teachers/lecturers are likely to be excluded from promotion.

Similarly, RSAs do not have only a repressive function. They have an ideological function and effect, too. They attempt to secure significant internal unity and wider social authority through ideology (for example, through their ideologies of patriotism and national integrity, or, in the case of education statute/legislation, through propagating the ideology of technical efficiency and school effectiveness as 'the answer' to educational and economic problems). Every RSA therefore has an ideological moment, propagating a version of common sense and attempting to legitimate it under threat of sanction.

For example, by means of the Council for the Accreditation of Teacher Education (CATE) and the Teacher Training Agency (TTA) circulars and education Acts, higher education institutions (HEIs) and education departments/faculties can have their resources reduced, their staff contracted and their specializations (in 'race', social class, gender, disability, sexuality) thereby altered. By means of Ofsted schools can be closed. Oppositional teachers and teacher educators can lose heart and lose pay; schools and HEIs can lose pupils/students and therefore income and therefore teachers'/lecturers' jobs; their successors are likely to be appointed because of their expertise in the National Curriculum rather than in equal opportunities issues.

It is no coincidence that trade union activists are often top of the list when school or college redundancies are about or that schools[9] clinging to what Ofsted now regards as 'outdated' (mixed-ability) methods are likely to be 'failed' at their Ofsted inspection. A school, such as the Earl Marshall Comprehensive school in Sheffield can have its head teacher (Chris Searle) removed for refusing to stick to the National Curriculum (Searle, 1996, 1997).

For Althusser, the difference between an ideological and a repressive apparatus of state is one of degree, a matter of whether force or idea predominates in the functioning of particular apparatus (see Benton, 1984:101-102). Ofsted and the Teacher Training Agency (TTA) are primarily ideological state apparatuses, but have considerable repressive capacity.

## Conforming teachers and student teachers

Government policy has attempted to 'conform' both the *existing* teacher workforce and the *future* teacher workforce (student teachers) by various means – a mix of the ideological and repressive aspects and functions of the education state apparatuses. Alongside legislation and statutory circulars – such as the

Education Reform Act of 1988, the 1994 Education Act (setting up the Teacher Training Agency) and the various requirements for initial teacher education – there has been:

- A discourse of sustained criticism, under both Conservative and New Labour governments of 'trendy' and 'politically correct' liberal-progressive and socialist-egalitarian forms of schooling, teacher education (for example, Woodhead, 1999) and of education research. Such criticism is also directed at academic disciplines such as sociology and the education studies with which they are associated.
- Sustained ministerial and media 'spinning', slanted presentation of government advisory reports such as the HMI and Ofsted *New Teacher in School* reports of 1988 and 1993 respectively (see Blake and Hill, 1995) and such as Teacher Training Agency reports and consultations (Mahoney and Hextall, 2000).
- The weakening of teachers' union power, the diminution of their national pay, conditions and negotiating arrangements.
- The diminution of the 'core' of full-time teachers in all sectors of education on permanent contracts and the accompanying increase of the 'peripheral' teachers on part-time and short-term contracts, and the stratification of the teaching force through the introduction of different pay scales and performance-related pay (Ainley, 1999; Chitty and Dunford, 2000).
- The abolition of corporatist arrangements with a majority of teacher union members, such as the Schools Council, which endorsed and prioritized the input of teachers' unions and representatives to curriculum developments. New Labour's General Teaching Council is a body with fewer powers and little intended corporatism.
- The substantial control of teachers' work via the selection of educational content through the National Curriculum and its associated publishable assessment results. This is even more apparent under New Labour with the heavily prescriptive 'literacy hour' and 'numeracy hour' in primary schools. It also applies to the ever more prescriptive 'national curriculum for teacher training', with its very tightly prescribed 'standards' under the Circular 4/98 (DfEE, 1998).
- The prescription of curriculum content has been accompanied by a virtual exclusion from the teacher education/training curriculum of the study of equal opportunities issues, and of the sociological, political and psychological aspects and contexts of learning, teaching and schooling. Spaces for the development of 'critical reflection' have been virtually squeezed out, a development exacerbated by the partial replacement of four-year by three-year and other, shorter, undergraduate ITE courses.
- The insistence on a subject-based, as opposed to topic-based interdisciplinary primary curriculum (DFE, 1993). New Labour has extended this pedagogical control by insisting that unless mixed-ability methods are being markedly successful in a particular school then the setting of children by ability should

become the norm (see Woods and Jeffrey, 1998; The Government, 1999: 10).

- The increased managerialization of schooling and intensification of teachers' work, with 'teachers. . . driven to burnout' (Whitty, 1997: 305). School managements increasingly insist that teachers concentrate primarily on improving pupils' National Curriculum standardized test results, in particular GCSE results at grades A to C. This is because, through competitive open enrolment and through the age-related per capita funding of schools by the 1988 Education Reform Act, schools can lose numbers, income, and thereby staff, if their test results appear poor in relation to competitor schools.

- The proletarianization of teachers in schools and teacher education, whereby the conditions of work in education approximate much more to manual working-class jobs than was formerly the case (Braverman, 1974; Harris, 1982, 1994; Ainley, 2000). Aspects of proletarianization are: the increased degree of surveillance, the reduced degree of autonomy left in decision-making (for example, with the curriculum), the increasingly repetitive and preordained nature of much of the work, the increased 'boss–worker' relations of subordination and domination between management and shop-floor teacher/lecturer workers, diminished security of tenure in work contracts, and reduced pay levels. To expand on one of these, the professional autonomy of teachers and teacher educators has been drastically reduced by the deluge of instructions and rapidly changing National Curriculum requirements about programmes of study. For Whitty, 'both state and market forces imply a "low trust" relationship between society and its teachers' with a resulting denigration of professional autonomy (Whitty, 1997: 307).

## Conclusion

Schools and the education system in general are commonly seen as part of a larger universe of symbolic institutions that do not overtly impose docility and oppression. They are largely seen as neutral and as meritocratic. However, using the insights of Bourdieu and Althusser, it can be seen that schools play a major role in reproducing existing power relations subtly through the reproduction, distribution and validation of a dominant culture that tacitly confirms what it means to be educated. At the same time, they invalidate and disconfirm other cultures.

The particular theoretical insights of Bourdieu and Althusser (among others) referred to in this chapter show how the current National Curriculum, a political construct ultimately designed by politicians, and the hidden curriculum, which is just as ideological even though hidden, are central to a grossly unequal schooling and education system that in very many ways reproduces and justifies the economic inequalities of an elitist hierarchy, along with the cultural and ideological discrimination that supports it.

The analysis presented here is based on and contributes to the Marxist and neo-Marxist traditions of analysis, which require the critical development of radical strategies for resistance and alternative procedures. Progressives and egalitarians might wish to consider that in place of a culturally exclusionary National Curriculum there should indeed be a common curriculum (see Hillcole Group, 1991, 1997), but that it should be *inclusionary* (as well as being critical – promoting critical reflection). The *Promoting Equality in Schools* books (Cole, Hill and Shan, 1997; Hill and Cole, 1999) and others (such as Pumfrey and Verma, 1994; Verma and Pumfrey, 1994) do attempt to do this for each of the National Curriculum subjects. A new curriculum could be validating, speaking to, speaking about and representing a range of cultures, rather than being restricted – overwhelmingly and fundamentally – to the cultural forms traditionally associated with those who rule our society. The formal and the hidden curricula should also develop critical reflection in pupils and students, and themselves be part of a wide-ranging comprehensivization of the structures of the schooling and education systems that seek to maximize both equality of opportunity and a far greater degree of equality of outcome.

## Notes

1.  Cited in Docking (1996: 10). Several of the subject-by-subject chapters in Cole, Hill and Shan (eds) (1997) and Hill and Cole (eds) (1999) detail some of these disputes. For a theoretical analysis of the relationship between the state, ideology and the curriculum, see Hill (2001).
2.  See Benn and Simon (1970) and Benn and Chitty (1997) for major works on selection in schooling, comprehensivization and social class. Also see the long-running education magazine *Forum for the Promotion of Comprehensive Education*. For journalistic accounts of the effects of selection on the author and his twin brother, see, for example, Buckle (2001) and Haymer (2001).
3.  Left-wing critiques of liberal-progressive and socially differentiated schooling and curricula draw primarily on the work of Gramsci (see Epstein 1993; Hill, Cole and Williams, 1997). Gramsci considered that schooling is and should be hard work, that while developing a critical perspective and attitude, working-class children need to study and become inducted into and familiar with the elite, dominant culture. Sarup's summary and discussion of Gramsci (Sarup, 1983) is very clear. See Chapter 2 and the Conclusion for a delineation of liberal-progressivism in education.
4.  Bourdieu's work has been criticized by culturalist neo-Marxists as over-deterministic (see for example Sarup, 1983; Giroux, 1983; Whitty, 1985; Cole, 1988. With specific reference to Bourdieu, see also Jenkins, 1982, 1992; Hatcher, 1998). For a discussion of the differences between culturalist and structuralist neo-Marxism see Hill, 1999, 2001.

5.  These are actual examples from the life of Zubeda Khan from her secondary schooling. On deciding to affirm her Muslim identity through adopting Islamic dress in place of Western dress she was astonished to be faced with a widespread change of attitude towards her by a number of her teachers (Khan, 1998).
6.  The word subaltern is used here and throughout in the sense prevalent in the United States, of being oppressed, treated as inferior, rather than in the (opposite) British sense of pertaining to the junior officer class.
7.  For Bourdieu, *pedagogic action* produces misrecognition of the objective truth of the culture as a cultural arbitrary. *Pedagogic agencies*, such as schools and further and higher education colleges, have pedagogic authority to reproduce the cultural arbitrary delegated to them by the dominant class. *Pedagogic agents*, such as teachers, are those who have authority in home and school. Their job, in Bourdieu's view, whether they like it or not, is to pass on dominant values by teaching the curriculum. Such *pedagogic work* has the function of keeping order − that is, to reproduce the structure of power relations.
8.  As stated, it is not the intention of this chapter to validate the complete corpus of Althusser's work, which is widely perceived to be deterministic and an apparent denial of 'human agency' − the ability of people to success-fully struggle to change things. He has also been criticized for the internally contradictory nature of both his ISA essay and his corpus of works. See, for example, Callinicos, 1976; Larrain, 1979; Benton, 1984; Liston, 1988; Elliot, 1993a,b; Barrett, 1993. However, the particular Althusserian concepts referred to in this chapter are illuminating, in particular with respect to the National Curriculum and to restructuring of other education state appara-tuses, such as Initial Teacher Education (see Hill, 1989) and to the restructur-ing of education in general (see Hill, 2001).
9.  For instances, see the publications of the Campaign for Academic Freedom and of NATFHE Rank and File.

## References

Ainley, P (1999) Left in a Right State: Towards a new alternative, *Education and Social Justice*, **2** (1), pp 74–78

Ainley, P (2000) *From Earning to Learning: What is Happening to Education and the Welfare State?* Tufnell Press, London

Althusser, L (1971) Ideology and state apparatus, in *Lenin and Philosophy and Other Essays*, New Left Books, London

Baker, K (1993) *The Turbulent Years: My life in politics*, Faber, London

Barber, M (1996) *The Learning Game: Arguments for an education revolution*, Victor Gollancz, London

Barrett, M (1993) Althusser's Marx, Althusser's Lacan, in *The Althusserian Legacy*, eds E Kaplan and M Sprinkler, Verso, London

Benn, C and Simon, B (1970) *Half-Way There: Report on the British comprehensive school,* McGraw-Hill, London

Benn, C and Chitty, C (1997) *Thirty Years On: Is comprehensive education alive and well or struggling to survive?* Penguin, London

Benton, T (1984) *The Rise and Fall of Structural Marxism: Althusser and his influence,* Macmillan, London

Blake, D and Hill, D (1995) The newly qualified teacher in school, *Research Papers in Education,* **10** (3), pp 309–39

Bourdieu, R (1976) The school as a conservative force in scholastic and cultural inequalities, in *Schooling and Capitalism,* eds R Dale *et al,* Routledge & Kegan Paul, London

Bourdieu, R and Passeron, J (1977) *Reproduction in Education, Society and Culture,* Sage, London

Bourdieu, R (1990) *In Other Words,* Polity Press, Cambridge

Braverman, H (1974) *Labour and Monopoly Capitalism,* Monthly Review Press, New York

Buckle, C (2001) Twins torn apart by elite system *Evening Argus* (Brighton), 2 March

Callinicos, A (1976) *Althusser's Marxism,* Pluto, London

Chitty, C and Dunford, J (eds) (2000) *State Schools: New Labour and the Conservative legacy,* Woburn Press, London

Cole, M (ed) (1988) *Bowles And Gintis Revisited,* Falmer Press, London

Cole, M, Hill, D and Shan, S (eds) (1997) *Promoting Equality In Primary Schools,* Cassell, London

Davies, A, Holland, J and Minhas, R (1992) *Equal Opportunities In The New ERA,* Tufnell Press, London

Department for Education (DFE) (1993) *Curriculum Organisation and Classroom Practice in Primary Schools. A Discussion Paper,* eds R Alexander, J Rose and C Woodhead, HMSO, London

Department for Education and Employment (DfEE) (1998) *DfEE Circular 4/ 98: Teaching: High status, high standards − requirements for courses of initial teacher training,* DfEE, London

DfEE (2001a) *Green Paper: Schools: building on success,* DfEE, London

Docking, J (ed) (1996) *National School Policy: Major issues in education policy for schools in England and Wales, 1979 onwards,* David Fulton, London

Elliot, G (1993a) Althusser's solitude, in *The Althusserian Legacy,* eds E Kaplan and M Sprinkler, Verso, London

Elliot, G (1993b) The lonely hour of the last instance: Louis Pierre Althusser 1918–1990, in *The Althusserian Legacy,* eds E Kaplan and M Sprinkler, Verso, London

Epstein, D (1993) *Changing Classroom Cultures: Anti-racism, politics and schools,* Trentham Books, Stoke-on-Trent

Gaine, C (1995) *Still No Problem Here,* Trentham Books, Stoke-on-Trent

Giroux, H (1983) Theories of reproduction and resistance in the new sociology of education: a critical analysis, *Harvard Educational Review,* 53 (3), pp 257–93

The Government (1999) *The Government's Annual Report 98/99,* The Stationery Office, London

Graham, D and Tytler, D (1993) *A Lesson for Us All: The making of the National Curriculum,* Routledge, London

Grenfell, M and James, D with Hodkinson, P, Reay, D and Robbins, D (1998) *Bourdieu And Education: Acts of practical theory,* Falmer Press, London

Harris, K (1982) *Teachers and Classes: A Marxist analysis,* Routledge & Kegan Paul, London

Harris, K (1994) *Teachers: Constructing the future,* Falmer Press, London

Hatcher, R (1995) The limitations of the new social democratic agendas: class, equality and agency, in *Education after the Conservatives,* eds R Hatcher and K Jones, Trentham Books, Stoke-on-Trent

Hatcher, R (1998) Class differentiation in education: rational choices? *British Journal Of Sociology of Education,* 19 (1), pp 5–24

Haymer, R (2001) How 11-plus divided twin brothers with the same IQ, *Sunday Mirror,* 18 February

Hill, D (1989) *Charge of The Right Brigade: The radical Right's attack on teacher education,* Institute for Education Policy Studies, Brighton

Hill, D (1997a) Equality and primary schooling: the policy context, intentions and effects of the Conservative 'reforms', in *Equality And The National Curriculum In Primary Schools,* eds M Cole, D Hill and S Shan, Cassell, London

Hill, D (1997b) Reflection in teacher education, in *Educational Dilemmas: Debate and diversity: teacher education and training, Vol 1,* eds K Watson, S Modgil and C Modgil, Cassell, London

Hill, D (1997c) Critical research and the death of dissent, *Research Intelligence,* 59 pp 25–26

Hill, D (1997d) Brief autobiography of a Bolshie dismissed, *General Educator,* 44 pp 15–17

Hill, D (1999) Social class, in *An Introduction to the Study of Education,* eds D Matheson and I Grosvenor, David Fulton, London

Hill, D (2001) State theory and the neo-liberal reconstruction of schooling and teacher education: a structuralist neo-Marxist critique of postmodernist, quasi-postmodernist, and culturalist neo-Marxist theory, *The British Journal of Sociology of Education,* 22 (1), pp 137–57.

Hill, D and Cole, M (eds) (1999a) *Promoting Equality in Secondary Schools,* Cassell, London

Hill, D and Cole, M (1999b) Introduction; education, education, education-equality and 'New Labour' in government, in *Promoting Equality In Secondary Schools,* eds D Hill and M Cole, Cassell, London

Hill, D, Cole, M and Williams, C (1997) Equality and primary teacher education, in *Promoting Equality In Primary Schools,* eds M Cole, D Hill and S Shan, Cassell, London

Hill, D, Saunders, M and Hankin, T (2001) Class analysis and education theory, in *Marxism Against Postmodernism in Educational Theory*, eds D Hill *et al*, Lexington Press, Lanham, MD

Hillcole Group (1991) *Changing the Future: Redprint for education*, Tufnell Press, London

Hillcole Group (1997*) Rethinking Education and Democracy: Education for the twenty first century*, Tufnell Press, London

Jenkins, R (1982) Pierre Bourdieu and the reproduction of determinism, *Sociology*, **16**

Jenkins, R (1992) *Pierre Bourdieu*, Routledge, London

Jones, K (1989) *Right Turn – the Conservative revolution in education?* Hutchinson, London

Jones, N and Docking, J (1992) *Special Educational Needs and the Education Reform Act*, Trentham Books, Stoke-on-Trent

Kelly, J (1999) Reworking gender and education, in *Postmodernism in Educational Theory: Education and the politics of human resistance*, eds D Hill *et al*, Tufnell Press, London

Khan, Z (1998) *Multicultural Education*, final year dissertation, Nene University College, Northampton, unpublished

Lareau, A (1997) Social class differences in family–school relationships: the importance of cultural capital, in *Education: Culture, economy, society*, ed A Halsey *et al*, Oxford University Press, Oxford

Larrain, J (1979) *The Concept Of Ideology*, Hutchinson, London

Lawton, D and Chitty, C (1987) Towards a National Curriculum, *Forum*, **30** (1)

Liston, D (1988) *Capitalist Schools: Explanation and ethics in radical studies of schooling*, Routledge, London

Mahoney, P and Hextall, I (2000) *Reconstructing Teaching: Standards, performance and accountability*, RoutledgeFalmer, London

Pollard, A *et al* (1994) *Changing English Primary Schools? The impact of the Education Reform Act at Key Stage One*, Cassell, London

Pumfrey, P and Verma, G (eds) (1994) *Cultural Diversity And The Curriculum, Vol 1: The Foundation Subjects and Religious Education in Secondary Schools*, Falmer Press, London

Sarup, M (1983*) Marxism/Structuralism/Education*, Falmer Press, Lewes

Sanders, M, Hill, D and Hankin, T (1999) Education theory and the return to class analysis, in *Postmodern Excess in Education Theory: Education and the politics of human resistance*, eds D Hill *et al*, Tufnell Press, London

Searle, C (1996) OFSTEDed, 'Blunketted and permanently excluded': an experience of English education, *Race and Class*, **38** (1)

Searle, C (1997) *Living Community, Living School*, Tufnell Press, London

Searle, C (1998) Book Review of Hillcole Group, 1997, *Forum*, **40** pp 30–31

Shor, I (1986) *Culture Wars: School and society in the Conservative Restoration 1969–1984*, Routledge and Kegan Paul, London

Simon, B (1992) *What Future For Education?* Lawrence & Wishart, London

Social Trends (2001) *Social Trends no 31*, The Stationery Office, London

Thatcher, M (1993) *The Downing Street Years*, HarperCollins, London

Tomlinson, S and Craft, M (1995) *Ethnic Relations and Schooling*, Athlone, London

Toynbee, P and Walker, D (2001) *Did Things Get Better? An Audit of Labour's Successes and Failures*, Penguin, London

Troyna, B (1995) The local management of schools and racial equality, in *Relations and Schooling*, ed S Tomlinson, Athlone, London

Turner, E, Riddell, S and Brown, S (1995) *Gender Equality In Scottish Schools: The impact of recent educational reforms*, Equal Opportunities Commission, Manchester

Verma, G and Pumfrey, P (1994) *Cultural Diversity and The Curriculum, Vol 3: The foundation subjects and religious education in secondary schools*, Falmer Press, London

Weiner, G, Arnot, M and David, M (1997) Is the future female? Female success, male disadvantage and changing gender patterns in education, in *Education: Culture, economy, society*, eds A Halsey *et al*, Oxford University Press, Oxford

Whitty, G (1985) *Sociology And School Knowledge: Curriculum theory, research and policy*, Methuen, London

Whitty, G (1997) Marketization, the State, and the Re-Formation of the Teaching Profession, in *Education, Culture and Economy*, eds A H Halsey *et al*, Oxford University Press, Oxford

Whitty, G, Power, S and Halpin, D (1998) *Devolution and Choice in Education: The school, the state and the market*, Open University Press, Buckingham

Woodhead, C (1999) quoted in BBC News, Education: Woodhead joins attack on 'liberal' attitudes. HYPERLINK http://news2.thls.bbc.co.uk/hi/english/ education/specials/education http://news2.thls.bbc.co.uk/hi/english/ education/specials/education/newsid%5F399000/399093.stm. 20 July.

Woods, P and Jeffrey, B (1998) Choosing Positions: living the contradictions of OFSTED, *The British Journal of Sociology of Education*, **19** (4), pp 547–70

# 6

# Promoting equality and equal opportunities: school policies

*Chris Gaine*

## Editors' introduction

*A policy may be developed to ensure the provision of equality and equal opportunities within education, and that policy may receive the most widespread support from the education community, but could it therefore be implemented, to full and true effect? Chris Gaine takes issue with the management of change. An array of evidence from national and international educational research illustrates the dubious interface between the stipulations of policy and the support systems in schools (the processes and personnel) that are required if the policy is to be implemented thoroughly and completely. The chapter thereby maps the crucial areas where policy has failed to effect change in the past and where it can succeed in the future, particularly in relation to equality.*

## Introduction

This chapter focuses on the obstacles, hazards and misunderstandings that stand in the way of policies, because they are many. Policies are about change; they are not about static situations. Their production and formal adoption are critical stages in sharing and developing understanding and commitment, and the whole point of adopting them is to legitimize and formalize the school's engagement with *something that needs changing*, or at least constant scrutiny. The same is true of any policy: if guidelines, procedures, considerations and key ideas were widely shared and second nature they would not need writing down or monitoring. It is because taken-for-granted assumptions, 'common sense' and first reactions are often *not* what produce the best longer-term benefits for students that policies are needed. Policies legitimate certain concerns, provide resources to further them, and provide a basis for evaluation and refinement.

Rather than suggest blueprints for ideal policies, then, this chapter relates the existing literature on managing change to the history of equality policies in education. This includes considering the processes and factors that are important in understanding, analysing and encouraging egalitarian change in schools and classrooms. The two fields are not usually linked in the literature, perhaps because equality activists in the past were often not 'managers' and because managers are often more centrally concerned with other sorts of change.

## Recent policy and response

In the late 1970s there was barely a school in the land with an equal opportunities policy worthy of the name. From the early 1980s some London schools began to formulate school policies about 'race' and by the mid-1980s several local education authorities (LEAs) encouraged or even enjoined their schools to have anti-racist policies, with some extending this to anti-sexist policies (concerns about disability were still enmeshed in recent special needs legislation and sexuality was not even on the agenda – see Gaine, 1987, chapter 9). By the late 1980s and early 1990s, however, two contradictory forces were at work: on the one hand many committed teachers (and heads and LEAs too) were concerned to keep egalitarian policies alive and active, whereas on the other the mounting discourse of derision about equality, the prioritizing of the subject concerns of the National Curriculum with its attendant testing regime, and the attrition of LEA powers, all made this much harder to do.

At the same time there was some disenchantment with policies. When there had been none at all, then even getting a policy written and formally accepted, gaining the prestige of official text, was sometimes seen as a panacea. Of course it was not, as those who worked in schools were soon aware, and 'were policies worth the paper they were written on?' became a common, if rhetorical, question.

After the accumulated effect of 17 years of Conservative rule, it is possible to detect some easing of the hostility towards equality policies. For Labour, 'social exclusion' is at times a coded way of expressing concern about social class without sounding like 'old Labour', and at other times a legitimization of concern (and action) about other excluded groups. Following the Stephen Lawrence Inquiry it has been possible (at least for a while) to acknowledge racism in institutions. Although Epstein (1998) and others would argue that the debate is misconceived, the government has expressed concern about boys' underachievement. As part of the 'performativity' approach to improving education, schools are obliged to monitor results of different groups amongst the students. In one way, Ofsted has co-opted the notion of policies to the extent that prior to inspections schools are sometimes to be observed frantically writing or 'updating' policies about half a dozen issues, 'equal opportunities' included, but many suspect that this reflects more a concern on Ofsted's part with what is measurable and observable than a consistent concern to engage with equality issues critically (CRE, 2000). In another way, since 1997 Ofsted has published a report on ethnic minority achievement that explicitly states that schools that recognize 'race' and ethnicity as issues are more likely to be successful in serving minority pupils' needs than a 'colour blind' approach (Ofsted, 1999).

Generally, recent history shows signs of a thaw that contends with a covert air surrounding equality measures. In response, the purpose of this chapter is not to attempt some formulaic recipe for reaching an agreed policy, and certainly not to produce a list of exhortations about what it 'must' contain. Those who are committed to equality in education will not need to be persuaded by such a list, and the uncommitted are seldom convinced by phrases beginning 'all schools must' or 'what is needed is for teachers to'. A comprehensive checklist of what a policy ought to consider has already been drawn up, in the Runnymede Trust's *Equality Assurance* (1993), written predominantly with 'race' in mind but structured in such a way that provisions aimed at other inequalities can be added.

# Policy-induced change

Egalitarian policies directed at change within schools are subject to specific limitations. Inequalities operate at structural, institutional, cultural and personal levels and hence egalitarian change has to address itself to all these levels. Schools, however, cannot directly affect the structural level of national funding, curricular priorities, laws even. Although schools may engage with it and often will feel themselves constrained and undermined by it, their effective sphere of influence is at the level of personal, cultural and institutional inequality. *A realistic policy addresses itself to change at these levels and recognizes its limits.* In order to relate policy to the context of implementation, the three main areas to be considered are *where and how* effective change is made, *who are the initiators and implementers*, and the allocation of *time* involved.

## Where and how

Egalitarian change, just like any other, can in principle be initiated and/or driven by school staff, the school, the local authority, or central government. The most striking egalitarian policies in post-war education have been state originated (see Gaine, 1990), focusing upon social class and resulting in the promotion, from the mid–1960s onwards, of non-selective secondary education. Later changes focusing on 'race' and gender have been initiated at school level, indeed at individual teacher level, where at times they have met formidable difficulties. At worst, trying to initiate this kind of change 'from the bottom up' was to work at a particularly difficult kind of innovation with none of the positive factors usually associated with success: there was no access to existing similar work, no one was actively promoting it, there was no policy or funds from the authorities at any level, virtually no external change agents on whom to rely for help or support, and at times no community pressure for change. We can reasonably speculate that many such initiatives before the 1980s (when some of the positive factors became more in evidence) did not progress very far.

When there was support from the local authority it helped, because its advocacy could then be invoked for legitimacy as well as resourcing, financial, personal and 'expert' support. Logic suggests, however, that the level of LEA support in many areas was inherently limited in proportion to the electoral gains in the high profiling of egalitarian reforms (and this became more of a limitation in the late 1980s and the 1990s).

Similarly, support from the centre cannot but help in some way. This is not to say that state-led initiatives are always better or to imply that somehow egalitarian work would be more effective if centrally instigated and led. Clearly, the central and local state can issue guidelines, policies, even directives, but we have no reason whatsoever to imagine that these actions in their own right produce any results. Besides, such centrally instigated reform is inevitably driven by a blend of different pressures and while it is usually

> accompanied by greater commitment of leaders, the power of new ideas, and additional resources. . . it also produces overload, unrealistic time-lines, unco-ordinated demands, simplistic solutions, misdirected efforts, inconsistencies and underestimation of what it takes to bring about reform.
>
> (Fullan, 1991: 27)

Researchers also seem to agree that large-scale curriculum projects (like the Humanities Curriculum Project in the 1970s) are often unsuccessful. This is despite the resulting time, resources and legitimization, mainly because they tend to assume a common value system, one that treats teachers only as technicians and passive recipients of programmes that they were not convinced they needed (Tompkins, 1986). This is a powerful factor in any reform where there is a high level of disenchantment with government-led initiatives.

If adequate responsiveness between the different key actors and agencies in education is a necessary condition for change to come about, then a crucial condition is adequate support from teachers and others working in schools. *If proposed changes are not meaningful to staff they will founder*, but the difficulty of the task of making them meaningful is almost always underestimated. Change cannot be assimilated unless its meaning is shared.

For staff to begin to take them to heart changes need to be perceived as clearly offering some improvement to themselves and their students. This sounds like a matter of rational appraisal, but actually it is rooted in the fact that change is seldom emotionally easy and therefore *needs justifying*. Marris (1975) puts it much more strongly than this, stressing that any significant change involves loss, anxiety and struggle and that would-be change agents need to recognize and understand this:

> When those who have the power to manipulate changes act as if they have only to explain, and when their explanations are not at once accepted, shrug off opposition as opposition or prejudice, they express a profound contempt for the meaning of lives other than their own. For the reformers have already assimilated these changes to their purposes, and worked out a reformulation which makes sense to them, perhaps through months or years of analysis and debate. If they deny others the chance to do the same, they treat them as puppets dangling by the threads of their own preconceptions.
>
> (Marris, 1975: 166)

This may seem like an apologia for relatively impervious racist, sexist, homophobic or other oppressive attitudes and assumptions, but it makes the point that in some respects such attitudes are like any others: they make sense of the world for individuals, and they interlock with, shore up and are in turn shored up by other constructs and meanings. They matter, and they do not respond well to attack. Looked at this way, simple human conservatism is necessarily tenacious and has to be regarded more respectfully than 'mere' stupidity or stubbornness. Fullan (1991) echoes Marris's point, stating that 'changes in beliefs are even more difficult: they challenge the core values held by individuals regarding the purposes of education; moreover, beliefs are often not explicit, discussed or understood, but rather are buried at the level of unstated assumptions' (1991: 42).

Some examples of what can happen when unstated assumptions are challenged are given in Rudduck's study of gender policies in secondary schools (1994), and an Australian study of anti-sexist initiatives (Kenway, 1995). Rudduck's book contains some striking accounts of the resistance activists met, even to (apparently) minor changes and when the change agent was in a relatively senior position (the flat refusal of one man, for instance, to comply with a direct instruction simply to write registers alphabetically). Kenway, too, had to confront trivialization, uncooperativeness and antipathy from teachers who felt their masculinity to be 'under siege'. Deep changes call for corresponding changes in a teacher's occupational identity, which 'represents the accumulated wisdom of how to handle the job, derived from their own experience and the experience of all who have had the job before or share it with them. Change threatens to invalidate this experience' (Marris, 1975: 16).

In some occupations and spheres it may be possible to devise procedures that promote equal treatment, such as applying careful and explicit criteria for council housing allocations or job recruitment. With regard to racial attitudes, it has been argued that in such circumstances a change in attitude can follow a change in behaviour, rather than the other way round, but in schools the problem for the change agent can be altogether more abstract, intangible and intractable than

that. The content of lessons and implicit messages conveyed by staff are pro-
foundly personal, buried well beneath assumptions embodied in the register.

Huberman (1983) indicates another set of reasons why teachers find change
difficult, based on a summary of key demands in their daily lives, as follows:

> *Immediacy and concreteness:* Teachers engage in an estimated 200,000 interchanges a
> year, most of them spontaneous and requiring action.
>
> *Multidimensionality and simultaneity:* Teachers must carry on a range of operations
> simultaneously, providing materials, interacting with one pupil and monitoring the
> others, assessing progress, attending to needs and behaviour.
>
> *Unpredictability:* Anything can happen. Schools are reactive partly because they
> must deal with unstable input – classes have different 'personalities' from year to
> year; a well-planned lesson may fall flat; what works with one child is ineffective
> for another; what works one day may not work the next.
>
> *Personal involvement with students:* Teachers discover that they need to develop
> and maintain personal relationships and that for most students meaningful interaction
> is a precursor to academic learning
>
> (Huberman, 1983: 482–83)

Thus 'the rational assumptions, abstraction and descriptions of a proposed new
curriculum do not make sense in the capricious world of the teacher' (Fullan,
1991: 34), and the potential costs of change for teachers in terms of time and
emotional investment are likely to be high. This results in one of the many
unproductive states into which teachers can be pushed, that of 'painful unclarity
– when unclear innovations are attempted under conditions that do not support
development of the subjective meaning of change' (1991: 35). Gross *et al* (1971)
illustrate this in their account of unrealized change in a school where, on the
face of it, the climate was supportive but where the real fundamentals of what
was required of them was simply unclear to teachers.

The familiar way of avoiding this, and other states such as false clarity (where
people think they have changed but in fact have only assimilated superficialities)
is by some process of in-service training, about which Fullan (1991) provides a
pessimistic summary:

> Pre-implementation training in which even intensive sessions are used. . . does not
> work. . . One-shot workshops prior to and even during implementation are not
> very helpful. Workshop trainers. . . are frequently ineffective. Consultants inside
> the district are often unclear about their roles. Teachers say they learn best from
> other teachers but research shows that they interact with each other infrequently. . .
> concrete and skill-specific training is effective, but only for the short run.
>
> (1991: 85)

Yet to combine pre-implementation training with assistance during implementation can be effective, as can be training of teachers as staff developers and the
provision of direct, practical, concrete outside help, supporting ongoing,

interactive, cumulative learning of new ideas, skills and behaviour. Telling people what they *ought* to do does not work.

It was exactly this kind of ongoing and interactive development that was missing in the study by Gross *et al* (1971), leading to teachers applying minimal effort towards change because they felt they did not have the necessary skills and knowledge. *The more complex the change, the more interaction is required during implementation*, and equality is complex.

Similar challenges present themselves when we look at the features of change or non-change at school level. Fullan suggests three Rs: *relevance, readiness* and *resources*. Changes are perceived to be relevant when they clearly have something to offer teachers and students (and to do so they have to be meaningful subjectively, as already discussed). Readiness is the school's capacity to 'use' reform. For individuals this means the proposed change must meet a perceived need and use their knowledge and skills; for schools it means there must be an appropriate cultural climate, available time and attention free from other concerns, and hence the third R, available resources. Schools vary in their promotion and support of a climate of change. The quality of interaction and the exchange of ideas, support and positive feelings about their work (not surprisingly) have an effect on staff morale and resulting orientation towards change (Mortimore *et al*, 1988; Rosenholtz, 1989). Analysis of recurring themes in the improvement of urban high schools suggests six elements: vision building, initiative taking and empowerment, staff development/resources assistance, restructuring, monitoring/problem coping, and the presence of evolutionary planning (Louis and Miles, 1990). When the balance is right then the school and the teachers can deal with the inevitable but nonetheless uncomfortable 'internal turbulence' (Huberman, 1992). Similarly, Ainscow and Hopkins (1994) state:

> Many research studies have found that, without a period of destabilisation, successful, long lasting change is unlikely to occur. Yet it is at this point that most change fails to progress beyond early implementation. In these cases, when the change hits the wall of individual learning or institutional resistance, internal turbulence begins to occur and developmental work begins to impact on all staff. . . this, we find, is the predictable pathology of educational change.
>
> (1994: 170)

While one might predict that attempting to promote egalitarian change would promote conflict, it should be remembered that conflict almost certainly exists in any case. Education is by definition a field of value divergence and dispute, not least about what it means to be educated. In recent years there has been a borrowing from industrial and commercial management theory of the idea of 'vision' and of schools having (or a good leader creating) a sense of mission and common purpose. While this may be possible and seems to be particularly attractive to the school effectiveness and school improvement movements, it can run the risk of ignoring the inherent conflicts in schools. *Change-makers should not be over-rational about school systems that are not*, being guided as they are by multiple and sometimes competing goals, with power located at various points in the system making decisions which can amount to bargains with several (sometimes unpredictable) constituencies.

Ball (1987: 8) develops this theme much more, conceptualizing schools not as organizations with coherent missions but through notions of power, goal diversity, ideological disputation, conflict, political activity and control. Different groups of pupils receive differing priorities within and between schools, differing philosophies are never far away. There is no understanding of schools, he suggests, without a recognition that they are arenas of struggle and hence no understanding of change in schools without a recognition of the role of power and control, ideologies, differing goals – and micro-politics. In secondary schools (Ball's main focus) amalgamations to form comprehensives in the 1970s meant that many were still riven with the resulting internal factions well into the 1980s, with divides between the former grammar and secondary modern camps, between subject departments and between changing subject missions within them, and between pastoral and academic structures. This must have militated against a shared perspective on the equality policies, let alone the subsequent changes brought about by the Education Reform Act. Thus equality has to be seen in the context of a school's existing micro-political arena, to which it may represent a potential challenge, for instance to the autonomy of subject or pastoral groupings and their associated hierarchies, career paths, and control of resources in the shape of money, staffing, time and territory.

Other work suggests that assessments similar to those made by Ball can also be made about primary schools. Southworth (1994) discusses very effective head teachers who had established pervasive cultures in their schools, but also indicates that it may take a head 10 years of work, including a series of careful appointments, to bring the school to a common set of values (and even then they may be his/her values, rather than genuinely conceived by the staff).

> Cultures of collegiality, mutual support and continuous critical development clearly cannot be taken for granted, and changes sought for reasons rooted in educational philosophy may either become entangled in pre-existing conflicts or get nowhere at all if they do not match with the head's (or the dominant group's) vision.
>
> (Gaine, 2000: 77)

In tactical terms, any change agent would have to examine his or her own colleagues for the different kinds of teachers identified by Ball as *believers*, for whom ideologies are important, *non-believers* to whom they are largely irrelevant, and *cynics*, who ridicule, reject or manipulate (1987: 16). Baldridge (1971) suggests officials, activists, attentives and apathetics, while for particular initiatives Lyseight-Jones (1990) lists supporters, blockers, opinion leaders, don't knows, laggards and band-wagoners. As these labels indicate, in micro-politics *influence is at least as useful a concept as power*, and influence can be related to several features of an individual such as age or gender.

The motive for egalitarian work is a problem. There are strategic, pragmatic, one might almost say selfish, motives for individuals (promotion, resources) or institutions (market advantage, profile) in other words, 'There are many reasons other than educational merit that influence decisions to change' (Fullan, 1991: 28). But there *are* principled motives: sometimes the motivation is provided by direct and obvious beneficiaries, and there are altruistic motives based on educational principles and values. Those who seek to persuade need to be clear which motives they are appealing to.

## Initiators and implementers

At this juncture, it is useful to consider the evidence for the effectiveness of different actors in the formulation and implementation of change-orientated policies.

Outside forces, of course, have a part to play. Although it is difficult to quantify the effect, outside policy statements and guidelines can confer legitimacy on initiatives taken at teacher or school level. To an extent, resources can be directed towards existing or prioritized initiatives. The curriculum (in its widest sense) could be changed on paper by LEAs for much of the 1980s, and has been changed by the government in major ways since 1988, but any such change still has to deal with teacher implementation. Evidence already cited suggests that facilitating (in a variety of ways) well-designed in-service training (INSET) that supports the process of implementation is more effective than almost anything else that agencies outside the school can do. Yet we know that centrally initiated changes have a poor record of success, especially when a government wants to address a need that is not recognized at school level, in accordance with agendas of its own. Two different worlds are interacting, and for Fullan (1991) to 'the extent that each side is ignorant of the *subjective* world of the other, reform will fail' (1991: 79, original emphasis). We have yet to see the extent of long-lasting change in teacher beliefs and behaviour resulting from the 'reforms' of the 1980s and 1990s, but it should be remembered that it was achieved by *force majeur*, with enormous attendant costs in terms of morale, teacher autonomy, illness and early retirement, as well as money.

At the school level, research from a variety of perspectives suggests that the role of the head is crucial, his or her active support being one of the single most important factors in successful change (Berman and McLaughlin, 1977). Head teachers have a role in creating the climate or 'readiness' for innovation, but seldom lead it. This is partly because a key part of their role is also to maintain stability – 'no news is good news, as long as everything is relatively quiet' – and partly because they are often (albeit against their better judgement) engaged in troubleshooting, crisis and containment. As House and Lapan (1978) state, the 'Principal cannot be a change agent or leader under these conditions' (1978: 145). For the same reasons the head can be the most effective 'blocker', even unintentionally: having initiated or supported change, heads have to back it in ways that teachers need. Failing to realize a need for new materials, skills development, ongoing evaluation, or revised organizational arrangements can turn initially positive teachers into resistant cynics or non-believers (Gross *et al*, 1971).

A degree of unrecorded change may exist, change attempted by individual teachers in the past that stood little chance of success, due to isolation. There must be many unmarked graves of attempts to do anti-racist or anti-sexist work in the 1970s, let alone earlier (although at the time there was more support at different levels in the system to combat class inequalities, evidenced by the number of progressive comprehensives created at that time – for instance in Leicestershire). Quite apart from the difficulties of the specifically egalitarian change we are examining, the conditions of teachers' work do not always allow them to be effective change agents (see Huberman, 1992) unless they are in schools where their energies and aims are supported, rewarded and revitalized. All commentators seem to agree that, whatever the change, *enormous and unusual personal commitment and energy are necessary on the part of the committed teacher* if they are to be successful. Dadds (1994) describes 'Carol', the initiator, in her account of a school innovation, as the 'heroine' of the story, and she means it. Suffice it to say that from the wealth of evidence about change, while teachers can be effective at changing what they do in their own classrooms, they will only be effective in bringing about wider change under certain conditions.

The first of these almost amounts to a precondition set by the school: opportunities need to exist for frequent interaction with others, especially if this involves engaging in shared reflection upon the higher-order skills in their work. In a very large study of teachers' work in the United States, Goodlad (1984) concludes that their 'autonomy seemed to be exercised in a context more of isolation than of rich professional dialogue' (1984: 186). This theme of isolation is echoed by others (for example, Rosenholtz, 1989) and its opposite, meaningful collaboration, is more often noted as a feature of effective schools (Mortimore *et al*, 1988). Thus, teachers can effect change upon other teachers if the school climate already facilitates dialogue or if the change process promotes it. In other words, teachers 'need to have one-to-one and group opportunities to receive and give help and more simply to *converse* about the meaning of change' (Fullan, 1991: 132, original emphasis).

A teacher innovator also needs to be a reflective practitioner (Schon, 1983). We have already seen that no real change happens unless it is internalized at a deep level, so teachers need to be able to reflect constantly upon and make links between apparently mundane classroom events and their meanings in relation to broader concerns. Bussis *et al* (1976) illustrate this with the introduction of 'progressive' primary practice and Sarason (1982) with the mainstreaming of special needs in the United States. Teachers who emphasize either technique or ideals at the expense of the other is unlikely to carry colleagues with them.

A third feature related to teacher innovation is the teachers' own career cycle. In a Swiss study Huberman (1978, cited by Fullan) found that the period for experimentation and diversifying tended to be between teachers' 7th and 18th years in the job, although this could be considerably shorter. Other phases (survival, stabilization and finally, focusing down) are self-evidently not conducive to making changes. However, because careers are made or enhanced by being noted as an innovator there is a strong risk that unless change is consolidated by becoming fundamentally owned by colleagues, it will never mature once its 'parent' has left.

Finally, innovating teachers need to beware of the commonest trap fallen into by outsiders, namely, ignoring the daily world of their colleagues. This requires them to be highly skilled interpersonally and tactically:

> If the teacher as advocate can become skilled at integrating the change and the change process, he or she can become one of the most powerful forces of change. . .
> It will require confronting norms of isolation. . . avoiding the imposition of solutions, premature forging of consensus, and failure to take into account the personal situations of those with whom the teacher-leaders wish to work.
>
> (Fullan, 1991: 139)

Advocates not skilled in this way risk what might be called *the change agent's paradox* – the more committed they are (or appear) the *less* likely they may be to accomplish the desired change.

School students could in principle also have a role in initiating and implementing change: after all, whatever the power of the staff, norms and values among pupils are both pervasive and can be fairly autonomous. Given their majority in any school, when students press for change about energy use, paper recycling, litter, wet breaks, or bullying they certainly elicit some response and there is no reason why this should not be true of equality issues. Yet given also the prevailing cultural attitudes in many (but not all) schools, students concerned about inequality are unlikely to be other than a minority.

A small number of the least powerful and inevitably temporary members of an institution may not be in a strong position to press for change, but they are critical in its implementation: any intended change involving, say, racist or homophobic language, which did not actively involve students would be seriously flawed, to say the least. If change is a process in which the staff's understanding has to be engaged, then the same has to be true of their students. It sounds like a truism, but any effective change in education has to be *educational*.

Lastly, it is worth considering briefly the role of teacher unions in innovation. In *No Problem Here* I suggested to teachers:

> Where there is an active union branch in a school they are clearly a group to work with. As the unions are sometimes the only cross-curricular groups who are allowed to meet without the hierarchy setting the agenda, and often have clear national guidelines to back them up, union members are a potential force for change.
>
> (Gaine, 1987: 138)

There is little general research on the efficacy of union-sponsored change. McDonnell and Pascal (1988) dispute the common charge that unions function as obstacles to reform, and it is worth noting that the three main UK teacher unions all produced guidance documents about 'race' during the 1980s and the

NUT continued to do so in the early 1990s (AMMA, 1986; NAS/UWT, 1986; NUT, 1978; 1984; 1986; 1989; 1992). All have produced new guidance documents for teachers since 1997. The NUT has also been far more active than the others have with respect to anti-sexist work.

The issue of who leads or initiates policy development makes a great difference to its effectiveness. *Government-induced change*, even if well funded and legitimated, does not necessarily produce anything that lasts. The same can apply to local *district-initiated change*. *School climate* and the *role of the head* can be crucial, and *teachers' working conditions* make it very difficult for them to initiate anything radical and sustained. In addition, without effective, responsive *interaction between these different spheres* of influence and power within education, effective change will not take place.

### Time to change

Given the complexity and multi-layered nature of true change, it is clear that it will never happen quickly. Three (not necessarily linear) phases are generally identified:

- initiation/mobilization/adoption;
- implementation/initial use;
- continuation/routinization/institutionalization.

There are *no* studies giving accounts of effective changes in education that have come about quickly. Despite the (theoretical) speed of communication and the massive funding and effort expended, according to Rogers and Shoemaker (1971) 'the average American school lags 25 years behind the best practice' (1971: 59). What is worse (from the point of view of the innovator) is that there is often an 'implementation dip': things get worse before they get better (and clearer). Southworth probably sums things up best, when stating that 'Change needs to be understood not as a Damascus road but as an endurance race' (1994: 22).

## Conclusions from research

In summary, the key criteria for evaluating a policy and its potential effectiveness in bringing about change are as follows:

- True change must be multi-level. School policies have to work within constraints and limits set by outside forces, but they will need to interact with these forces to be effective.
- Change initiated by the government or the LEA may have lasting effects in continuing to confer legitimacy.

- In classroom terms, significant change will not have been achieved unless materials have been revised, there are new teaching approaches, and there has been an alteration in teachers' beliefs, in other words, personal and cultural change is a critical target.
- Merely technical or documentary changes are likely to be ineffective.
- Outcomes for students are unlikely to be discernible in terms of assessments or easily quantifiable measures (see Gaine and George, 1999: 87–8 for an elaboration of this argument).

It has become very clear that change of any significance and duration is stubbornly difficult to bring about. We have the descriptions from Fullan (1991) of many kinds of non-change: technical modifications without any corresponding change in beliefs; 'false clarity', when people think they have changed but have only adopted trappings; 'painful unclarity' when people are confused and resentful; changes which quickly die with the ending of funding, the loss of the head's support, or the departure of a key figure.

## Final practicalities

A synthesis of the existing research and the analysis in this chapter suggest that effective egalitarian school policies (policies that produce and promote change):

- need *pressure* to initiate and to implement, ideally at several levels at once;
- require deep and shared *understanding* of the changes required on the part of staff involving a spiral of reflective *learning*;
- involve risks and so create anxiety, uncertainty and the need for *support*;
- are helped or hindered by the *climate* and micro-political features of the school;
- almost always need the clear support of the *head*;
- can be nurtured and legitimated, or undermined, by *key players outside the school*;
- take *time* to develop and to work (usually years).

These constituents of potentially effective policy can each be related to specific areas of consideration. A key strategic question in relation to *pressure* is what kind of pressure will be effective and on whom? Are there specific groups within the school that can be shown to be losing out through present practices? If this can be shown to have outcomes in disruption, attainment, staying-on rates and published results then it can be persuasive. Can pressure be brought to bear from different sources – students, parents, governors, teachers, non-teaching staff, trade unions, religious or pressure groups? Can useful alliances be made between groups disadvantaged in different ways? Can pressure be brought to bear at different levels: individual classrooms, counselling systems, pupils' councils, posters and displays, language used in staff meetings, representation on the governing body? Can pressure be brought to bear in terms of motive? Is there a significant mismatch between ideals and actuality that might stir some into action?

For the task of developing *understanding* it is possible to single out staff because they are the permanent members of any educational institution, and we could single out further those who have the most intense, varied and subtle interactions with students: primarily but not exclusively teachers. The task is to develop teachers' understanding of (and willingness to understand) what equal opportunities might really mean. Any policy needs to build in opportunities for the progressive development of understanding and insight through explicit INSET but also through any other opportunities that arise – department meetings, materials reviews, prospectus production, interaction with other schools and endless informal discussions and arguments. Procedures and rules can only govern overt and usually obvious behaviour; commitment comes from understanding, and understanding can sometimes only come slowly. Key people may need to be on a permanent monitoring group, although they may have rather different starting points. While many can identify with the description by Stephen Ball (1987) of a working party as 'a *cul de sac* down which ideas are lured and then quietly strangled', they can be made to be an effective source of developing commitment and understanding.

The need for *support* follows from the previous point. Patience and respect for seemingly intransigent colleagues or students can be hard to find but, for many, these aspects will determine whether they come to understand equal opportunities concerns. This does not have to mean being endlessly forgiving of bigots, but neither does it mean expecting everyone to travel at the same pace or with the same insights. Recognition of this can help to avoid the change agent's paradox of apparent 'overcommitment' leading to less effectiveness (although this really is a paradox: who has the resolve for this kind of work without enormous commitment?). In this connection, it should not be forgotten that support is needed for the change agents as well as for everyone else. This can come from allies within the school, senior staff, students, colleagues from other schools, networks and organizations, or from friends. It is much harder to be effective without it.

It is worth assessing the overall *climate* of one's school with regard to openness to change and innovation. How have other changes worked? Where did they start? Are there significant barriers in the form of nervous senior staff, rabid governors, or a generally obstructive and negative clique of staff? It is also worth examining formal and informal power structures – not least in terms of the balance between white and ethnic minority staff, young and old, male and female and those with working- and middle-class roots.

The need for the support of *the head* will make many readers' hearts sink. Nonetheless, it is necessary to emphasize the point that egalitarian change is fundamental to most if not all aspects of school life. A school that is critically engaged with these issues is a radically different kind of school from one that is not, so the head's role is central and, ultimately, cannot be sidestepped. However, to those working in an unpromising situation in this respect the key word may be 'ultimately'. The effects of pressure, learning and understanding, support and time can make themselves felt on heads too.

Key players outside the school in the 1990s are less likely to include the LEA than they were a decade ago, although they may still have their influence. As for parents with enhanced 'parental choice', groups bent on affecting the school's intake or profile with regard to class, special needs, ethnicity or gender may either legitimate or undermine egalitarian policies, and local media image and 'reputation' can similarly work for or against equal opportunities: 'political correctness' and homophobia still make powerful and easy local newspaper copy. As a key player the government, too, can work for or against the development of equal opportunities policies. Published league tables seem to have increased schools' anxiety about white and middle-class flight rather than concentrate everyone's minds on improving schooling for everyone. Yet Ofsted's inspection guidelines can be used to legitimate equal opportunities measures, and although there is no evidence yet of them becoming radical in their interpretation of the promotion of moral and spiritual development or citizenship, they can be a powerful source of pressure (or threatened pressure) if significant groups within a school are not being well served.

*Time* is what individual students do not have; yet it is crucial for them, their educators and their schools to find the time to fundamentally change the way they do things. This circle cannot be squared. This unpalatable, sometimes infuriating and always frustrating fact needs to be acknowledged in all policy planning, otherwise disillusionment or even despair will result. The implication of this is not that committed people simply wait for something to happen but that policies take account of the need for time and build in interim steps, stages and targets as well as mechanisms that take account of the other factors I have listed, many of which are dependent upon time.

Clearly, this chapter has not presented a simple and inspiring checklist of stages towards an effective equal opportunities policy, and there is always an element of dissatisfaction with this, a sense that the brief of the chapter (and the book) has not been fulfilled. Many readers will recognize, however, that no such checklist exists and that principle and commitment need to be informed by the experiences, successes and failures of others. If we are to advance the cause of equality in schooling, there are things we can learn from more general research about forces and processes involved in change. These things are worth at least as much consideration as the ideal content of a policy.

# References

Ainscow, M and Hopkins, D (1994) Understanding the moving school, in *Readings In Primary School Development*, ed G Southworth, Falmer Press, London

Assistant Masters and Mistresses Association (1986) *Our Multicultural Society, The Educational Response*, AMMA, London

Baldridge, V (1971) *Power and Conflict in the University*, Wiley, New York

Ball, S (1987) *The Micropolitics of the School*, Routledge, London

Berman, P and McLaughlin, M (1977) *Federal Programmes Supporting Education Change*, **3**, Rand Corporation, Santa Monica, CA

Bussis, A *et al* (1976) *Beyond Surface Curriculum*, Westview Press, Boulder, CO

Commission for Racial Equality (CRE) (2000) *Inspecting Schools For Race Equality: Ofsted's strengths and weaknesses*, CRE, London

Cuban, L (1988) A fundamental puzzle of school reform, *Phi Delta Kappa*, **70** (5), pp 341–44

Department of Education and Science (1985) *Education For All*, HMSO, London

Dadds, M (1994) Becoming someone other: teacher professional development and the management of change through INSET, in *Readings In Primary School Development*, ed G Southworth, Falmer Press, London

Epstein, D (1998) *Failing Boys?* Open University Press, Buckingham

Fullan, M (1985) Change process and strategies at local level, *Elementary School Journal*, **85** (3), pp 391–421

Fullan, M (1991) *The New Meaning Of Educational Change*, Cassell, London

Gaine, C (1987) *No Problem Here*, Hutchinson, London

Gaine, C (1990) On getting equal opportunities policies, and keeping them, in *Education For Equality*, ed M Cole, Routledge, London

Gaine, C (2000) Anti-racist education in 'white' areas: the limits and possibilities of change, *Race, Ethnicity and Education*, **3** (1), pp 65–81

Goodlad, J (1984) *A Place Called School: Prospects for the future*, McGraw Hill, New York

Gross, N, Giacquinta, J and Bernstein, M (1971) *Implementing Organisational Innovations*, Harper International, New York

House, E and Lapan, S (1978) *Survival in the Classroom*, Allyn & Bacon, Boston, MA

Huberman, M (1983) Recipes for busy kitchens, *Knowledge, Creation, Diffusion, Utilization*, **4**, pp 478–510

Huberman, M (1992) Critical Introduction, in *Successful School Improvement*, ed M Fullan, Open University Press, Milton Keynes

Kenway, J (1995) Masculinities in schools: under siege, on the defensive and under reconstruction, *Discourse*, **16** (1), pp 59–80

Levin, H (1976) Educational change, its meaning, in *The Limits of Educational Reform*, eds M Carnoy and H Levin, McKay, New York

Louis, K and Miles, M (1990) *Improving The Urban High School: What works and why*, Teachers College Press, New York

Lyseight-Jones, P (1990) A management of change perspective: turning the whole school around, in *Education for Equality*, ed M Cole, Routledge, London

McDonnell, L and Pascall, A (1988) *Teacher Unions And Educational Reform*, Rand Corporation, Santa Monica, CA

Marris, P (1975) *Loss And Change*, Doubleday, New York

Mortimore, P *et al* (1988*) School Matters: The junior years*, Open Books, Wells

National Association of Schoolmasters/Union of Woman Teachers (1986) *Multi-Ethnic Education*, NAS/UWT, Birmingham

National Union of Teachers (NUT) (1978) *All Our Children*, NUT, London

NUT (1984) *Combating Racism in Schools*, NUT, London

NUT (1986) *Education for Equality*, NUT, London

NUT (1989) *Anti-Racism in Education*, NUT, London

NUT (1992) *Anti-Racist Curriculum Guidelines*, NUT, London

Ofsted, (1999) *Raising the Achievement of Minority Ethnic Pupils,* Ofsted, London

Reay, D (1991) Working with boys, *Gender And Education*, **3** (3), pp 269–82

Rogers, E and Shoemaker, F (1971) *Communication of Innovations*, 2nd edn, Free Press, New York

Rosenholtz, S (1989) *Teachers' Workplace: the social organization of schools*, Longman, New York

Rudduck, J (1994) *Developing a Gender Policy in Secondary Schools,* Open University Press, Milton Keynes

Runnymede Trust (1993) *Equality Assurance,* Runnymede Trust/Trentham Books, London

Sarason, S (1982) *The Culture of the School and the Problem of Change,* Allyn & Bacon, Boston, MA

Sarason, S (1990) *The Predictable Failure of School Reform,* Jossey Bass, San Francisco, CA

Schon, D (1983) *The Reflective Practitioner,* Temple Smith, London

Southworth, G (1994) *Readings in Primary School Development*, Falmer Press, London

Tompkins, G (1986) *A Common Countenance: Stability and change in the Canadian curriculum*, Prentice-Hall, Toronto

Part II

# Facts and Concepts

# 7

# Social class

## Dave Hill and Mike Cole

### Editors' introduction

*In this chapter, Hill and Cole examine the overall economic context in which inequalities are reproduced. The context is a class-based capitalist mode of production. They apply three different theoretical perspectives, functionalism, Marxism and post-modernism to analyse, firstly, social class per se and, secondly, the relationship between social class and education. In doing so, they critique consumption/life-style-based social class classifications. They present and discuss the persistent social class related inequalities in society and in the education system.*

### Introduction

In this chapter, we demonstrate the social class inequalities that characterize British society and the education system in England and Wales. We present a Marxist analysis of these inequalities and of the classifications that are commonly used to sort people into occupational and life-style/consumption-based groupings. We conclude briefly by calling for an egalitarian and critical education system, a theme that is elaborated in the concluding chapter.

### Social class and society

The degree to which the UK is a class-divided society is apparent from following statistics:

- Looking at the very poorest, 8.75 million people were in households with less than 40 per cent of average income. This is half a million higher than in 1996/97 and four times the level of the early 1980s (Rahman *et al*, 2000: 3).
- As of 1998/99 there were 4.5 million children in households with below half-average income after housing costs. This represents a threefold rise over the last 20 years. Around two million children live in households where there is no adult in paid employment (Rahman *et al*, 2000: 5).
- The differences in health between different social classes remains striking: children in the manual social classes are twice as likely to die in an accident as those in the non-manual classes, and girls in the manual social classes are around five times as likely to become mothers as those in non-manual classes (Rahman *et al*, 2000: 6).
- 'Lone parents and households with an unemployed head are twice as likely to get burgled as the average, and much less likely to have any household insurance. And one in six of the poorest households do not have any type of bank or building society account, compared with 1 in 20 households on average incomes' (Rahman *et al*, 2000: 6).
- 'Based on a survey in September 1999. . . more than two-fifths of [lone parents] with one child said they had incomes below £163 a week, the amount needed to buy the goods and services that most people regarded as essentials. . . More than half lone parents with two or more children had incomes below. . . £227 a week' (Gordon and Townsend, 2001, reported in Carvel, 2001b).
- '[The] distribution of income became more unequal in the 80s, stabilised in the early 90s and began to widen again in 1997. In 1997–8 the income of the richest 10% rose 4% to £559.70 a week while for the poorest it rose only 1.8% to £136.10' (*Social Trends*, 2001, reported in Carvel, 2001a).
- As regards the distribution of wealth, the poorest half of the population owns only 5– 6 per cent of the total national wealth. The most wealthy 1 per cent, on the other hand, owns around a quarter of all wealth. This is apparent from Table 7.1.

These figures are before the effects of the national minimum wage and the working families tax credit, introduced by the New Labour government, whose stated intention is to abolish child poverty completely by 2020. The New Labour government increased the minimum wage from £3.70 an hour to £4.10 an hour for adults as from 1 October 2001, boosting the pay of between 1.3 and 1.5 million low-paid workers.

Poverty – low income and the lack of wealth – is overwhelmingly a function of social class position. There are certainly examples of distressed gentlefolk who have attended the most prestigious and expensive private schools such as Eton or Roedean, and while there are many highly paid professionals and senior managers whose weekly income is less than their weekly expenditure, poverty is not the typical characteristic of graduates of Eton or Roedean, nor of senior

**Table 7.1** *Distribution of wealth in the UK, 1976 and 1998 (Social Trends, 2001: 109)*

| | Percentages | | | |
| --- | --- | --- | --- | --- |
| | **1976** | **1991** | **1997** | **1998** |
| **Marketable wealth** | | | | |
| Percentage of wealth owned by:[1] | | | | |
| Most wealthy 1% | 21 | 17 | 22 | 23 |
| Most wealthy 5% | 38 | 35 | 43 | 44 |
| Most wealthy 10% | 50 | 47 | 55 | 56 |
| Most wealthy 25% | 71 | 71 | 75 | 75 |
| Most wealthy 50% | 92 | 92 | 93 | 94 |
| Total marketable wealth (£ billion) | £280bn | £1,711bn | £2,280bn | £2,543bn |
| **Marketable wealth less value of dwellings** | | | | |
| Percentage of wealth owned by:[1] | | | | |
| Most wealthy 1% | 29 | 29 | 30 | 26 |
| Most wealthy 5% | 47 | 51 | 55 | 50 |
| Most wealthy 10% | 57 | 64 | 67 | 65 |
| Most wealthy 25% | 73 | 80 | 84 | 86 |
| Most wealthy 50% | 88 | 93 | 95 | 95 |

[1] Adults aged 18 and over

managers or media moguls. Poverty *is*, however, the typical characteristic of the unemployed and the unskilled white- and blue-collar working classes.

Adonis and Pollard's *A Class Act, The Myth of Britain's Classless Society* (1997) also shows how Britain is still a deeply divided society, characterized by class distinctions. In particular, Adonis and Pollard focus on the system of secondary education, which is rigidly separated into a flourishing, lavishly funded private sector, as compared to a demoralized, under-financed public sector. They point out that those who benefit from private education are almost invariably from privileged backgrounds: the fact that they attend the best schools in the country merely entrenches their privileges and enhances their prospects still further. Inequality, Adonis and Pollard insist, thus remains deeply rooted in British society.

## Social class and education: what are the facts?

*Guardian* writer Dave Hill (no relation to one of the co-writers of this chapter) has described the London Borough of Hackney as follows:

A typical Hackney class register contains a mosaic of names: Mbarek, Bianca, Yaseen, Timothy, Sidra, Dilek – a small sample that speaks volumes about the complex, polyglot neighbourhood where they all live. Hackney is a human kaleidoscope, where a hundred different languages from every continent is spoken. But while the borough is flush with cultural diversity, the potential this creates is cruelly underfulfilled thanks to Hackney's other defining feature, its ingrained poverty. Hackney is one of the poorest places in the whole of western Europe, a slough of want whose southern borders lie painfully adjacent to the vast wealth of the City. It is hard to overstate the hardship that exists there. In 1993, a third of all Hackney's households had a gross income of less than £5,000 a year.

Unemployment rates have exceeded 20 per cent for a generation. A quarter of its homes contain no bathroom or toilet. Such is the economic environment in which too many of Hackney's children live. No wonder that two thirds of its primary school pupils qualify for free school meals, the highest in the land. Children in such circumstances live in every corner of the borough, from Stoke Newington which adjoins Islington in the half gentrified north, where you can see thirty-something women in leggings and ankle bootees and even men in corduroys, to Homerton in the damp stained south-east, with its penitential, inter war council blocks and mentally disordered out patients from the old Hackney hospital wandering the streets.

(Hill, 1997)

And so, children from Hackney stand less chance of getting to university, or of learning to read than do children from Huntingdon. *Social Trends* (2001) points out that large differences remain between socio-economic groups. For example, 'around two thirds of young people with parents in non-manual occupations attained five or more GCSEs at grades A* to C in year 11 in 2000, compared with a third of those with parents in skilled and semi-skilled manual occupations' (p 68). Tables 7.2 and 7.3 show starkly the relationship between social class, educational success and income. The 'league tables' of various assessment and examination results in effect represent a social map of Britain.

The 1997 report on university entrance, commissioned by the Higher Education Funding Council for England (HEFCE) was headlined as 'University intake startlingly biased towards rich incomes' (Carvel, 1997). It noted that young people whose parents have postcodes in more privileged areas are five times more likely to get to university than contemporaries from working-class neighbourhoods with low–average incomes. The methodology attempted to match the postcodes of students applying to enter university with an analysis of the latest national census to provide a sharp-focus description of small neighbourhoods of about 150 households.

The report showed that the wealthiest quarter of young people, from areas with affluent lifestyles and with a high proportion of non-manual workers in those postal districts, have about a 50 per cent chance of becoming undergraduates before age 21. This is in marked contrast to the poorest quarter of postal districts – areas of high unemployment with a high proportion of manual workers. Young people here have an 11 per cent chance of going to university. Brian Fender, chief executive of HEFCE said that the 'startlingly wide variation'

**Table 7.2** *Highest qualification held in Great Britain by socio-economic group, 1996–97*

| | Professional | Employers and managers | Intermediate non-manual | Junior non-manual | Skilled manual and own account non-professional | Semi-skilled manual and personal service | Unskilled manual | All socio-economic |
|---|---|---|---|---|---|---|---|---|
| Degree | 66 | 24 | 26 | 5 | 2 | 1 | - | 14 |
| Higher Education | 16 | 19 | 25 | 6 | 9 | 5 | 1 | 12 |
| GCE A level[2] | 7 | 16 | 12 | 14 | 14 | 9 | 5 | 12 |
| GCSE Grades A-C[1] | 5 | 20 | 20 | 37 | 25 | 23 | 16 | 24 |
| GCSE Grades D-G[1,2] | 1 | 6 | 6 | 16 | 14 | 12 | 11 | 11 |
| Foreign | 4 | 2 | 3 | 2 | 2 | 3 | 2 | 2 |
| No qualifications | 2 | 12 | 8 | 20 | 34 | 47 | 65 | 25 |

[1] Excludes members of the armed forces, economically active full-time students and those who were unemployed and had never worked.
[2] Or equivalent.

From *Social Trends 28* (1998:67) London: HMSO Source: General Household Survey, Office for National Statistics; Continuous Household Survey; Northern Ireland Statistics and Research Agency

**Table 7.3** *Usual gross weekly earnings of all employees: by highest qualification level attained and age, Spring 2000*

| | 16–24 | 25–34 | 35–44 | 45–54 | 55–59/64 | All of working age |
|---|---|---|---|---|---|---|
| Degree or equivalent | £280 | £470 | £600 | £610 | £560 | £520 |
| Higher Education below degree level | £230 | £370 | £410 | £400 | £460 | £390 |
| GCE A level or equivalent | £180 | £340 | £390 | £360 | £330 | £320 |
| GCSE grades A★–C | £140 | £270 | £270 | £300 | £270 | £240 |
| Other, (including GCSE below grade C) | £180 | £260 | £280 | £260 | £290 | £260 |
| No qualifications | £100 | £220 | £200 | £210 | £210 | £200 |
| All | £170 | £340 | £370 | £360 | £320 | £320 |

*Source: Social Trends,* **31** (2001: 99)

in entry rates of rich and poor had important implications for the number of university places that might eventually be required if more young people went to university. He suggested that if children from more deprived backgrounds reached this average rate, more than 100,000 additional higher education places would be needed, raising the number of undergraduates by a fifth.

In more detail, the HEFCE report found that young people from very high-income professional neighbourhoods in exclusive areas had a 75 per cent chance of getting to university. In neighbourhoods of families with large detached properties in the stockbroker belts, the chance was 57 per cent. For military or white-collar families in owner-occupied suburban semis it was 33 per cent. At the bottom of the scale, young people from blue-collar families in council homes in areas of high unemployment had only a 7 per cent chance of getting to university. This suggested that the 30 per cent now going to university 'should not be viewed as a natural maximum but as a composite of very different rates' (Carvel, 1997).

Updated figures for entry in the academic year 1998–9, showing the percent-age of each social class gaining entry into higher education, is given in Table 7.4.

**Table 7.4** *Estimated participation rates in higher education by social class (Sanders, Tysome and Wojtas, 2001)*

| | Percentages | |
|---|---|---|
| | **1991–92** | **1998–99** |
| Professional | 55 | 72 |
| Intermediate | 36 | 45 |
| Skilled non-manual | 22 | 29 |
| Skilled manual | 11 | 17 |
| Partly skilled | 12 | 17 |
| Unskilled | 6 | 13 |

Although *Guardian* writer Dave Hill highlights the *problems* of the inner cities – they did after all, go up in flames in the inner city riots/risings of the early and mid-1980s, in Brixton, Toxteth, Handsworth – it is important to recall that most medium-sized and small towns in Britain have their own mini inner cities – their own heavily policed 'sink' or deprived housing estates. The 1993 Ofsted report *Access and Achievement in Urban Education* investigated educational provision in seven sample 'disadvantaged urban areas' (Ofsted 1993:6). These were Hartcliffe in Bristol, West Chaddesden in Derby, Thamesmead in the London Borough of Greenwich, Orchard Park in Hull, Wythenshawe in Manchester, Britwell and Northborough in Slough, and Tilbury in Thurrock. These areas are characterized by a high proportion of rented accommodation, usually local authority, over-crowding, low car ownership, high levels of litter, graffiti, the effects of vandalism, drug abuse and crime, and, in schools, a high percentage of pupils receiving free school meals. Ofsted could have chosen estates in a hundred other towns. They are also generally characterized by poor levels of educational achievement, attendance and expectation.

## Why social class is still a classroom issue

Children and teenagers bring their social class backgrounds into school with them (as well as other aspects of their subjectivities). As such they tend to meet with socially differentiated (social class-related) teacher expectations, as discussed in Chapter 5. This is primarily through 'the hidden curriculum' – the values and attitudes and desired social and work behaviours that is expected of them. Teenagers attending working-class secondary schools such as Hackney Downs School in London, or Ramsgate Secondary Modern in Kent, or The Ridings in Halifax tend to have different expectations, labelling, and stereotyped work futures than those attending prestigious selective secondary-age schools such as the London Oratory School.

As part of this social class-based differentiation between schools via 'the hidden curriculum', there is evidence that the pedagogies – the teaching and learning methods used by teachers and pupils – vary according to the pupils' social class. Sally Brown, Sheila Riddell and Jill Duffield's *Classroom Approaches to Learning and Teaching: The social class dimension* (1997) was based on following two classes in each of four schools through their first two years of secondary education, observing 204 lessons. Their findings were that children in the two working-class schools spent between 3 and 6 per cent of their time in discussion compared with 17 to 25 per cent in the middle-class schools. They observed that pupils in predominantly working-class secondary schools appear to be given more time-consuming reading and writing tasks than do children in middle-class schools and have less opportunity for classroom discussions. Their two-year study of four schools in a Scottish education authority demonstrated that teachers of English in the two middle-class schools were more likely to give a reading or writing assignment as homework leaving time in class for feedback and redrafting written work. Brown *et al* related this difference to the teachers' desire to maintain order in the classroom. They suggested that the long writing tasks were very much associated with control and the lack of discussion. This was, they suggested, to do with teachers thinking that the children couldn't really manage to discuss things among themselves.

According to this research, children at the middle-class schools were positive about the individual help they received. This was in contrast to a typical response from a pupil in a working-class school: 'I'd rather get right into it, get on and let them mark it and if there is something wrong, do it again.' Brown *et al* concluded added that although social class had been pushed off the *research* agenda by the focus on school effectiveness and improvement, this particular study indicated that it still needed to be investigated. It seems in many ways to replicate the findings of Bowles and Gintis's *Schooling in Capitalist America* referred to below, concerning the social class-based reproductive nature of the curriculum of schools.

## Social class: theoretical issues

Sociologists have been interested in social class for over one hundred years.[1] Oversimplifying matters, we can draw a broad distinction between three theoretical perspectives: functionalism, Marxism and post-modernism.

### Functionalism

> Different occupations can co-exist without being obliged mutually to destroy one another, for they pursue different objectives. . . Each of them can attain his [sic] end without preventing the others from attaining theirs. . . Since they perform

different services, they can perform them together. . . [T]hese different functions [can be] pictured as a series of branches issuing from a common trunk.

(Emile Durkheim, cited in Anthias and Kelly 1995: 184–85)

Functionalists have traditionally focused on the maintenance of stability in societies and the way in which values are shared, and on the way in which societies tend towards integration rather than disintegration – hence the metaphor 'branches from a common trunk'. Elements that are dysfunctional to given societies can be 'sorted out' and made functional without recourse to basic structural change. Thus, as far as social class is concerned, stratification (systematic structures of inequality) serves a necessary and definite function in all societies. Emile Durkheim, for example, although aware of the negative consequences of the division of classes in industrial society, argued that this division would ultimately have positive results, that it would lead to 'organic solidarity', that is solidarity through interdependence (Durkheim, 1968). Class inequality, therefore, according to the functionalists, is legitimate, indeed *necessary and desirable*, in that, as people realize their various class functions in society, a value consensus will emerge, and societies will became stable and integrated. As such, functionalism is essentially a conservative school of thought in the sense that it upholds conserving the status quo.

## Functionalist theory and education

Functionalism in education is associated with the theories of Parsons (for example, 1960) and Davis and Moore (for example, 1967). They see the major roles of schooling and other tiers of education as the socialization of new citizens (children/school students, job trainees, undergraduates) into accepting a shared set of values, accepting the currently existing society and economy. The function of education is seen as socialization and role allocation.

Individual failure, for example in educational performance or criminal behaviour, is explained by pathologizing it, by relating it to problems with socialization or individual personality deficiency. If you fail, functionalists suggest, it is basically your own fault, or that of your parents, or the neighbourhood in which you were brought up. On the first account, failure is indicative of a lack of intelligence and/or a lack of effort. Secondly, (or in addition) your parents could have provided you with an 'inadequate' socialization (witness how single parents are stigmatized in the press on this issue). Finally (or in addition) it may be because of your 'defective', 'feckless', deviant' social class location or subculture with which you identify – those inner-city council estates in national press stereotypes. Thus working class underachievement is attributed to dysfunctional elements in the system such as dysfunctional families or role models, or ineffective individual schools, rather than to structural inequalities in society. Functionalists assume that, once some changes are made, for example setting up a properly meritocratic schooling system, everyone will have the same chance to succeed.

Functionalists have inherent faith in the existence of meritocracies (the ability to be upwardly or downwardly mobile based on individual merit) in capitalist societies, or at least in those with liberal pluralist democracies and characterized by open social mobility. And they are quite happy for social and economic inequalities to remain.

## Marx and Marxism

> The history of all hitherto existing society is the history of class struggles. . . oppressor and oppressed stood in constant opposition to one another, carried on an uninterrupted, now hidden, now open fight, a fight that each time ended, either in a revolutionary re-constitution of society at large, or in the common ruin of the contending classes. . . Our epoch. . . has simplified the class antagonisms. . . into two great hostile camps, into two great classes directly facing each other: Bourgeoisie and Proletariat.
>
> (Karl Marx 1977: 35, 36)

It is Karl Marx more than anyone else who developed a comprehensive theory about the relationship between social class and social structures; in particular social class and capitalism. By capitalism, Marx meant that mode of production which followed feudalism and in which the means of production (raw materials, machinery and so on) are concentrated into a few hands, a world order predicated on a few owning the means of production – the bourgeoisie or the capitalist class – and the vast majority being force to sell their labour power in order to survive – the proletariat or the working class.

It is clear from the above quotations from Durkheim and Marx that the differences between functionalism, which centralizes *shared* values and consensus on the one hand, and Marxism on the other, are quite profound. Marx not only believed that capitalist society was inherently *conflict ridden* (contrast this belief with functionalism), but that class action though history is all apparent and inevitable. For Marx, class means exploitation and domination, which is grounded in *production* (social relations in factories and offices, for example). Despite attempts by academics at one level, and radical Right and New Labour politicians at another, to confine Marxism to the dustbin of history, we believe that Marx's works remain crucially significant for an analysis of contemporary capitalism (a view shared by increasing numbers of analysts writing in British and US broadsheet newspapers).

Marxists analyse events in terms of how they exemplify the class-based exploitative nature of the capitalist mode of production, and resistance to that exploitation and oppression. Marx believed that the workers and capitalists are in objective conflict with each other: the former are materially exploited by the latter whether they subjectively know it or not, or indeed whether they care or not.

In order to understand why Marx and Marxists believe this to be so, we need to examine a central theme in Marx's writings that has become known as the labour theory of value (LTV). According to Marx, workers' labour is embodied in goods that they produce. The finished products are appropriated by the capitalists and eventually sold at a profit. However the worker is paid only a fraction of the value he or she creates in productive labour; the wage does not represent the *total* value he or she creates. We *appear* to be paid for every single second we work. However, underneath this appearance the working day/week is split into socially necessary labour (and the wage represents *this*) and surplus labour, labour that is not reflected in the wage, the basis of surplus value out of which comes the capitalist's profit. Therefore, the capitalist mode of production is a system of exploitation of one class (the working class) by another (the capitalist class).

Issues of nomenclature, the way we refer to people or things, are crucial in understanding the nature of social class. For example, the use of the terms 'upper class' and 'lower class' can imply a justification for the existence of differentiated social classes and says nothing about the relationship between these classes. 'Ruling' and/or 'capitalist class', on the one hand, and 'working class', on the other, however, implies a specific relationship between them.

Marx's solution to what he saw as the exploitative nature of capitalism was its overthrow and its replacement by a socialist system throughout the world. This socialist society would be one in which, according to Marx, 'we shall have an association, in which the free development of each is the condition for the free development of all' (1977: 53). In such a society, the working class, instead of the capitalist class, would democratically own and control the means of production. Marx believed that such a society could only come about when the working class, in addition to being a 'class-in-itself' (an *objective* fact because of the shared exploitation inherent as a result of the LTV) became a 'class-for-itself' (Marx, 1847). By this, Marx meant a class with a *subjective* awareness of its social class position, that is to say, with 'class consciousness' – including an awareness of its exploitation. Marx presumed that, with this consciousness, the working class would seize control of the means of production, the economy. He also understood that to do this the working class would also need to take political power. Seizure of the economy and the political apparatus would constitute a socialist revolution. Here is not the place to rehearse the various arguments about whether a socialist society, based on Marxist principles, or indeed a socialist world, is possible, nor, if possible, what form it should take (but see, for example, Foot 1990, 1993, 2001; Birchall, 2000).[2] (For counter arguments, see, for example, Scruton 1980.)

## Marxism and education

Marxist sociology of education has been a major force from the mid-1970s onwards. (for example Sarup, 1983; Cole (ed), 1988; Livingstone, 1995; Rikowski, 1997, 2001a, b; Hill *et al*, 1999, 2001; Cole *et al*, 2001). In 1976, the very influential book *Schooling in Capitalist America*, by Sam Bowles and Herb Gintis was published. For the purposes of this chapter, it is only necessary to be aware of one of the central tenets of this seminal work namely *the correspondence principle*.[3] According to this principle working-class failure is seen as the *raison d'être* of the capitalist system. According to Bowles and Gintis, schools do not fail working-class pupils/students for reasons of dysfunction in the education system (which functionalists claim). On the contrary, according to Bowles and Gintis, capitalism *relies* on schools slotting certain young people in certain sectors of the capitalist economy, and others in other sectors. As they put it:

> The educational system helps integrate youth into the economic system. . . through a structural correspondence between its social relations and those of production. The structure of social relations in education not only inures the student to the discipline of the work place, but also develops the types of personal demeanour, modes of self-presentation, self-image, and social-class identifications which are the crucial ingredients of job adequacy. Specifically, the social relationships of education – the relationships between administrators and teachers, teachers and students, students and students, and students and their work – replicate the hierarchical division of labor. . . By attuning young people to a set of social relationships similar to those of the work place, schooling attempts to gear the development of personal needs to its requirements. . . Different levels of education feed workers into different levels within the occupational structure.
>
> (Bowles and Gintis, 1976, cited in Cole (ed) 1988: 2–3)[4]

The work of Bowles and Gintis, as with the other 'reproduction theorists' such as Althusser and Bourdieu, discussed in Chapter 5, has been the subject of considerable debate, since the publication of *Schooling in Capitalist America*. Most of this debate has been from within a Marxist perspective (see for example, Sarup 1983; Cole (ed) 1988; Livingstone 1995; Rikowski 1997 (2001a, b).[5] Reproduction theorists can be termed *structuralist* neo-Marxist, because they focus primarily on the power of economic structures to heavily affect education and social structures. They analyse and, ironically, agree with the (conservative) structural functionalists that schools *do* serve to separate and allocate children and students and socialize them into accepting the current structure of society and their places within it. However, (unlike functionalists), rather than welcoming this ideological hegemonizing, this use of schools by the ruling capitalist class to reproduce society culturally, economically and ideologically, Marxists critique it and regard this reproduction as immoral and in need of radical change.

One of the main critiques of the reproduction theorists has been the seeming lack of space credited, for example by Bowles and Gintis, to resistance to the reproduction of the capitalist system. Although Marxist in intent, and even though they do provide a chapter on how to resist and ultimately, by revolution to overthrow capitalism and replace it with socialism, Bowles and Gintis's theoretical line of argument, is functionalist in effect. This is because of the way it centralizes the 'inevitable' reproduction of the capitalist system within education. Their work lacks a concern with 'agency' – the capacity of people to change or transform substantially the situation they live in. Thus, a number of writers, such as Henry

Giroux, Peter McLaren, Paula Allman, and Richard Hatcher have stressed the role, actual and potential, of teachers and students resisting the reproduction of capitalism and agitating for progressive social change.

## Post-modernism

> Resistance towards certainty and resolution. Rejection of fixed notions or reality, knowledge, or method. Acceptance of complexity, of lack of clarity and of multiplicity. Acknowledgement of subjectivity, contradiction and irony. Irreverence for traditions of philosophy or morality. Deliberate intent to unsettle assumptions and presuppositions. Refusal to accept boundaries or hierarchies in ways of thinking. Disruption of binaries which define things as either/or.
>
> (Elizabeth Atkinson, 2001)

This is how Elizabeth Atkinson defines post-modern thinking. An eclectic concept, broadly speaking, it is the convergence of three separate strands of thought:

- A mixture of styles within forms of art. These are derived both from the past and from popular culture (for example, certain architectural forms, Warhol's Pop Art, 'hip hop' music, Salman Rushdie's novels, the work of film directors such as David Lynch and TV programmes such as Channel 4's *Big Breakfast Show*).
- The 'post-structuralist' writings of French theorists, such as Foucault, which reject structuralist explanations of society – the determining power of structures like capitalism or patriarchy – in favour of multiple sites of power.
- The conception of society as being 'post-industrial' or 'post-capitalist'.

It is the last two of these strands that are particularly relevant to social class. Post-modernists do not believe that any overarching theory (such as Marxism) can explain society. Post-modernists reject 'dualisms' (for example, the notion that there are two major classes in society that are fundamentally in conflict) in favour of 'multiple identities'. Thus, they claim, the class struggle has been superseded by the 'new social movements' (animal rights, gay and lesbian movements, the disability movements and so on). Since (following Foucault) they consider that power is everywhere and there is no possibility of generalized struggle, all forms of action, they consider, must be local and small scale. Post-modernists reject any notions of absolute truth or certainty in favour of multivocality (believing that no one view is any more true than another) and undecidability.

## Post-modernism and education

For post-modernists, the function of education is not seen as socializing individuals into a shared set of values (functionalism) since there are none. Rather post-modernism celebrates a multiplicity of forms of education, and of values.

While some post-modernists, because of their 'deliberate attempt to unsettle assumptions and presuppositions' (see the above quote by Atkinson) claim to share the belief of Marxists in social justice, by definition they have no programme for action nor vision of the future. Thus:

> Postmodernism's. . . myopic limitations have particular consequences when it comes to (their). . . inability to agree on and define a re-constructive socially and economically transformatory vision of the future (and to their). . . inability to define what *effective* and solidaristic role radical educators might play in that political strategy. . . no post-modernist theorist. . . has gone beyond *de*construction into constructing a coherent programme for *re*construction. This is precluded by a post-modern theoretical orientation. This applies to Giroux's. . . recent work (1999) as much as to his tentative suggestions of what a post-modern school might look like (in Aronowitz and Giroux, 1991, critiqued in Hill, 1993). It also applies to his first avowedly post-Marxist, post-modern book (1993). Similarly, Usher and Edwards (1994) suggest that any 'reconfiguration is provisional and open to question'. What this 'reconfiguration' looks like, in both cases, is redolent of 1960s individualistic, student-centred ultra-pluralism with its attendant dangers of separat(e)ist development.

(Hill, 2001: 140–41)

## Social class and the Registrar-General's classification

While we believe that Marxism provides the best explanation of social class, in order to understand sociological (and other) analyses, we need to turn to classifications of occupations used also for official government purposes. Here, we examine both the Registrar General's Classification, used since the census of 1911, and the new Office for Population and Census Studies (OPCS) classification, which updates it, and was used in the census of 2001.

In both these classifications occupational groups have been grouped into a number of broad categories. In the Registrar-General's classification (see Table 7.5), unskilled, semi-skilled, and skilled manual workers were denoted 'working class'. The 'working class' were differentiated from 'the lower middle class' – employees such as those in 'routine', low-paid white-collar jobs, who were in turn differentiated from other, better paid/higher status/more highly educated sections of the middle class. These official classes (Classes 1–5) have been used in recent decades as the basis for the A, B, C1, C2, D and E social class/consumption group indicators in sociological research, and by market research bureaux, opinion pollsters, and advertisers. They are still used in editions of *Social Trends* produced annually by the government National Statistics Office (for example, *Social Trends*, 2001).[6]

The OPCS classification of occupations developed in 1998 altered and replaced the Registrar-General's classification. It takes into account some recent changes in the occupational structure of the labour force. For example the new

**Table 7.5**  *The Registrar-General's classification of occupations*

| Class 1 | Professional | Accountant; architect, clergyman [sic], doctor, lawyer, university teacher | 5% |
|---------|--------------|---------------------------------------------------------------------------|-----|
| Class 2 | Intermediate | Aircraft pilot; chiropodist; MP; nurse; police officer; teacher | 14% |
| Class 3a | Skilled non-manual | Clerical worker; draughtsman [sic]; secretary | 10% |
| Class 3b | Skilled manual | Driver; butcher; bricklayer; cook | 44% |
| Class 4 | Semi-skilled | Bus conductor; postman [sic]; telephone operator | 17% |
| Class 5 | Unskilled | Labourer; messenger; cleaner; porter | 6% |

classification includes a new category, Class 8, which can be equated with 'the underclass'. (For a detailed Marxist critique of this concept of 'underclass', see Hickey, 2000: 170).[6]

This classification was revised in 2001 (Woodward, 2001). Based on criteria including employment contract, working conditions, prospects and security, teachers were demoted from Class 1 (Higher managerial and professional) to Class 2 (Lower managerial and professional). Also demoted were social workers, police constables and branch bank managers. Higher education lecturers remain in Class 1 'because they generally have more freedom and better conditions than teachers' (Woodward, 2001).

The 2001 revised socio-economic classification of occupations, with percentage of working population in brackets is given in Table 7.6.

### A Marxist critique[7]

These occupations are based not only on income but also on notions of status and associated consumption patterns and lifestyles (derived from the work of sociologist Max Weber – see Weber, 1979).

The classifications may be interesting sociologically, but Marxists would criticize them on three grounds. First, they ignore – indeed hide – the existence of the capitalist class – the class that dominates society economically and politically. This class own the means of production (and the means of distribution and exchange) – they are the owners of factories, transport companies, industry, finance, the media. In other words, these consumption-based patterns mask the existence of capitalists, including the super rich and the super powerful – the ruling class. The occupational, familial, educational and other interconnections of this class have been well documented, including, for example by Jeremy Paxman (1990) and Anthony Sampson (1982). In such classifications, the ultra-wealthy John Paul Getty, Richard Branson and the Duke of Westminster are placed in the same class as, for example, university lecturers, journalists, and solicitors, an employer of 25 workers, in the same class as an employer of 25,000.

**Table 7.6** *The 2001 reclassification of occupations*

---

*Class 1: Higher managerial and professional (11%)*. Higher managerial: employers of more than 25 staff, and senior managers (eg plumber, carpenter, dressmaker who employs more than 25). Higher professional: doctors, dentists, lawyers, university teachers.

*Class 2: Lower managerial and professional (23.5%)*. Junior managers, police sergeants, teachers, social workers, journalists.

*Class 3: Intermediate (14%)*. Police constables, firefighters, junior prison officers.

*Class 4: Small employers and own account workers (9.9%)*. Non-professionals who employ fewer than 25 employees (eg plumber, carpenter or dressmaker who employs fewer than 25 or who is self-employed).

*Class 5: Lower supervisory and technical (9.8%)* Factory foreman [sic], supervisors, train drivers (e.g. plumber, carpenter or dress maker who is employed by somebody else).

*Class 6 Semi-routine (18.6%)*. Shop assistants, call-centre workers.

*Class 7 Routine (12.7%)*. Drivers, cleaners, lorry and van drivers.

*Class 8* Never worked, unemployed, long-term sick.

---

Secondly, and more fundamentally, consumption-based classifications of social class gloss over and hide the fundamentally antagonistic relationship between the two main classes in society, the working class and the capitalist class. In Marxist analysis, the working class includes not only manual workers but also millions of white-collar workers – such as bank clerks and supermarket checkout operators, as well, whose conditions of work are similar to those of manual workers. They are exploited in fundamentally the same way as are the manual working classes. While it may be of sociological interest to be informed of, for example, the different leisure pursuits of, say, bank clerks and building labourers, research based on occupational hierarchies tells us little, if anything, about the *relationship* between social classes. This relationship, following Marx, is based fundamentally on conflict generated out of the conflicting interests of workers and capitalists.

The third criticism of consumption-based classifications is that, by segmenting the working class, they both hide the existence of *a* working class and they also serve the purpose of 'dividing and ruling' the working class – that, by segmenting different groups of workers, for example white-collar and blue-collar workers, and workers in work and the so-called 'underclass' workers (see note 6). These subdivisions of the working class can be termed class fractions or segments (Ainley, 1993). Such classifications hide and work to inhibit or disguise the common interests of these different groups comprising the working class. They serve, in various ways, to inhibit the development of a common (class) consciousness against the exploiting capitalist class. (In a similar way, Marxists note that the promotion of ethnic or 'racial' divisions between black and white workers also serves to weaken the solidarity and 'muscle' of the working class.)

## The way forward

So far, we have been very critical of the way in which schools are run. We would like to finish on a positive note. We believe that school students should be made aware of all the major possible ways that have been suggested to run local, national and international economies and societies. This book is written in the spirit of challenging the restrictive ethos of current conservative developments in schools (whatever the name of the government in power) and replacing it with one that encourages rather than obstructs critical thinking. Let us be very clear: we are not advocating that only socialist theories *should be* given critical attention in schools. This would amount to bias, just as we believe the present National Curriculum and hidden curriculum system amounts to bias. What we are suggesting is that schools should encourage critical thinking. This should include an awareness of ideas such as socialism and Marxism, which challenge capitalism, in addition to those ideas (currently virtually the only ones examined in schools) that uphold it.

We share the concerns of tens of thousands of teachers, student teachers, and others involved in schooling, that, in terms of the consideration of alternatives, and in terms of the development of 'critical thinking',[8] British schooling is in danger of being 'dumbed down'. Although there are some differences in policy, we see 'New Labour's' education policy as being essentially the same as that of the Conservative government (see Chapter 1 of this volume; Cole and Hill, 1997; Hill, 1999a, 2000; Power and Whitty, 1999).

At present, the ongoing education revolution in Britain, for example, the establishment of a competitive market in schooling, the imposition of ever more prescriptive curricula, guidelines for the National Curriculum core subjects and for 'teacher training' (see Chapters 1 and 4 of this volume), initiated by Margaret Thatcher and continued with a vengeance by New Labour (Cole and Hill, 1997; Whitty, 1998; Hill, 1999; Rikowski, 2001a) accords very much with the theoretical tenets of functionalism, not only in terms of educational policy (globalized capitalism is taken as given and schools and teachers are required to function efficiently to prepare pupils/students for their future roles in the division of labour in capitalist Britain) (Cole, 1999), but also in terms of content (again the free market economy is taken as given and debate about alternatives is stifled). Through the hidden curriculum, via the expectations of teachers and other school staff, by the respective roles of staff in the schools, schooling reflects and reinforces the social class hierarchy of the wider society.

However, schools, or other parts of the education system, do not have to be places where students are encouraged to think in one-dimensional ways. Indeed, were this the case, there would be no point in this book. Schools can and should be arenas for the encouragement of critical thought, where young people are provided with a number of ways of interpreting the world, not just the dominant perspectives.

In addition, the National Curriculum Council, responsible for organizing the first version of the National Curriculum after the 1988 Education Reform Act, stressed that pupils/students should be able to acquire value systems that are their own, 'rather than simply transmitted by others and accepted uncritically' (NCC, 1991: 10). School education should ensure that it gives 'systematic attention to a range of moral and social issues and. . . avoid the danger of indoctrination' (p 11). If this is seen in the context of 'understanding. . . society in all its aspects: its institutions, structures and characteristics, including economic and political organisation, and principles and life as a citizen, parent or worker in a community' (p 15) and of schools helping pupils/students 'understand about the 'political' aspects of living in society: human rights; decision-making processes: democratic participation' (p 15), then clearly students have a statutory right, even in the present political climate, to be introduced to the ideas of Karl Marx, as well as those of Emile Durkheim, Max Weber, Freidrich Hayek and Adam Smith. We are doing young people a serious disservice if, through our teaching, market capitalism – with its hierarchies of social class, of gender, of 'race' and ethnicity, of able bodied and able mindedness, and of sexuality – is presented as God-given, natural and uncontested. If possible alternative systems, such as socialism (for example 'state interventionist', on the one hand, and 'democratic workers' control', on the other), are not fully addressed, then school students are being denied a choice – with alternative social, political and economic systems being, in effect, hidden from history. All students have a right to know that market capitalism is simply one way, albeit globally the dominant one, of running economies, nationally and globally.

In order to begin to understand the changes occurring in industry and in the economy and society in general in any meaningful way, students need a thorough awareness of the significance, conceptually and empirically, of social class.

## Notes

1. See, for example, Lee and Newby (1984); Marshall *et al* (1989); Edgell (1993); Crompton (1994, 2000); German (1996); for thorough analyses of socio-logical debates surrounding social class.
2. Birchall cogently reveals the illogicallity of the anti-Marxists who proclaim that Marxism is fraudulent because it sees human history in terms of

scientific laws by which societies are consecutively replaced one by one (slavery by feudalism, feudalism by capitalism and capitalism by socialism). No such laws of history are possible, they proclaim. A few minutes later, by some strange sleight of hand, it emerges that after all there is one absolute law – all revolutions lead to tyranny (Birchall, 2000: 22). As Birchall points out, there have actually been only a few major revolutions in modern history, far too few to permit us to deduce any absolute principles. 'No self-respecting scientist would base a scientific law on so few experiments' (Birchall, 2000: 22). As he puts it, 'I can spin a coin and get "tails" five times in a row – but that scarcely proves all coins will come down tails' (2000: 22). Analysing the French and Russian revolutions and the Spanish Civil War, Birchall concludes that if any general lesson can be drawn, it is not that revolution leads to tyranny, but rather that failure to complete a revolution opens the way to tyranny (2000: 22).

Rikowski (2001a) explores how the 'Battle in Seattle', in late 1999, where radical students were much in evidence, incorporated a struggle against the World Trade Organization's education agenda. This agenda is an aspect of neo-liberalism – freeing up all public services to corporate capital (see Hill, 1999a).

3. Extracts from Bowles and Gintis (1976) that most clearly demonstrate the correspondence principle are reproduced in the prologue of Cole (ed) (1988). It should be mentioned that since the publication of *Schooling in Capitalist America*, Bowles and Gintis have moved their position theoretically from revolutionary socialism to what they describe as post-liberal democracy (see, for example, Bowles and Gintis, 1986; for a discussion see Cole 1988).

4. See Chapter 5 for a discussion of culturalist, or humanist, neo-Marxist critique of 'reproduction theory' texts such as *Schooling in Capitalist America*. Hill also discusses the differences been 'culturalist neo-Marxists' on the one hand, and the more deterministic 'structuralist neo-Marxists' (typified by the reproduction theorists) in Hill (1999b, 2001). (See also Sanders, Hill and Hankin, 1999; Hill, Sanders and Hankin, 2001).

5. These are also used in lifestyle selling Web sites. For example www.fish4 homes.co.uk, www.upmystreet.co.uk and www.move.co.uk show the social class breakdown for individual postcode areas, using the Registrar-General's Classification

6. Hickey argues against the use of the designation, 'underclass' because it has the effect of excluding its members from the working class. In addition, it implies that all other classes share a common feature (being 'included' in society) that distinguishes them from the long-term or periodically unemployed (who are said to be 'excluded'). This gives the impression that all other classes share something in common, or are even one social grouping, with interests that differ from the 'underclass'. This view is captured by the descriptive slogan, 'a two-thirds, one-third society'.

By contrast, Marxists argue that this is a false and misleading characterization. Hickey gives three reasons for this. First, the interests of a marginalized group vary directly, not indirectly, with the level of struggle and success of the working class as a whole. The achievement of the better-organized sections of the working class in raising the general level of wages, defending jobs and influencing government welfare policy benefits all. Second, there is no reason why marginalized groups should not be drawn into the organized working class; they can be at any time and have an interest in so doing. Third, social commentary generates a systematically distorted picture by conflating those who are marginalized and demeaned by unemployment and casual labour with those who are only seeking part-time or casual work. Most of those included as part of a marginalized 'underclass' are members of the working class who are either in part-time or short-term work by choice or are keen to secure full-time or permanent jobs. In either case, their interests are not opposed to those of full-time, permanently contracted workers, as is implied by the term, 'underclass'. The number of the truly marginal members of society is therefore systematically overestimated. Fourth, the deep divisions and incompatible class interests within the 'two-thirds' society (between the capitalist class and the working class) are ignored by the analysis (Hickey, 2000: 170).

7. See Hill (1999b) for a development of this critique.

8. For an elaboration of the concept and practice of 'critical thinking' and 'critical reflection' see Hill (1997) and the delineation of radical Left principles for education in Chapter 1. For a brief discussion of the concept of 'teachers as critical transformative intellectuals', see the Conclusion to this volume.

# References

Adonis, A and Pollard, S (1997) *A Class Act, The Myth of Britain's Classless Society*, Hamish Hamilton, London

Ainley, P (1993) *Class and Skill: Changing divisions of knowledge and labour*, Cassell, London

Anthias, F and Kelly, M (eds) (1995) *Sociological Debates: Thinking about 'the social'*, Greenwich University Press, Dartford

Aronowitz, S and Giroux, G (1991) *Postmodern Education: Politics, culture and social criticism*, University of Minnesota Press, Minneapolis, MN

Atkinson, E (2001, in press) The responsible anarchist: postmodernism and social change, *British Journal of Sociology of Education*

Birchall, I (2000) Revolution? You Must Be Crazy! *Socialist Review*, 247, December, pp 20–22

Bowles, S and Gintis, H (1976) *Schooling in Capitalist America*, Routledge & Kegan Paul, London.

Bowles, S and Gintis, H (1986) *Democracy and Capitalism*, Basic Books, New York

Brown, S, Riddell, S and Duffield, J (1997) Classroom approaches to learning and teaching: the social class dimension, Paper delivered to the ECER (European Educational Research Association Annual Conference, Seville)

Carvel, J (1997) University intake startlingly biased towards rich, *Guardian*, 19 April

Carvel, J (2000a) Immigration rise main social trend of 1990s. *The Guardian*, 25 January

Carvel, J (2000b) 5m Britons living on the breadline, *The Guardian*, 8 March

Cole, M (ed) (1988) *Bowles and Gintis Revisited: Correspondence and contradiction in educational theory*, Falmer Press, Lewes

Cole, M (1988) From reductionist Marxism and revolutionary socialism to post-liberal democracy and ambiguity: some comments on the changing political philosophy of Bowles and Gintis, *British Journal of Sociology*, 23

Cole, M (1998) Globalisation, modernisation and competitiveness: a critique of the New Labour project in education, *International Studies in the Sociology of Education*, 8 (3), pp 315–32

Cole, M and Hill, D (1995) Games of despair and rhetorics of resistance: post-modernism, education and reaction, *British Journal of Sociology of Education*, 16 (2), pp 165–82

Cole, M and Hill, D (1996a) Resistance postmodernism: emancipatory politics for a new era or academic chic for a defeatist intelligentsia? in *Information Society: New Media, Ethics and Postmodernism,* ed K S Gill, Springer-Verlag, London

Cole, M and Hill, D (1996b) Postmodernism, education and contemporary capitalism: a materialist critique, in *Values and Education,* eds O Valente, A Barrios, V Teodoro and A Gaspar, Faculty of Science, Department of Education, University of Lisbon

Cole, M and Hill, D (1997) 'New Labour', old policies: Tony Blair's 'vision' for education in Britain, *Education Australia*, 37 pp 17–19

Cole, M, Hill, D, McLaren, P and Rikowski, G (2001) *Red Chalk: On schooling, capitalism and politics,* Institute for Education Policy Studies, Brighton

Cole, M, Hill, D and Rikowski, G (1997) Between postmodernism and nowhere: the predicament of the postmodernist, *British Journal of Education Studies*, 45 (2), pp 187–200

Crompton, R (1994) *Class and Stratification: An Introduction to Current Debates,* Pluto Press, Oxford

Crompton, R (2000) *Renewing Class Analysis,* Blackwell, London

Davis, K and Moore, W (1967) Some principles of stratification, in *Class, Status and Power*, eds R Bendix and S Lipset, 2nd edn, Routledge & Kegan Paul, London

Durkheim, E (1968) *The Division of Labour in Society,* Free Press, New York

Edgell, S (1993) *Class,* Routledge, London

Foot, P (1990) *The Case for Socialism,* The Socialist Workers Party, London

Foot, P (1993) *Why You Should Join the Socialists,* Bookmarks, London

Foot, P (2001) *Why You Should Vote Socialist,* Bookmarks, London

German, L (1996) *A Question of Class,* Bookmarks, London

Giroux, H (1999) Border Youth, Difference and Postmodern Education, in *Critical Education in the New Information Age,* eds M Castells, R Flecha, P Freire, H Giroux, D Macedo and P Willis, Rowman & Littlefield, Lanham, MD

Hickey, T (2000) Class and class analysis for the twenty-first century, in *Education, Equality and Human Rights: Issues of gender, 'race', sexuality, special needs and social class,* ed M Cole, Routledge Falmer, London

Hill, D (1993) Book review of S Aronowitz and H Giroux, Postmodern Education: Politics, Culture and Social Criticism, *Journal of Education Policy,* **8** (1), pp 97–99

Hill, D (1997) The Happiest Days? *Guardian Weekend,* 22 November

Hill, D (1997) Reflection in teacher education, in *Educational Dilemmas: Debate and Diversity, vol. 1: Teacher Education and Training,* eds K Watson, S Modgil and C Modgil, Cassell, London

Hill, D (1999a) *New Labour and Education: Politics, ideology and the Third Way,* Tufnell Press, London

Hill, D (1999b) Social class and education, in *An Introducton to the Study of Education,* eds D Matheson and I Grosvenor, David Fulton, London

Hill, D (2000) New Labour's neo-liberal education policy, *Forum for Promoting Comprehensive Education,* **42** (1), pp 4–7

Hill, D (2001) State theory and the neo-liberal reconstruction of schooling and teacher education: a structuralist neo–Marxist critique of postmodernist, quasi-postmodernist, and culturalist neo–Marxist theory, *The British Journal of Sociology of Education,* **22** (1), pp 137–57

Hill, D, McLaren, P, Cole, M and Rikowski, G (eds) (1999) *Postmodernism in Education Theory: Towards a politics of human resistance,* Tufnell Press, London

Hill, D, McLaren, P, Cole, M and Rikowski, G (eds) (2001) *Marxism against Postmodernism in Educational Theory,* Lexington Press, Lanham, MD

Hill, D, Sanders, M and Hankin, T (2001) Class Analysis and Education Theory, in *Marxism Against Postmodernism in Educational Theory,* eds D Hill *et al,* Lexington Press, Lanham, MD

Lee, D and Newby, H (1984) *The Problem of Sociology,* Hutchinson, London

Livingstone, D (1997) Searching for the Missing links: neo-Marxist theories of education, *British Journal of Sociology of Education,* **16**

Marshall, G *et al* (1989) *Social Class in Modern Britain,* Unwin Hyman, London

Marx, K (1976) *Capital: A Critical Analysis of Capitalist Production Vol. 1,* Penguin, Harmondsworth

Marx, K (various editions) *The Communist Manifesto,* Introduction

Marx. K (1847) *The Poverty of Philosophy*

National Curriculum Council (1991) *Managing Economic and Industrial Understanding in Schools,* National Curriculum Council, York

Office for Standards in Education (Ofsted) (1993) *Access and Achievement in Urban Education,* HMSO, London

Parsons, T (1960) *Structure and Process in Modern Societies,* The Free Press, Chicago, IL

Paxman, J (1990) *The English*, Penguin, London

Power, S and Whitty, G (1999) New Labour's education policy: first, second or third way? *Journal of Education Policy*, **14** (5), pp 535–46

Rahman, M *et al* (2000) *Monitoring Poverty and Social Exclusion 2000*, Joseph Rowntree Foundation, York, www.jrf.org.uk/knowledge/findings/social policy/d20.htm

Reid, I (1978) *Sociological Perspectives on School and Education*, Open Books, London

Rikowski, G (1997) Scorched Earth: prelude to rebuilding Marxist educational theory, *British Journal of Sociology of Education*, **18** (4), pp 551–74

Rikowski, G (2001a) *The Battle in Seattle: Its significance for education*, Tufnell Press, London

Rikowski, G (2001b) Prelude: Marxist educational theory after postmodernism in *Marxism against Postmodernism in Educational Theory*, eds D Hill, P McLaren, M Cole and G Rikowski, Lexington Press, Lanham, MD

Sampson, A (1982) *The Changing Anatomy of Britain*, Hodder & Stoughton, London

Sanders, M, Hill, D and Hankin, T (1999) Education theory and the return to class analysis, in *Postmodern Excess in Education Theory: Education and the politics of human resistance*, eds D Hill *et al*, Tufnell Press, London

Sarup, M (1983) *Marxism and Education*, Routledge, London

Social Trends (1998) *Social Trends 28*, HMSO, London

Social Trends (2001) *Social Trends 31*, The Stationery Office, London

Scruton, R (1980) *The Meaning of Conservatism*. Penguin, London

*Times Educational Supplement* (1996) Why class is still a classroom issue, *TES*, 4 October

Usher, R and Edwards, R (1994) *Postmodernism and Education: Different voices, different worlds*, Routledge, London

Weber, M (1979) *Economy and Society*, University of California Press, Berkeley, CA

Whitty, G (1998) New Labour, Education and Social Justice, *Socialist Teacher*, **65**

Woodward, W (2001) Teachers demoted in class structure, *Guardian*, 16 March

# 8

# 'Race'

## Tim Waller, Mike Cole and Dave Hill

### Editors' introduction

This chapter has five aims:

- *to provide a conceptual overview of 'race' and racism in relation to society in general;*
- *to look at 'race', racism and legislation;*
- *to analyse data on ethnic background and achievement and performance at school;*
- *to look at the issue of racial harassment;*
- *to draw out some implications for schooling with reference to a number of recent reports.*

*The chapter makes a number of policy suggestions for racial equality in education.*

### Introduction

The British public is deeply concerned about 'race' and immigration issues. According to a MORI survey conducted in November 2000: (www.readers digest.co.uk) (Bouquet and Moller, 2000: 62–63):

- 80 per cent of adults believe that refugees come to Britain because they regard it as a 'soft touch';
- 66 per cent think there are too many immigrants in Britain (11 per cent up on a MORI poll conducted in 1999);

- 63 per cent say too much is done to help immigrants – respondents overestimate the financial aid asylum seekers receive (£113 per week, whereas in fact a single adult gets £36.54 a week in vouchers to be spent at designated shops, just £10 of which can be converted to cash);
- respondents believe that 20 per cent of the population are immigrants (the real figure is 4 per cent);
- respondents believe 26 per cent of the population belongs to an ethnic minority (the real figure is around 7 per cent);
- 37 per cent feel that there is more racial prejudice in Britain than five years ago and 38 per cent believe it will grow worse in the next five years.

# 'Race' and racism: concepts and theories

In this section, we will develop our own definition of racism, but first we will consider the concept of 'race'. Robert Miles has argued cogently against the notion that there exist distinct 'races' (1982: 9–16). He gives three reasons for this. First, the extent of genetic variation within any population is usually greater than the average difference between populations; second, while the frequency of occurrence of possible forms taken by genes does vary from one so-called 'race' to another, any particular genetic combination can be found in almost any 'race'; third, owing to inter-breeding and large-scale migrations, the distinction between 'races', identified in terms of dominant gene frequencies, are often blurred (Miles 1982: 16; see also Leicester 1989; Gillborn and Youdell, 2000: 4).

If 'race' has no genetic validity, it still has use as an analytic concept (in comparing and contrasting 'race' with other equality issues, for example). In addition, it does, of course, also exist as 'a social construct' in discourse. It is, therefore, still necessary to use the term. When this is the case, for the reasons outlined above, we believe it should be put in inverted commas.

The (false) belief that there exist distinct 'races' is the genesis of the concept of *racism*. Racism describes far more accurately and substantially historical and current realities than the more popular but nebulous and overgeneralized notion of prejudice.

Racism has traditionally referred to a situation where people are seen as causing *negative consequences* for other groups or as possessing certain negatively evaluated characteristics *because of their biology*. This has seemingly been the dominant form of racism throughout history. However, since the early 20th century, there have been major changes in the way in which 'race' and nation have been conceived. The colonial empires of European states, once legitimated by racism, have been broken up. The 19th-century doctrine of scientific racism (genetic or biological inferiority) has been discredited – although not eliminated – thus making the explicit expression of forms of 19th-century racism in the formal political arena difficult (Miles 1993: 71). It is necessary, therefore, to extend this definition in three major ways. First there is a need to include 'seemingly positive characteristics' in any definition of racism; second it is necessary to enlarge the definition to include cultural factors (cf Cope and Poynting, 1989; Modood, 1992,[1] 1994; Cole 1996, 1997a, 1997b); third there is a need to consider unintentional racism.

## Evaluated characteristics

Negatively evaluated characteristics include such instances of racist discourse as 'black people are not as clever as white people' but excludes such seemingly positive statements as 'black people are good at sports'.[2] While such assertions can lead to individual and/or short-term group enhancement (an unmerited place in the school football team for the individual or enhanced status for the group as a whole in an environment where prowess at sport is highly regarded), it is potentially racist and likely to have racist consequences. This is because, like most stereotypes, it is distorted and misleading and typically appears as part of a discourse that works to justify black school students' exclusion from academic activities.

Distinguishing between 'seemingly positive' and 'ultimately damaging' discourse is important. Nazi propaganda portrayed Jewish people as alien and morally subhuman and, therefore, a threat to the Aryan 'race' – a description that was part of a process that led eventually to the Holocaust. However, Jews were also characterized as a clever 'race', and (at least implicitly), possessing superhuman abilities. Thus, along with perceived threats of German 'racial degeneration' were fears that, through having superordinate skills of organization, the ability to dominate and act collectively as one entity, the Jews were able to control the world. This 'clever', 'super-able' stereotype, a perception that, on the surface, could seem positive, led to allegations that Jewish people were part of a conspiracy to take over the world, a notion that was also in part responsible for the Holocaust.

To take another example, people of South Asian or Chinese origin tend to be stereotyped as having a 'strong culture', an attribute that is used to pathologize people of African/Caribbean origin, who are in turn stereotyped (ridiculously) as having a weak culture or as having no culture at all! While this may serve to enhance the status of the former at the expense of the latter, in the context of racist discourse, it can result in accusations that people of Asian origin are failing to integrate or are 'taking over', which can lead to violence and other forms of hostility.

## Cultural racism

David Mason has argued that 'new racisms' depend for their power on the continued influence of biologically determinist modes of conceptualizing human difference (1994: 845-858). Although biological racism is still a powerful force, so too is cultural racism. Perhaps contemporary racism might best be thought of as a matrix of biological *and cultural racism* (cf Cole 1997a). In that matrix racism can be based purely on biology (for example, such statements as 'blacks are not as intelligent as whites') or purely on culture, as in the case of Islamophobia (for example, in Peregrine Worsthorne's (1991) words, 'Islam. . . has degenerated into a primitive enemy' (cited in Richardson 1992: xi).

Quite often, it is not easily identifiable as either. The racist term 'Paki' is a curious case in point. Relatively unrelated to Pakistan, it has become a generic term for anyone who is perceived to be from a specific alien stock *and/or* is believed to engage in certain alien cultural practices, based, for example, around religion, dress or food. The fact that it is being written by racists as 'packy' in the singular and 'packies' in the plural (*Guardian*, 1995) is indicative of how far it has become removed from the geographical area of Pakistan. Even when 'Pakistani' is used in racist discourse, it is highly unlikely that it is used in a knowledgeable way to refer to a (former) inhabitant of that particular South Asian country.

## Intentional and unintentional racism

Racism can be both intentional and unintentional. A distinction needs to be made between those people who, by their words or actions, openly advocate, or promote in various ways, notions of biological and/or cultural inferiority on the one hand, and those, on the other, who *out of ignorance* are being racist without realizing it. Unintentional racism might include, for example, using expressions like 'the Paki shop' (although such expressions could well be intentionally racist) or making stereotypical generalizations about minority ethnic communities. Intentional racism needs to be dealt with in a more challenging way; unintentional racism in a more gentle and supportive way. Education, it should be stressed, has a role to play in challenging both intentional and unintentional racism.

## Definition of racism

Racism may thus be redefined, following Cole (1997b) to include intentional and unintentional racism; seemingly positive characteristics; and biological and cultural racism.

Racism is a process, which can be intentional or unintentional, whereby social relations between people are structured by perceived biological and/or cultural differences in such a way as define and construct different social groups. Such groups are assumed to have a natural, unchanging origin and status. They are seen as being inherently different and as causing negative consequences for other groups and/or as possessing certain evaluated characteristics. These evaluated characteristics are stereotypes so they are likely to be distorted and misleading. If they are at first seemingly positive rather than negative, they are likely to be ultimately negative (cf Cole 1997b).[3]

## Nomenclature

Nomenclature, the way we refer to people, is important and is a hotly contested issue. The first point to make is that it is not to do with that invention of the radical Right – 'political correctness'; it is to do with respect for people. The second point to make is that it is perhaps easier to establish terms that are not acceptable than those that are preferred. The nomenclature 'coloured', for example, is unacceptable to most people in Britain. The third point to make is that there are no accurate and fixed definitions of a minority ethnic group. 'The notion of where and how the boundary [between groups] is constructed is diverse, contextual and relational', with the boundaries often changing 'over time, and in response to concrete economic, political or ideological conditions' (Anthias 1992: 423).

Ideally, one should adhere to ethnic self-definition. However, there is, inevitably, as with other equality issues, disagreement over what nomenclature is and is not appropriate (for example, Modood 1988; 1994). Many people of Asian and other minority ethnic origin do not self-describe as 'black'. Also the term 'ethnic minority', in practice, means that members of the dominant majority group are not referred to in terms of their ethnicity. This implies that they do not have ethnicity (Leicester, 1989: 17). Hence, *at the present time in Britain*, the formulation 'Asian, black and other minority ethnic' is preferable. 'Ethnic' or 'ethnics' should not be used in isolation and needs to be prefigured by 'minority' (or 'majority') and followed by a noun such as community (ies) or group(s). It needs to be stressed that we all have ethnicity, whether we are a minority or the majority.[4]

## 'Race', racism and education policy

There are three broadly identifiable approaches to education in multicultural Britain: *monocultural*, *multicultural* and *anti-racist* education respectively. Monocultural education attempts to make everyone 'socially and culturally British'. It is the traditional and historically most practised form of education in Britain and, in many ways, has been given a boost by the National Curriculum. It is exclusive, not inclusive – it excludes minority ethnic cultures. Multicultural education, on the other hand, starts from the premise that education should use the rich cultural heritage of Britain and celebrate difference. Traditional multicultural educators set out to teach about other people's cultures, other people's ways of life, thereby hoping to improve Asian, black and other minority ethnic people's self-image and instil respect for minority ethnic cultures. Modern multicultural educators hopefully adopt a less missionary-type approach and genuinely attempt to forge greater understanding of diverse cultures. Finally, anti-racist education's starting point is that Britain is a fundamentally racist society, that racism cannot be understood without reference to economic, political and ideological factors, nor without reference to other inequality issues, and that education should play a role in attempting to dismantle that racism.[5]

The main problem with *monocultural* education is that it has the tendency to reinforce biological and cultural racism, by implicitly and explicitly championing British colonial history and by exalting the supposed superiority of British cultural institutions and 'the British character'. *Multicultural* education, in concentrating on safe 'cultural sites' – the arts, religion and food – allows the teacher to avoid examining her/his own racism and can have a tendency to be patronizing. Elsewhere Cole (1997a) has asked how the vast majority of a predominantly white teaching force can be capable of teaching about the dynamic and multifaceted cultures of Britain.[6] The strength of *anti-racist education* is that, in contrast to monocultural and multicultural education, it *requires* teachers and teacher educators to engage in 'critical reflection', to question their own practice and that of their schools, with a commitment to working within a morality of social justice and egalitarianism and a concomitant determination to raise issues of, for example, racism and anti-racism within the classroom, the school and society (see Hill, 1992; 1994; 1997a).

## 'Race', racism and legislation

Teachers and student teachers need to be aware of the legislation with regard to all the issues of equality. Indeed, student teachers are *required* by Circular 4/98 Annex A, Section D to have an 'understanding that current legislation on race obliges schools to provide all pupils with an education free from racial discrimination' (TTA 2000:15).[7]

The Race Relations Act of 1976 makes it unlawful to discriminate against a person on grounds of 'race', colour or ethnic origin or nationality. This can be either indirect or direct. Indirect racism involves treating a person *on racial grounds* less favourably than others would be treated in the same or similar circumstances. Direct racism, on the other hand, can vary from crude racist jokes to subtle differences in, for example, expectation, provision or treatment. It may be intentional or unintentional or even well meaning, but it is still unlawful. It is, of course, also hurtful – especially when it is repeated thousands of times in an individual's experience: daily name calling, for example.

Codes of practice have been issued by the Commission for Racial Equality (CRE) relating to employment and for the elimination of racial discrimination in education (CRE 1989), which applies to all schools. This pamphlet covers such unlawful acts as segregation on racial grounds, instructing or pressuring others to unlawfully discriminate, victimizing or treating less favourably those who have brought proceedings under the Race Relations Act, have given evidence or information relating to proceedings, or have alleged that discrimination occurred (CRE 1989: 11). It also deals with unlawful practices relating to admission policies, exclusions, assessment, allocation to teaching groups, work experience, careers advice, grants, fees and residential accommodation (pp 14–27) and lays down the obligations of local education authorities and governors (pp 12–13). The pamphlet has an appendix, which deals with other relevant sections of the Race Relations Act (pp 29–36). For example, it points out that it is unlawful under the Public Order Act of 1986 to incite racial hatred. This would include, for example, the distribution of racially inflammatory publications to pupils or students (p 32).

There have been a number of more recent changes. For example, the incorporation of the European Convention of Human Rights into British law occurred in October 2000. Article 14 of the Convention says that Human Rights must be available without discrimination on grounds of 'race', sex, religion and other status. The Race Relations Amendment Act (2000), in addition to bringing previously excluded organizations, including the police, the prison service, the Health and Safety Executive, immigration and all government departments within the scope of the Race Relations Act, will also make it a legal duty for all public bodies, including schools, colleges and universities, to take positive steps to promote racial equality. In an effort to combat institutional racism, these bodies will have to consider the effect on race relations of any new policies or procedures that they produce (NATFHE, 2000).

With respect to racist incidents, the Home Office Code of Practice on Recording and Reporting Racial Incidents (April 2000) states that 'the definition of a racist incident that should be used by all agencies is that recommended by the Stephen Lawrence Inquiry' (cited in Wheathampstead Education Centre, 2001: 4) (see below, for a discussion of this inquiry).

According to this definition, a racist incident is 'any incident which is perceived to be racist by the victim or any other person'. Under this definition, any such incident will be investigated, recorded and monitored as such (Wheathampstead Education Centre, 2001: 4). It is important to note that this does not pre-empt the outcome of the ensuing investigation, which should be based on the objective assessment of evidence. Racial harassment can occur whether it is intentional or not (see below for a discussion of intentional and unintentional racism). In investigating any incident as defined above, schools will seek to establish whether any act or expression directed by a member or members of one racial or ethnic group to another or others has occurred that causes harm or offence, where the motivation *or effect* is to create racial dislike or hatred. Ethnic groups include European groups and Travellers (Wheathampstead Education Centre, 2001: 4). It is important to note that racist incidents can occur without a victim or target being present (for example, telling racist jokes) (Wheathampstead Education Centre, 2001: 5).[8]

Finally, a European 'Race' Directive, to be implemented by 2003, will have the effect of specifically outlawing racial harassment. This Directive shifts the burden of proof in 'race' discrimination cases on to the employer to prove that they have not discriminated against the complainant (NATFHE, 2000).

## Current data on ethnic background, performance and achievement at school

The Swann report (DES, 1985), and other investigations supported by the Commission for Racial Equality (CRE) focused attention on the effects of racial discrimination on minority ethnic groups in the British education system in the 1980s. However, until the inquiry into the racist murder of Stephen Lawrence (Macpherson, 1999), the effects of institutional racism and black underachievement exposed by Swann were largely (and deliberately) ignored by subsequent government legislation and policy. For example, a serious weakness of all National Curriculum orders, and in particular English, has been the lack of attention given to the needs of bilingual and multilingual pupils (see Leicester, 1989). Despite the September 2000 curriculum review and the advent of 'citizenship' education by 2002 the curriculum remains, in Grosvenor's words, 'English, white and Christian' (1995: 81; also Grosvenor, 1997, and Chapter 12 of this volume). Clearly, it is not only the curriculum but the whole context, organization and structure of education that has failed to address racism, and it is through the apparatuses of the state that racism becomes institutionalized.

## Ethnic origin and teacher pupil interaction

Research discussed in Gillborn and Gipps (1996: 54) has recorded an unusually high degree of tension and conflict between white teachers and African-Caribbean pupils. The same tension and conflict does not appear in teacher–student relationships where the students are from other minority ethnic backgrounds. The research undertaken in the 1970s, 1980s and 1990s highlighted the fact that even teachers who said they were committed to equality were more likely to have negative views about students of African-Caribbean origin. Black pupils of both sexes are therefore more likely to be disciplined and disproportionately criticized by white teachers. There is a clear link between these circumstances and the overly high number of African-Caribbean students who are excluded from schools.

School case studies (see Chapters 4, 5 and 12 of this volume) describe processes where, despite their best intentions, teachers' actions can create and amplify conflict with African–Caribbean pupils (see, for example, Sollis, 1996). In comparison with African-Caribbean school students, teachers often have more positive expectations of (South) Asians – as relatively quiet, well behaved and highly motivated. However, Gillborn and Gipps argue that Asian pupils are sometimes subject to negative and patronizing stereotypes – especially concerning language abilities and the nature of their home communities. They suggest that these stereotypes can be especially damaging for Asian girls.

Relationships between white teachers and minority ethnic students are not determined solely by a racist education system acting to constrain and exclude non-white groups. In fact, in spite of all the institutional racism that appears to be present at all levels within education in the UK, (middle class) minority ethnic students from Indian, Chinese, and black African backgrounds have achieved very good results in public examinations over a number of years. Farrar (1992: 55) suggested that 'racism is an inadequate summary of the experience of black people in Britain'. In other words, we should not see minority ethnic groups as casualties. He goes on to suggest that 'there is a growing catalogue of high achievement which bursts the boundaries unwittingly set by those who see nothing but persecution and humiliation in the black experience' (1992: 55).

## Exclusion from school

African-Caribbean children are four to six times more likely to be excluded than their white and Asian counterparts, for fewer offences, less serious offences and at a younger age German (1999: 1). They are also less likely to be restored to the mainstream. In some London boroughs they are up to 10 to 15 times more likely to be excluded. Sir Herman Ouseley has pointed out that, as there are 10,000–14,000 permanent exclusions every year, schools are discarding the equivalent of the population of a small town each year.

According to Osler (1997), for Black Caribbean families this situation amounts to an 'educational crisis'. Once excluded, a pupil has only a 15 per cent chance of returning to mainstream education. While the overall proportion of girls excluded is relatively small, black Caribbean girls are also particularly affected. They account for 8.8 per cent of excluded girls, but only 1.1 per cent of the total number of girls in school.

Gillborn and Gipps (1996) point out that qualitative research has documented individual cases where racial discrimination has occurred. It seems clear, despite the 1976 Race Relations Act and policies for equal opportunity at school and local authority level, that institutional racism is still very much a factor (see Gillborn and Mirza, 2000: 28–29).

## Progress and achievement at school

The present circumstances regarding progress, achievement and ethnic background in schooling are informed by the extensive report made by Gillborn and Gipps on behalf of Ofsted (1996), by Ofsted (1999) and by Gillborn and Mirza (2000).

## Comparisons between key stages

On average African-Caribbean pupils tend to achieve less well than whites although the national assessment results at Key Stage 1 showed that in 1992 and 1994 African-Caribbean children were ahead of white children in Birmingham. Gillborn and Gipps summarize the position as follows: 'At the end of junior school ethnic minority pupils' attainments often lag behind those of white pupils. There is some evidence that the gaps widen during the junior years' (1996: 41).

The general pattern of achievement that emerges is that for some African-Caribbean pupils, particularly boys, achievement at Key Stage 1 is better than that of their white peers but during the rest of their school career their achievements are below those of their white peers. What happens to African-Caribbean boys is that, according to Gillborn and Gipps, teachers and schools play an active, if unintended, role in the creation of conflict between teachers and schools on the one hand and African-Caribbean pupils on the other. This reduces the black young people's opportunity to achieve.

By the time African-Caribbean students take GCSE exams they achieve the lowest scores of any ethnic group – on average about five exam points lower than white students. The proportion of African-Caribbean students achieving five good GCSEs (grades A-C) is less than half the national average. Pupils of Bangladeshi and Pakistani ethnic origin are below the national average at age 11, but then steadily close the gap between themselves and the rest. In some local education authorities they perform at or above the national GCSE average (Commission on the Future of Multi-Ethnic Britain, 2000). Gillborn and Gipps argue that the situation is too varied for simple talk of black underachievement, however. Pupils of black African origin often achieve relatively higher results than their peers of black Caribbean origin.

## Achievement at the end of compulsory education

Performance at GCSE level is more affected by class and gender – see Table 8.1. Pupils from more economically advantaged backgrounds achieve the highest averages and girls tend to do better than boys from the same social class background.

**Table 8.1** *Average exam scores: by 'race', class and gender (percentage gaining five or more GCSEs at Grades A-C) England and Wales 1995*

|  | African-Caribbean female | Asian female | White female | African-Caribbean male | Asian male | White male |
|---|---|---|---|---|---|---|
| Manual | 15 | 22 | 20 | 14 | 23 | 18 |
| Intermediate | 18 | 26 | 25 | 21 | 27 | 24 |
| Professional | 25 | 28 | 32 | 27 | 31 | 30 |

Adapted from Gillborn and Gipps (1996: 17)

Although it is important to consider the effects of 'race' and class and gender, what Gillborn and Gipps do not point out is that many children from minority ethnic backgrounds are economically disadvantaged as a result of the institutional racism that provides the families with poorer housing, health, employment and life chances and so forth.

Gillborn and Gipps (1996: 2), however, do provide a useful summary of data for achievement at GCSE level. They establish that:

- school students of Indian origin achieve more highly, on average, than pupils from other South Asian backgrounds;
- school students of Indian origin achieve higher rates of success than their white counterparts in some (but not all) urban areas;
- there is no single pattern of achievement for school students of Pakistani origin although they tend to achieve less well than whites in many areas;
- school students of Bangladeshi origin are known to experience greater levels of poverty than other South Asian groups. Their relative achievements are often less than those of other ethnic groups. In one London borough, however, Bangladeshi pupils are now the highest achieving of all ethnic groups;
- school students of African-Caribbean origin have not shared equally the increasing rates of educational achievement;
- the achievements of young men of African-Caribbean origin are a particular cause for concern;
- the situation is too varied for simple talk of black underachievement – school students of black African origin often achieve relatively higher results than their peers of black Caribbean origin.

Gillborn and Mirza (2000) show that 'all can achieve: of the six minority ethnic categories. . . analysed, every one is the highest attaining of all in at least one LEA' (p 9). For example 'although at national level Pakistani youth are less likely to attain five higher grade GCSEs than their white peers, this pattern is reversed in some areas . . . in four out of ten LEAs that monitor by ethnic origin, Pakistani pupils are more likely to attain this benchmark than white pupils locally' (p 10).

Similarly, Bangladeshi attainments still lag behind white averages nationally but at the local level there are many cases where this pattern is challenged (p 11). However, they do conclude that despite the variation between different LEAs, significant and consistent inequalities of attainment emerge for many of the principal minority groups (p 11). 'African-Caribbean and Pakistani pupils have drawn least benefit from rising levels of attainment: the gap between them and their white peers is bigger now than a decade ago' (p 14).

Gillborn and Mirza's (2000) conclusion is that 'social class and gender differences are. . . associated with differences in attainment but neither can account for persistent underlying ethnic inequalities: comparing like with like, African-Caribbean, Pakistani and Bangladeshi pupils do not enjoy equal opportunities' (p 27).

## Post-compulsory education

For post-16 education, Gillborn and Gipps (1996: 5) suggest that, although there is a general trend of increasing participation, young people from all minority ethnic backgrounds have a higher participation than their white peers. *Social Trends* (2001) points out that young people from most minority ethnic groups in England and Wales are likely to be in post-16 education and training. In 2000, 96 per cent of Indian 16-year-olds were in education and training compared with 85 per cent of white young people of the same age (2001: 65). Gillborn and Gipps note that generally, Asian young people tend to follow traditional 'academic' courses and are the most highly qualified of all groups (including whites). African-Caribbean young people are more likely to follow vocational courses. Class and ethnicity need to be taken into account. Young people of Indian origin from professional backgrounds have the highest participation rates in post-16 education whereas white young people from semi-skilled backgrounds are least represented. This pattern of participation suggests two possible underlying causes. White youngsters from semi-skilled backgrounds are more likely to gain employment at 16, due to institutional racism aimed at young people from Asian, black and other non-white minority ethnic groups, and/or other class and ethnic groups put a higher value on post-16 education. The position remains similar to that reported by Gillborn and Gipps in 1996 in Table 8.2, showing very clearly the relationship between race and class – the racialized nature of the class system and the social class nature of minority ethnic groups.

## Access to higher education

Relatively more students from minority ethnic backgrounds apply to higher education courses. However, white students are more likely to be accepted by

**Table 8.2** *Post-compulsory education (percentage of each cohort of 16–19-year-olds in full-time post-compulsory education) broken down into ethnic group and social class, 1991 figures*

| | Bangladeshi | Black Caribbean | Indian | White African | Black | Pakistani, other | Black |
|---|---|---|---|---|---|---|---|
| Professional | 88 | 61 | 82 | 62 | 80 | 69 | 72 |
| Skilled | 65 | 52 | 76 | 38 | 79 | 63 | 48 |
| Semi-skilled | 60 | 48 | 70 | 30 | 75 | 60 | 36 |

Adapted from Gillborn and Gipps 1996: 67

the 'old' universities and black Caribbean and African applicants are accepted least often.

Certain ethnic groups experience significantly different rates of admission to all universities: Chinese young people are more likely to be admitted than other groups, whereas black Caribbeans and Pakistanis are least likely to gain a place at university. Considering that Indians from all class backgrounds, black Africans from all class backgrounds, Pakistanis from professional and skilled backgrounds and black others from professional backgrounds all have a higher rate of participation in 16–19 education than white students from all backgrounds – questions need to be asked as to why minority ethnic students are not represented in anything like the same proportion at university.

It would seem that university education is still a preserve of mainly white students and that despite the rhetoric of 'wider access' and the adoption of equal opportunities policies by some universities over the last two decades, institutional racism is still a factor in the admission of students to university. Past research summarized in Allen (1996) suggests that 'biased and selective practices' by university admissions tutors still exist. The underlying cultural perspective in education is, as Grosvenor (1997) argues, still one of assimilation. Some minority ethnic groups do not gain admission because they do not appear 'British' enough.

The Ofsted report (1999) *Raising the Attainment of Minority Ethnic Pupils* suggested that school initiatives to combat racism were patchy and inconsistent. For example, 'very few schools review their curricular and pastoral strategies to ensure that they are sensitive to ethnic groups in the student population' (1996: 12). Ofsted suggested that the more successful schools, ones in which minority ethnic pupils flourish:

understand the hostility that these pupils often face (especially Gypsy Travellers). These schools have developed successful strategies for countering stereotyping which have had a tangible impact on the pupils confidence and self esteem, but have also influenced the attitudes of the majority.

(Ofsted 1999: 14)

The report emphasizes that a crucial feature of combating racism is 'a school ethos which is open and vigilant, in which pupils can talk about their concerns and share in the development of strategies for their resolution' (1999: 18).

Ofsted (1999) also reviewed LEA initiatives and found that fewer than a quarter of the 25 LEAs visited had a clear strategy for raising the attainment of minority ethnic groups (1999: 19). The report argued that 'most of the authorities are conscious of their responsibility for promoting good race relations and combating racial harassment. Most have written policies. . . but few monitor the implementation of these strategies or the extent of racial harassment' (1999: 23). This report, together with Gilborn and Mirza (2000), suggests that the many of the findings of Gillborn and Gipps (1996) are still valid and that there is an urgent need for all schools to monitor racial harassment and to counter it through anti-racist policy and practice.

## Racial harassment

Klein (1997: 16) argued that 'racial harassment, most frequently by white working-class boys, is a growing concern'. The charity Childline reported in 1996 that of over 1,600 calls made to their helpline one in four callers said they had experienced racist bullying. The fact that some schools have difficulty identifying racist bullying was highlighted by the case of 13-year-old Vijay Singh who on 12 October 1996 hanged himself after being bullied by white boys.

His diary reads:

I shall remember this eternity and will never forget.
Monday: My money was taken.
Tuesday: Names called.
Wednesday: My uniform torn.
Thursday: My body pouring with blood.
Friday: It's ended.
Saturday: Freedom.

On Sunday Vijay was dead.

There is also significant evidence from qualitative studies, as discussed in Gillborn and Gipps (1996) that highlights the widespread incidence of racist violence and harassment against some pupils, and the tremor, stress, and impact on the victims, their families, and their peers. However, Gillborn and Gipps argue that racist harassment is not always recognized by some teachers, who may mistakenly view it as simple boisterousness – and sometimes tell the victims to 'ignore it'. Asian pupils seem especially likely to be victimized by their white peers. This echoes the pattern in society more generally and points to the urgent need for action against racial violence and harassment.[9]

Some progress has been made. Section 4.29 of DfEE Circular 10/99, states that:

> [t]he emotional distress caused by bullying – whatever form – *be it racial* or as a result of a child's appearance, behaviour or special educational needs, or related to sexual orientation – can prejudice school achievement, lead to lateness or truancy and, in some extreme cases, end with suicide [our emphasis].

Section 4.30 of the same Circular states that '[h]ead teachers have a legal duty to take measures to prevent all forms of bullying among students'.

## Islamophobia

Britain is also turning into a nation of Muslim-haters, according to the Runnymede Trust (1997). Their report suggests that the religious *fatwa* against the writer Salman Rushdie and the Gulf War have reinforced the stereotyping of Muslim cultures as 'intolerant and threatening'. The report argues that discrimination should be unlawful on religious as well as racial grounds and calls for education and employment initiatives to combat racism. Since the publication of the Runnymede Trust report, after a change of government and a campaign for over 15 years by the Muslim community, the state has finally agreed to provide funding for two Islamic schools.

An interim report by Parker-Jenkins *et al* (1999), based on interviews with 100 subjects, suggests that young Muslim women feel that they have to work twice as hard to succeed. They face indifference at school, hostility at college, discrimination at work and a cultural-versus-religious struggle within their communities.

## The Stephen Lawrence Inquiry report (Macpherson 1999)

As a result of a lengthy public campaign by his parents this report was finally published in February 1999, nearly six years after Stephen Lawrence's murder. The report provided a definition of institutional racism that was accepted by some, but crucially not all, chief police officers in the UK. It concludes that racism exists within all organizations and institutions and that the problem is thus deeply ingrained. It called for radical thinking and sustained action to tackle it in all organizations particularly in the fields of education and family life.

For Sivanandan (2000b: 1) Macpherson was 'not just a result but a learning process for the country at large'. He argues that through the course of the inquiry, 'the gravitational centre of race relations discourse was shifted from individual prejudice and ethnic need to systemic, institutional racial inequality and injustice.' Sivanandan asserts that institutional racism had never before been acknowledged by government or by official inquiry. He cites, as an example, Lord Scarman,[10] who declared that there was no such thing as institutional racism, only personal prejudice which 'does manifest itself occasionally in the behaviour of a few police officers on the street'.

## The Stephen Lawrence Inquiry report: recommendations for education

Macpherson (1999) made 70 recommendations for the prevention of racism, of which the following relate specifically to the role of education:

Recommendation 67. The National Curriculum is amended to promote the valuing of cultural diversity and the preventing of racism – in order better to reflect the needs of a diverse society.

Recommendation 68. Local education authorities and school governors have the duty to create and implement strategies in their schools to prevent and address racism. Such strategies should include that:

- schools record all racist incidents;
- all recorded incidents are reported to the pupils' parents or guardians, school governors and LEAs;
- the number of racist incidents is published annually, on a school-by-school basis;
- the numbers and self-defined ethnic identity of excluded pupils are published annually, on a school-by-school basis.

Recommendation 69. Ofsted inspections should include examination of the implementation of such strategies.

Macpherson has clearly endorsed an anti-racist view, which suggests that it is vital for teachers to establish practices that challenge racism. Following the report, the government has 'accepted Recommendation 67, accepted in part Recommendation 68 and accepted Recommendation 69' (CRE, 2000: 79).

The New Labour (September 2000) revision of the National Curriculum gives slightly greater emphasis to promoting racial tolerance and challenging racism through the introduction of the subject heading of 'citizenship'. For example, pupils will be taught about 'the origins and implications of the diverse national, regional, religious and ethnic identities in the United Kingdom and the need for mutual respect and understanding'. However, it is not until August 2002 that schools will have a statutory responsibility to teach the programmes of study for citizenship at Key Stages 3 and 4.[11] The introduction of 'citizenship' is certainly a move to be welcomed, and follows on from some of the recommendations of Macpherson, but many teachers and writers concerned about racism and social justice in education would suggest that the curriculum, in particular English and history, needs to be radically changed to reflect the nature and needs of a diverse and pluralist society (see Cole, Hill and Shan 1997; Cole 1998; Gaine 1995; Grosvenor 1995; Hatcher 1997; Hill 1997b; Troyna 1993; Hill and Cole 1999b, for example). Sivanandan, in particular, has been critical of the proposed citizenship programme in the National Curriculum and he states that 'all that the government has done is to set down a few vague statements about respecting cultural differences in the non-mandatory sections of the new Citizenship Studies course' (2000a: 4).

The Stephen Lawrence Inquiry report stressed the fundamental role that education has in eliminating racism and promoting cultural diversity. Following the report, the DfEE set up an Advisory Group on Raising Ethnic Minority Pupil Achievement and the Race, Education and Employment Forum. In March 2000 the document *Learning for All: Standards for racial equality* was published by the CRE and sent to all schools. The document was intended as 'guidance and a source of good practice in addressing issues of equality and cultural diversity' (CRE, 2000: 7). It sets standards for the range of school responsibilities within seven areas including; curriculum policy, leadership and management, admission, exclusion and partnership with parents and the community. The document also includes an audit form so that schools can audit themselves against the standards. The document is to be broadly welcomed, but teachers are expressing concern over the need for staff development before the audit to make the most of the guidance in the document.

## Inspecting schools for race equality: Ofsted's strengths and weaknesses

Osler and Morrison's (2000) report, carried out on behalf of the Commission for Racial Equality (CRE), reveals that Ofsted's leaders had never informed schools or contracted inspectors of Ofsted's government-assigned responsibility to monitor how schools implement strategies 'to prevent and address racism', following recommendations set out in the Stephen Lawrence Inquiry report (Osler, 2000: 22). Indeed, as ex-Chief Inspector of Schools, Chris Woodhead, admitted, in the 3,647 inspections carried out between the publication of the report and July 2000, only four include 'race' equality issues among the key action points (cited in Osler, 2000: 23). Osler reminds us that, although inspectors are required to report on the ethnic composition of schools and on differences in attainment between ethnic groups, schools are not required to monitor attainment by ethnicity. It was difficult for inspectors to carry out their work without this data (Osler, 2000: 24), hence inspection reports were littered with vague, confusing or meaningless statements. Despite the prevarications of Woodhead, all Ofsted inspectors were issued with new guidance, *Evaluating Educational Inclusion* (Ofsted, 2000), which addresses many of the recommendations in the *Inspecting Schools for Race Equality* report, including that Ofsted publicize its designated lead responsibility for monitoring strategies to address and prevent racism in schools (Osler, 2000: 25). There is now a two-day mandatory 'educational inclusion' training programme for Ofsted inspectors to be completed within the 2000/01 academic year.

## The Parekh report

The Commission on the Future of Multi-ethnic Britain (the Parekh report) (2000) identified, with respect to education, a number of 'points for immediate action'. These include:

- Forums in which government officials, academics, practitioners and representatives of non-governmental organizations can jointly review developments in education that have an impact on issues of 'race' equality and cultural diversity.
- Education for citizenship to include human rights principles; skills of deliberation; advocacy and campaigning; open-mindedness and tolerance of difference; knowledge of global interdependence; understanding of equality legislation, and opposition to racist beliefs and behaviour.
- Guidance on how each curriculum subject should have an international and multicultural dimension.
- Targets for reducing the numbers of exclusions experienced by pupils of particular community backgrounds.
- School inspections to report on issues of 'race' in the school and the attainment of minority ethnic groups. Ofsted inspectors to undergo a programme of appropriate training.
- Substantial programme of certificating training for specialists in teaching English as an additional language.

## Summary and conclusion

This chapter clearly demonstrates the existence and effects of racism within the British education system. As Osler and Morrison (2000) and Parekh (2000) note, the recommendations of the Stephen Lawrence Inquiry report are in danger of not being fully implemented. Of particular concern are the increasing incidents of racial harassment and violence and the number of exclusions from school (particularly of African-Caribbean boys). This information was unequivocally presented to the government by Gillborn and Gipps. The problem is that their evidence has been largely, and significantly ignored. Gillborn and Gipps conclude their report by stating that:

> One of the clearest findings of this review is that if ethnic diversity is ignored, if differences in educational achievement and experience are not examined, then considerable injustices will be sanctioned and enormous potential wasted.

> (Gillborn and Gipps1996: 7)

A number of writers, such as Hatcher and Jones (1996), Hatcher (1997), Hill and Cole (1999), and Whitty *et al* (1998), point out that the education agenda, since the election of New Labour remains 'standards', targets and 'value for money'. Education, as noted in Chapters 1, 3, 4, 5, 7 and 12 of this volume, continues to be organized to secure cultural reproduction, to give particular benefit to middle-class, mainly male, white pupils. Clearly a significant factor influencing the current position is the previous Conservative governments' education policies which were not only 'colour blind' but also overtly racist. The official emphasis on 'standard English', British history and Christian worship in schools has reinforced division through the formal and informal curriculum. As Grosvenor (1995) points out, the disproportionate number of black exclusions can be directly related to the Conservative restructuring of the education system so that white parents can exploit the 'market' for school places and avoid schools with significant numbers of minority ethnic pupils. This exacerbates the already pronounced inequalities in attainment between schools with a mainly white middle-class intake on the one hand, and those with a working-class, in particular a black working-class intake. A parent's right to choose school has become predominant over race relations legislation.

Gillborn and Gipps (1996), and Gillborn and Mirza (2000) have shown that 'race', class and gender are still factors in educational achievement. Students who live in the most economically deprived areas do less well in public examinations and league tables. There is a direct correlation between achievement and free school meals – schools with a high proportion of students claiming free school meals are at the bottom of the league tables. It is no accident that a significant proportion of students from minority ethnic communities live in areas that are economically deprived and attend schools at the lower end of league tables. The league tables were set up by the Conservative governments to reinforce and recreate divisions in schooling and in society.[12] Money, resources, status and power are transferred from the bottom to the top of the league tables. Any amount of tinkering with the mechanism of the tables by bringing in 'value added' data is misleading – the tables are a divisive legacy of the Thatcherite years and should be abolished.

The current structure for inspection has a similar divisive aim and effect. Most failing schools are in economically deprived areas and are treated in exactly the same 'objective' (culturally loaded – see Chapter 5) manner as schools in middle-class and wealthy areas of the country. Ouseley (in Pyke, 1995) argued that the Ofsted inspection system was significantly marginalizing issues of equality (only 16 percent of reports commented on equality in their list of key issues for action). A revised framework for inspection came into force in April 1996. The education system has a vital part to play in reducing the fragmentation of society by promoting inclusion, cohesion and equity. Government needs to be explicitly concerned with improving the life chances and achievements of all pupils.

There is a need to consider ethnic origin alongside social class and gender, and for schools to be supported in the development of an effective anti-racist education including anti-racist policies, which, as Grosvenor (1995) argues, challenge the routine reproduction of racism in education and embrace, rather than excluding, the views of all minority ethnic communities. Otherwise, Sir Hermann Ouseley's nightmare vision of 'educational apartheid' will surely become a reality. Such institutional racism, in addition to personal racism, must be resisted at all levels of society.

## Notes

1.  While we agree with Modood's arguments for racism having a cultural dimension, we are not in sympathy with his overall project in this book, which entails the wholesale rejection of historical materialism, along with the privileging of functionalist analysis, and the promotion of a liberal concept of 'ethnic pluralism' (Cole 1993a: 23).
2.  We are using the term 'black' in the British context to refer to children of African and African-Caribbean origin (see Cole 1993b).
3.  This definition is derived in part from the work of Robert Miles, and as the result of communications with Smina Akhtar. Our thanks to both of them.
4.  This is not to say, of course, that there is not differentiation within black communities – nor, equally importantly, within Asian communities. For a fuller discussion of nomenclature in Britain, see Cole 1993b. See also Virdee and Cole, 2000. For a discussion of nomenclature with respect to Britain and to some other (selected) countries in Europe, see Cole 1996. See Green and Grosvenor (1997) for a discussion of the concept of 'ethnicity' as 'invention'. Here, 'ethnicities' are conceived as generating and consolidating their 'selves' through signs, symbols, rituals, and institutional relations, in which people actively participate to define their group identities and solidarities (Conzen et al, 1992: 5). For Conzen et al, the idea of invention goes beyond the view that 'ethnic groups' are mere cultural constructs. Rather 'ethnicity. . . is a process of invention that incorporates, adapts, and amplifies pre-existing communal solidarities, cultural attributes and historical memories.' Furthermore, they claim that ethnicities are more than collective

fictions for they are 'grounded in real life contexts and social experience' (1992: 4–5).While one may question their ideas on communal solidarities (see Archer, 1998, especially chapter 1) what the authors capture is ethnicity as a cultural formation whose meaning is negotiated. (Green and Grosvenor, 1997: 889). For detail on the ethnic minority population in the UK see the Policy Studies Institute, 1997.

5.   Such approaches are, of course, also applicable to many other countries in the world, although the terminology may be different.

6.   For an extended critique of monocultural and multicultural (and an appraisal of anti-racist) education see Cole 1992 (see also Cole 1998 for an anti-racist critique of reconstructed multiculturalism). Some writers have suggested that multicultural and antiracist education *are* compatible, but only insofar as the former is part of the latter – by itself. See, for example, Hessari and Hill 1989; Leicester 1992. Hessari and Hill argue that anti-racism should include multiculturalism and that multiculturalism needs to be a part of anti-racism. For arguments that they *are not* compatible, see Cole 1992 and 1998; see also the many works of the late Barry Troyna, for example Troyna (1993). (At the end of Cole 1992, there is an 'Interchange of views between Leicester, a "new multiculturalist", and Cole, an anti-racist, as to whether or not the two approaches are compatible.')

It is worth noting that information technology has great potential in the passing on of accurate and authentic information pertaining to multicultural Britain, and this eventually could make certain forms of multicultural education a far more viable proposition (for a discussion, see Cooner and Loveless, 1997). See George 1993 for a useful handbook on equal opportunities regarding 'race' and education. See also Jones, 1999.

7.   For a comprehensive analysis of the other requirements of 4/98 A (D), see Cole (ed) 1999.

8.   For detailed advice on dealing with racial harassment, see Wheathampstead Education Centre 2001

9.   See the Institute for Race Relations 2000 for details of racist violence and murders in society.

10.  Lord Scarman was appointed by the Thatcher government to inquire into the causes of the Brixton anti-police riots of 1981.

11.  Research has consistently demonstrated that children can be racist at much earlier ages, in fact from age three onwards. Racist attitudes can be firmly entrenched and often need direct confrontation (but explanation rather than chastisement) with children as young as five (Connolly, 1999a, b).

12.  For a detailed analysis of the effect of Conservative education policy on the educational careers of minority ethnic students see Chapter 1 of this volume and Troyna and Carrington (1990); Sarup (1991); Hatcher, Troyna and Gewirtz (1996); Hill (1997b); Whitty, Power and Halpin (1998); Hill and Cole (1999a).

# References

Allen, P (1996) Black scepticality – black students in higher education, *Multicultural Teaching,* **14** (3)

Anthias, F (1992) Connecting 'race' and ethnic phenomena, *Sociology* **26** (3), pp 421–38

Archer, M (1992) *Culture and Agency: The place of culture in social theory,* Cambridge University Press, Cambridge

Bouquet, T and Moller, D (2000) Are we a tolerant nation? *Reader's Digest,* November, pp 62–67

Cole, M (1992) British values, liberal values or values of justice and education: three approaches to education in multicultural Britain, in *Cultural Diversity and the Schools Vol 3 Equity or Excellence? Education and Cultural Reproduction,* ed J Lynch, C Modgil and S Modgil, Falmer Press, London

Cole, M (1993a) Widening the cricket test, *The Times Higher Education Supplement,* 26 March

Cole, M (1993b) 'Black and ethnic minority' or 'Asian, Black and other minority ethnic': a further note on nomenclature, *Sociology* **27** (4), pp 671–73

Cole, M (1996) 'Race', racism and nomenclature: a conceptual analysis', in *Racism(s) and Xenophobia in European Football,* ed U Merkel, Meyer and Meyer, Aachen

Cole, M (1997a) Equality and primary education: what are the conceptual issues? in *Promoting Equality in Primary Schools,* eds M Cole, D Hill and S Shan, Cassell, London

Cole, M (1997b) 'Race' and racism, in *A Dictionary of Cultural and Critical Theory* 2nd edn, ed M Payne, Blackwell Publishers, Oxford*

Cole, M (1998) Racism, reconstructed multiculturalism and antiracist education, *Cambridge Journal of Education,* **28** (1), pp 37–48

Cole, M (ed) (1999) *Professional Issues for Teachers and Student Teachers,* David Fulton, London

Cole, M, Hill, D and Shan, S (eds) (1997) *Promoting Equality in Primary Schools,* Cassell, London

Commission for Racial Equality (CRE) (1988) *Medical School Admissions: Report of a formal investigation into St George's Hospital Medical School,* CRE, London

Commission on the Future of Multi-ethnic Britain (2000) *Report of the Commission on the Future of Multi-ethnic Britain* (the Parekh report), Profile Books, London

Connolly, P (1999a) Prejudice or play in primary pupils, *TES,* 29 October

Connolly, P (1999b) *Racism, Gender Identities and young children,* Routledge, London

CRE (1989) *Code of Practice for the Elimination of Racial Discrimination in Education,* CRE, London

CRE (1992) *Ethnic Monitoring in Education,* CRE, London

CRE (2000) *Learning for All: Standards for racial equality in schools,* CRE, London

Conzen, K, Gerber, D, Morawska, G, Pozzetta, G and Vecoli, R (1992) The Invention of Ethnicity: a Perspective from the USA, *Journal of American Ethnic History* **12** (1)

Cooner, Singh, T and Loveless, A (1997) Information technology, in *Promoting Equality in Primary Schools*, eds M Cole, D Hill and S Shan, Cassell, London

Cope, B and Poynting, S (1989) Class, gender and ethnicity as influences on Australian schooling, an overview, in *The Social Contexts of Schooling*, ed M Cole, The Falmer Press, Lewes

Department for Education and Employment (DfEE) (1999) *Social Inclusion: Student support*, HMSO, London

Department of Education and Science (DES) (1985) *Education For All (The Swann report)*, HMSO, London

Farrar (1992) Racism, education and Black self-organisation, *Critical Social Policy*, **36** (2/3)

Gaine, C (1995) *Still No Problem Here*, Trentham Books, Stoke-on-Trent

George, R (1993) *A Handbook on Equal Opportunities in Schools, Principles, Policy and Practice*, Longman, Harlow

German, G (1999) *School Exclusions and the Black Communities: A critique of government proposals*, The Working Group Against Racism in Children's Resources, London

Gillborn, D and Gipps, C (1996) *Recent Research on the Achievement of Ethnic Minority Pupils*, HMSO, London

Gillborn, D and Mirza, H (2000) *Educational Inequality; Mapping race, class and gender – a synthesis of research evidence*, Ofsted, London

Gillborn, D and Youdell, (2000) *Rationing Education: Policy, practice, reform and equity*, Open University Press, Buckingham

Gravelle, M. (2000) Planning for Bilingual Learners, Trentham Books, Stoke-on-Trent

Green, M and Grosvenor, I (1997) Making Subjects, History-Writing, Education and Race Categories, *Paedogogica Historica*, **23** (3)

Grosvenor, I (1995) 'Race', Racism and Black Exclusion, *Forum*, **37** (3)

Grosvenor, I (1997) *Assimilating Identities, Racism and Educational Policy in Post-1945 Britain*, Lawrence & Wishart, London

*Guardian*, (1995) 17 February

*Guardian*, (1996) 6 September

Hatcher, R (1997) New Labour, school improvement and racial equality, *Multicultural Teaching*, **15** (3), pp. 8–13

Hatcher, R and Jones, K (1996) Education After the Conservatives: The response to the New Agenda of Reform, Trentham Books, Stoke-on-Trent

Hatcher, R, Troyna, B and Gewirtz, D (1996) *Racial Equality and the Local Management of Schools*, Warwick Papers on Education Policy No 8, Warwick University

Hessari, R and Hill, D (1989) *Practical Ideas for Multicultural Learning and Teaching in the Primary Classroom*, Routledge, London

Hill, D (1992) What the radical Right is doing to teacher education, a radical Left critique, *Multicultural Teaching*, **10** (3), pp 31–34

Hill, D (1994) Cultural diversity and initial teacher education, in *Cultural Diversity and the Curriculum, Vol 4, Cross-Curricular Contexts, Themes and Dimensions in Primary Schools*, eds G Verma and P Pumphrey, Falmer Press, London

Hill, D (1997a) Reflection in Teacher Education, in *Educational Dilemmas, Debate and Diversity, Vol 1, Teacher Education and Training*, eds K Watson, S Modgil and C Modgil, Cassell, London

Hill, D (1997b) Equality in primary schooling, in *Promoting Equality in Primary Schools*, eds M Cole, D Hill, and S Shan, S, Cassell, London

Hill, D and Cole, M (1997) Introduction, in *Promoting Equality in Primary Schools*, eds M Cole, D Hill and S Shan, Cassell, London

Hill, D and Cole, M (1999a) Introduction, in *Promoting Equality in Secondary Schools*, eds D Hill and M Cole, Cassell, London

Hill, D and Cole M (eds) (1999b) *Promoting Equality in Secondary Schools*, Cassell, London

The Institute of Race Relations (IRR) (2000) *Racially Motivated Murders Since 1991*, IRR, London

Jones, R (1999) *Teaching Racism or Tackling It?* Trentham Books, Stoke-on-Trent

Klein, R (1996) Race inequality 'as bad as ever', *TES*, 10 October

Klein, R (1997) Rescuing the Lost Boys of Racism, *TES*, 14 November

Leicester, M (1989) *Multicultural Education, From Theory to Practice*, NFER-Nelson, Windsor

Leicester, M (1992) Antiracism versus the new multiculturalism, moving beyond the interminable debate, in *Cultural Diversity and the Schools Vol 3 Equity or Excellence? Education and Cultural Reproduction*, eds J Lynch, C Modgil, and S Modgil, Falmer Press, London

Macpherson, Sir W (1999) *The Stephen Lawrence Inquiry, Report of an inquiry*, The Stationery Office, London

Mason, D (1994) On the dangers of disconnecting race and racism, *Sociology* **28** (4), pp 845–58

Miles, R (1982) *Racism and Migrant Labour*, Routledge & Kegan Paul

Miles, R. (1993) *Racism after 'Race Relations'*, Routledge, London

Modood, T (1992) *Not Easy Being British, Colour, Culture and Citizenship*, Runneymede Trust and Trentham Books, London

Modood, T (1994) Political blackness and British Asians, *Sociology* **28** (4), pp 858–76

National Association of Teachers in Further and Higher Education (NATFHE) (2000) *Equality News No 3*, December

Office for Standards in Education (Ofsted) (1996) *Exclusions from Secondary School 1995/6*, Ofsted, London

Ofsted (1999) *Raising the Attainment of Minority Ethnic Pupils, School and LEA responses*, Ofsted, London

Ofsted (2000) *Evaluating Educational Inclusion: Guidance for Inspectors and Schools*, Ofsted, Inspection Quality Division, London

Ofsted (2001) *Improving Attendance and Behaviour in Secondary Schools*, <www.ofsted.gov.uk>

Osler, M (1997) Exclusions drama turns into a crisis for blacks, *Times Educational Supplement*, 10 October

Osler, A (2000) School inspection and racial justice: challenges facing Ofsted and Schools, *Multicultural Teaching*, **19** (1)

Osler, A and Morrison, M (2000) *Inspecting Schools for Racial Equality: Ofsted's Strengths and Weaknesses*, Trentham Books, for the Commission for Racial Equality, Stoke-on-Trent

Parekh, B (2000) Introduction to the Report of the Commission on the Future of Multi-ethnic Britain, *Multicultural Teaching* 19 (1), p 7

Parker-Jenkins, M, Haw, K, Khan, S and Irving, B (1999) *Muslim Women: Destinations and labour market implications* (official report), Leverhulme Trust, London

Policy Studies Institute (1997) *Ethnic Minorities in Britain*, PSI, London

Pyke, N (1995) Inspections 'neglect' racial equality, *TES*, 3 February

Richardson, R (1992) Preface to Modood, *Not Easy Being British, Colour, Culture and Citizenship*, Runnymede Trust and Trentham Books, London

Runnymede Trust (1997) *Islamophobia – its features and dangers*, The Runnymede Trust, London

Sarup, M (1991) *Education and the Ideologies of Racism*, Trentham Books, Stoke-on-Trent

Sivanandan, A (2000a) *Macpherson and After*, Institute of Race Relations, London

Sivanandan, A (2000b) *Outcast England, How Schools Exclude Black Children*, IRR, London

Smithers, R. (2001) Punishment for Black pupils appears harsher, *Guardian*, 1 March, p 11

Sollis, A (1996) The 'underachieving' African Caribbean boy, *Multicultural Teaching*, 14 (2), pp 32–36

Troyna, B and Carrington, B (1990) *Education, Racism and Reform*, Croom Helm, London

Troyna, B (1993) *Racism and Education*, Open University Press, Buckingham

TTA (2000) *Raising the Attainment of Minority Ethnic Pupils*, TTA, London

Virdee, S and Cole, M (2000) 'Race', racism and resistance, in *Education, Equality and Human Rights*, ed M Cole, Routledge Falmer, London

Wheathampstead Education Centre (2001) *Dealing with Racial Harassment: A guide for schools*, Wheathampstead Education Centre, Wheathampstead

Whitty, G, Power, S and Halpin, D (1998) *Devolution and Choice in Education, The School, the State and the Market*, Open University Press, Buckingham

*This is the second edition (paperback) – please note that the first edition (hardback) has a serious typographical error that alters the sense of what Cole is saying.

# 9

# Gender

## Kate Hirom

## Editors' introduction

*After the Sex Discrimination Act 1975, the academic achievement of girls increased to the point, in the late 1990s, where it exceeded boys' performance in certain areas. Concerns about the underachievements of boys are the starting point for Kate Hirom's feminist analysis of gender inequality. Strategies to promote equal opportunities in schooling since 1975 are tested against statistical evidence of an ongoing variety of gender differences – in examination performance (primary to A level), in classroom behaviours, exclusion procedures, provision for special educational needs and literacy. These distinctions are compared with evidence of changing formulations of inequality in society, from the development of 'masculinities' and the 'feminization of schools' to crime, employment opportunity and the economics of gender differentiation.*

## Introduction

As the 1990s drew to a close, the issue of gender in education was raised to the status of a national crisis.

A moral panic about boys and their future developed in the popular and educational press. Educational experts shifted their attention away from measures to promote girls' learning and on to strategies for improving the performance of boys. The underachievement of boys had become one of the 'biggest challenges' facing schools and society (Wragg, 1997). In 1998 the Minister for Schools, Stephen Byers, directed all schools to acknowledge this gender gap and develop strategies to tackle it.

The underachievement of any pupil is, of course, a matter of deep concern but the fact that girls' achievement has risen above that of boys is also a cause for celebration, given the legacy of discrimination they have inherited. The media panic and rapid response to the achievement of girls vis-à-vis boys suggests the backlash with which all advances in equal opportunities are met, as threatened power bases regroup and rearm in attempts to reimpose the status quo.

There is, however, a need to look behind the headlines and behind the statistics, to ask which girls are achieving and which boys are not.

## Sex, gender and theory

It is important to establish, initially, the difference between sex and gender. Whereas sex refers to basic physiological differences between males and females (differences in genitalia and respective roles in human reproduction, for example), gender relates to social and cultural differences, relative to time and place. For example, the 'acceptable modes of dress' or body language for males and females have varied dramatically throughout history and in different regions; and attributes such as aggression and passivity are not uniformly linked to one gender across different societies (Mead, 1950).[1]

The main problem with biological explanations is that they fail to account for these geographical and historical variations (Measor and Sikes, 1992: 7; see also La Fontaine, 1978). Those who argue that biology accounts for gender differences in society generally propose that human beings possess a genetically based programme – a 'biogrammar' – which predisposes them to behave in certain ways (cf Tiger and Fox, 1972). Research on the structure of the brain, for example, has been used to suggest that females have a physiological predisposition to a facility for language skills (Smith, 1996; Hannan, 1996). These arguments also fail to take into account the evidence that socialization into gender roles may begin at a very early stage in a child's life, in babyhood (cf Oakley, 1972).

## Socialization theories

Explanations based on socialization can be grouped into *social learning* theory (roles learnt from parents, peers and teachers), *cognitive development* theory (roles established in the child's quest for competence in a world where such competence is linked to being 'male' or 'female') and *psychoanalytic* theory (focused on the emotional aspects of a child's life).

The theories and investigative methods of Sigmund Freud, to which the word 'psychoanalysis' strictly refers, have been much criticized, particularly by feminists, for the way in which they seem to focus on the male as the norm and the female as deviant from it. Some feminists have concentrated criticism almost exclusively on Freud's description of little girls' supposed envy of boys' masculinity – so called 'penis envy'; others have found value in Freud's general theory that all humans share an original bisexuality and see his theories as supporting the view that it is in the construction of our social identities that individuals become gender divided. (cf Mitchell, 1974).

In feminist theories female 'difference' is seen not in a negative, inferior light but as a position of strength and resistance to a patriarchal society. Patriarchy has been defined by the feminist writer Adrienne Rich as:

> The power of the fathers; a familial – social, ideological and political system in which men – by force, direct pressure or through ritual, tradition, law and language, customs, etiquette, education, and the division of labour, determine which part women shall or shall not play and in which the female is everywhere subsumed under the male.
>
> (Cited in Eisenstein, 1981: 18–19)

According to the French psychoanalyst Jacques Lacan (1973), gender identity occurs at the same time as our entry into the language system and, indeed, it is constructed through the language system. 'He' or 'she', 'male' or 'female' become significant distinctions of one being from another. Studies of language have highlighted the way in which language discriminates against women. Many words give a view of women as a deviant, subordinate group – for example, in the basic use of the masculine as the root word with the feminine as a suffix (actor –actress). Spender (1980) extends the discussion of sexist language to differences in the style of discourse used by women and by men.

Gendered language (such as the generic 'he') is now discouraged in most academic and other institutions and most people accept the right of a woman to use 'Ms'. Yet attempts to redress the historical gender bias of our language are discounted by some, particularly on the right, as a trivial aspect of 'political correctness' (a term that has become pervasive in the anti-egalitarian backlash). This position itself indicates how important language is in the reproduction and maintenance of power relations for social institutions in society (such as the judiciary, police, industry and finance). Bourdieu's term 'symbolic violence' is a powerful metaphor for the way in which language can be used as a force of repression and exclusion. It is important, however, to recognize that boys also come under 'the rule of the father', and although they may be intended to inherit its power and privileges, the passage is by no means assured or easy.

Some theories have suggested that boys can also feel envious of girls' femininity and that boys' devaluing of girls and feminine things can be explained by their more difficult struggles to become masculine. According to Chodorow (1978), both males and females identify, initially, with the mother. For females it is relatively straightforward to continue to do so while boys have to undergo the more complicated process of detachment. Measor and Sikes (1992) suggest that socialization theory might be best seen as a combination of the various non-biological approaches (1992: 10–12), a recognition that gender is by definition a social construct, that appropriate gender roles are constructed not socially given.

Gender inequalities are reproduced, in large part, through the institution of the family where gender roles are constructed through the socialization process with respect to expectations, the division of household chores, dress, toys, children's literature and so on. However, inequalities are also reproduced by peer pressure, the media (cf Cole, Maguire and Bosowski, 1997), leisure and sport (cf Tomlinson, 1997), and, of course, by the education system.

## Feminist approaches

Feminist reactions to gender inequalities in society have been historically divided between *radical* or *revolutionary feminists*, who see patriarchy as the principle form of oppression (Millett, 1970; Firestone, 1972) and *socialist feminists*, who see gender inequality as the product of the capitalist system (Mitchell, 1971; Rowbotham, 1973; Barrett, 1980). The former tend to see the continuing domination of women by men as transcending the divisions of social class: Firestone (1972) wrote of 'sex class' as an additional category to economic class. The latter tend to focus on the subordination of women as serving a functional role in capitalism in providing a ready source of cheap (or in the home, free) labour from which few women profit: the basis of female oppression is economic. Both groups see that gender equality can only be achieved through a radical or revolutionary restructuring of society. In contrast, *liberal feminists* favour reform under the existing system, one step at a time. More recent feminist approaches see gender as part of an interconnecting web of different identities of class, race and gender (Nicholson (ed), 1990). *Black feminists* have been particularly critical of the exclusion of their experience from earlier versions of feminism. (Amos and Parmar, 1984; Bhavanani and Coulson, 1985; Lorde, 1984; Carby, 1982; Mohanty, 1988). *Post-modernist feminism* tends to emphasize the complex and local nature of inequality, rejecting a universal theory or 'metanarrative' of social change (for example Butler, 1990; Lather, 1991; Jones, 1993).

It has been argued by Cole and Hill (1995, 1996) and Kelly (1992, 1994, and 1998) that in concentrating on the local rather than the international, in accepting all voices as equally valid, post-modernism in its appropriation of feminism is not able to theorize nor to advance the cause of women in the modern world. In particular, as socialist feminist Jane Kelly (1994, 1999) argues, post-modern feminists have little to say about the situation of working-class women in the 21st century.

## Gender and legislation

The Sex Discrimination Act 1975 (SDA) makes it unlawful to discriminate against a person on grounds of sex. Discrimination means unfavourable treatment, either by *direct discrimination* where a person of one sex is treated less favourably, because of his or her sex than a person of the opposite sex in similar circumstances is or would be treated, or *indirect discrimination* where a condition or requirement is applied to both sexes, but disproportionately few people of one sex can comply with it, while the inability to comply with it is to the disadvantage of the individual concerned.

With relation to schools, section 22 of the SDA sets out the treatments of a pupil that could be regarded as discriminatory. It states that it is unlawful for the 'responsible body' to discriminate against a girl (or boy) on the ground of sex (a) in the terms in which it admits her/him to the establishment as a pupil (b) by refusing or deliberately omitting to accept an application to the establishment as a pupil. Where she/he is a pupil of the establishment, it is unlawful for the responsible body to discriminate in the way it affords access to any benefits, facilities or services, or by refusing or deliberately omitting to afford access to them, or by excluding her/him from the establishment or subjecting her/him to any detriment. Of particular importance is the requirement that girls and boys must have equal access to all the 'benefits, facilities, or services' offered by the school (SDA, 1975: Section 22c)

So what does this all mean? It is important to realize, firstly, that these requirements apply to co-educational schools. An exception is made for admission to single-sex schools, although the facilities available at such schools should not be less favourable than those at other schools. Secondly, it means that co-educational schools cannot attempt to balance their intake in terms of the sexes of applicants nor to increase their intake of girls now that, as Ball and Gewirtz (1997: 214) have pointed out, they are seen as 'a valuable and sought after resource'. Thirdly, the Act means precisely the same access to the curriculum and also to any other benefit offered by the school such as careers guidance and all extra-curricular and out of school activities organized by the school, including work experience and career visits.

## Educational implications

The Sex Discrimination Act of 1975, monitored by the Equal Opportunities Commission (EOC) with the power to intervene with local authorities to ensure equality of provision, has provided an important legitimization for strong equal opportunities policies in schools. According to Skelton (1993), the Act 'is a milestone in the history of women's education. The 1994 Education Act may have put equal opportunities on the agenda, but the Sex Discrimination Act took the theory and transformed it into a mode of practice.'

For some critics (see Arnot and Weiner, 1987) the legislation did little to actively improve the quality of experience in schools for female students and teachers, because few resources were provided to extend different subjects on the curriculum, such as technology for girls and modern languages for boys, to a larger constituency.

The legislation did, however, provide the impetus for working groups such as the Girls into Science and Technology Project (GIST) which attempted (with some success) to make science a more girl-friendly subject (cf Matthews, 1996). Above all, the legislation helped to raise the awareness of teachers of the extent of sex discrimination in schools, albeit that the work of feminist researchers such as Walkerdine (1981), Skelton (1989), Stanworth (1983) and Spender (1982, 1987, 1988) is often seen as more influential in raising awareness, particularly of the sex discrimination found in daily classroom interactions.

## The role of the school in the reproduction of gender inequality

Gender inequality is reproduced in schools in several ways, including the organization of the school, the organization and management of classrooms and lessons, students' experience of the curriculum (both actual or formal and hidden) and in teachers' activities and actions (Measor and Sikes, 1992: 53).

King (1978) exemplifies the ways in which for quite unnecessary reasons primary classrooms have employed gender as an organization device, for such activities as lining up. In secondary schools, female students are often encouraged to compete against males (Measor and Sikes, 1992: 55). It is difficult to see an educational rationale for such practices, which have the effect of reinforcing gender divisions rather than cooperation.

Strategies to promote anti-sexism (actions or behaviours consciously seeking to redress the current sexist nature of society) entail a careful consideration of such issues as the formal curriculum where history, for example, can give the impression of studying white ruling-class men – 'his-story' rather than 'her-story' (George 1993: 88). Women and girls should not be marginalized and the perpetuation of stereotypes should be avoided, yet through the hidden curriculum (through the gender expectations of teachers and other school staff and the respective roles of staff within schools) schooling also often reflects and reinforces the patriarchal hierarchy of the wider society.

Numerous research studies have shown that, in daily classroom interactions, teachers respond differently to boys and to girls. Boys are more disruptive and demanding of attention than girls (Fuller, 1980: Walkerdine, 1981; Stanworth, 1983; Measor and Sikes, 1992: 63–64). The teacher's common response is to give more attention to boys. Teachers are less likely to learn the names of their female students and are more likely to see girl students as a non-individuated group, particularly Asian girls who are typed as passive and docile and whose names are considered more difficult to pronounce (Brah and Minhas, 1988).

Teachers of both sexes are more likely to say that they enjoy teaching boys, that boys are more creative (Stanworth, 1983), whereas teachers' reports on lessons are more likely to focus on boys. Girls generally respond to boys' domination of classroom space and time by getting on with their work and supporting each other. However, their achievements are often dismissed as 'careful work' rather than 'flair'. Cohen (1998: 27) has pointed out that, historically, male lack of effort has been seen as natural, as 'healthy idleness', with female hard work pathologized as 'morbidity'. If boys tend to overestimate their own abilities (Barber, 1994; Myers, 2000: 6), this may go unchallenged.

# Gender and academic performance

## Primary and secondary

Although girls have suffered from adverse discrimination in classrooms for decades, their academic achievement in recent years has outstripped that of boys in most areas.

Analysis of baseline testing in the first term of primary school shows that in 1998 girls arrived in primary schools with the stronger grasp of the alphabet, of numbers and every other aspect of early learning. At age 7 girls continue to outperform boys across the board though the gap is more marked in English. For 11-year-olds, comparison by gender shows a gap of 18 per cent in writing (with 62 per cent of girls reaching Level 4 but only 44 per cent of boys); in reading there was a 9 per cent gap (National Literacy Trust, 2000). However, in the 1999 Standards Assessment Tests (SATs) the gender gaps in reading and writing were reported to have narrowed to 6 per cent and 16 per cent respectively. More startling is the wide regional variation: 5 per cent in more affluent Sutton, compared with 21 per cent in Hackney, a deprived inner-city catchment area.

Figures published by the school standards minister in November 1997 showed that about two-thirds of 14-year-old girls – but only half of boys – reached the expected level in history, geography, design and technology, modern foreign languages and music. Figures published in September 1999 showed that girls outperformed boys in English (Level 5 was reached by 72 per cent of girls but only 55 per cent of boys) but did no better in maths and slightly worse in science.

## Examination performance: GCSE and A level

In 1999, across all GCSE subjects, 17.7 per cent of female grades were an A* or A grade compared with 12.8 per cent of male grades, with 60.2 per cent of females' grades being A–C grades compared with 50.2 per cent of males' grades (DfEE, 2000). However, in 1978 a slightly higher number of boys (23.7 per cent) compared to girls (23.6 per cent) achieved the best grades. The increase since 1988 (the year of introduction of GCSE examinations) is marked and is greater for girls than it is for boys. In the final year of GCE O level and CSE (1987), the difference in favour of girls was 1.6 per cent. By 1990 it had increased to 7.6 per cent (a rapid change) and by 1999 to 10.6 per cent (SCAA, 1996; DfEE, 2000).

For A level, the School Curriculum and Assessment Authority (SCAA) figures show that, across all subjects, in 1995, boys were more likely to get an 'A' grade (16.6 per cent) than girls (15.1 per cent), and were more likely to get higher grades at supplementary level. The 1999 results indicate that the difference between males and females narrowed at the highest grades to a negligible difference, though not uniformly for all subjects (and females are slightly less likely to achieve at the top of the range) (DfEE, 2000).

In terms of grade profiles, Table 9.1 shows the gender difference in 1999, with 37.9 per cent of females being awarded two or more A levels and just under 30.8 per cent of males (with three or more passes awarded to 27.5 per cent of females, compared with 22 per cent of males) (DfEE, 2000).

**Table 9.1** *School leavers obtaining two or more A-level passes as a percentage of the 17-year-old age group by gender, 1977–1991, 1995, 1999*

|   | 77 | 80 | 85 | 90 | 95 | 99 |
|---|----|----|----|----|----|----|
| F | 11.2 | 12.0 | 12.9 | 17.6 | 21.0 | 37.9 |
| M | 13.7 | 13.1 | 14.2 | 16.6 | 18.9 | 30.9 |

SCAA 1996, DfEE 2000

## Single-sex education

Debates on the benefits of single-sex verses co-educational schooling have been taking place since the beginning of the century. As Skelton (1993) points out, there is no real evidence that single-sex schooling significantly improves the examination performance of either boys or girls. Many of the single-sex schools are available to mainly middle-class pupils and therefore social class as well as gender is a factor in performance.

Selective girls' schools, account to some extent for the consistently high levels of girls' achievement, and the biggest increase in the intake of Oxford and Cambridge between the 1970s and 1990s was among girls from independent schools (McCrum, 1996 in Arnot *et al* 1999: 108). However, Benn and Chitty (1996) found that girls' comprehensive schools achieve better examination results than equivalent boys' or mixed schools despite scoring higher than average on indices of social deprivation.

## Higher education

The Higher Education Statistics Agency's figures show that the gender division carries on at college and university. As with A-level results, men are more likely to gain a first (10.1 per cent as opposed to 9.4 per cent of women). However, there are more male mature full-time students than female and mature students are more likely to get a better degree. There are more women first year students in total (and have been since 1994) and the 1998 degree results show that slightly more women (53 per cent) than men graduated. However, the number of females on teacher training and nursing degree courses is disproportionately high, with a very small percentage in engineering and technology, architecture and mathematics.

Social class is a major factor in girls' performance. The majority of achieving females are still middle class in origin. In 1963 the Robbins report found that only 4 per cent of female graduates had fathers in skilled work, 5 per cent in semi-skilled or unskilled manual work. Dearing, in 1997, suggested little change in this position, (Arnot *et al*, 1999: 114). We may, therefore, really be talking about the rise of a female graduate elite composed of upper-middle and middle-class females, rather than an improvement in the position of women in general.

## Interpreting statistics

Information linking results and gender is relatively new and as the statistics are subjected to increasing scrutiny, more questions are being raised. Elwood and Coomber (1995) point out that changes in the makeup of the entry profile should be taken into account in comparative data over time. For example, it is likely that, given the link between GCSE and the National Curriculum, more underachieving boys are now entered for mathematics than formerly. Results of both boys and girls may be affected by the entry policy of schools. In mathematics, for example, teachers are more likely to enter girls for the middle tier in which they can only achieve a B because they confuse girls' lack of confidence in the subject with their actual ability to succeed.

This can have an effect on A-level choices. While 300,000 girls take maths GCSE only 20,000 take A-level maths. The National Curriculum has led to a wider subject base for both boys and girls, yet there remains a heavily gender-segmented pattern to pre- and post-16 subject choices, which continues into university (Croxford, 2000: 130). Where English is a core subject, 200,000 males take English GCSE but only 15,000 at A level. Women are less likely to pursue subjects associated with careers in science and technology.

In addition the published results only reflect differences by gender without taking into account socio-economic background. Regan (1998) points out that the difference in achievement at GCSE between pupils from middle-class areas like Kingston-on-Thames and those from inner city deprived areas such as Tower Hamlets is far more significant than the gap between boys and girls overall. The danger of knee-jerk reactions to statistics gathered over a relatively short time span is also illustrated by the much-heralded improvement in boys' reading on the basis of the 1999 Key Stage 2 SAT results, attributed initially to the immediate success of the literacy strategy, but later attributed by other commentators to the more 'boy friendly' subject matter of the comprehension test (spiders) (cf Wragg, 1999).

Statistics are relevant but they cannot tell the whole story, neither can they tell it immediately (see Davies, 1998). They are also as amenable to appropriation for political ends as any other form of evidence (Regan, 1998).

## Exclusion

Five times as many boys are permanently excluded from secondary school. At primary school the proportion is even larger (Parsons *et al*, 1995). From a study of 176 schools in Scotland, both primary and secondary, Lloyd (2000: 257) concludes that schools have gendered models of deviance. Girls' deviance is seen as less confrontational and less challenging to the system, and girls are seen to be 'better at taking a telling off'. The high proportion of African-Caribbean boys excluded suggests that race is also a factor. Raphael Reed (1999) suggests that the rise in exclusions is inextricably linked to the drive for 'school improvement'.

## Special educational needs (SEN)

The fact that more boys than girls are likely to be reported as having special educational needs is often given as evidence that more boys are unable to cope in schools, but this also needs careful examination.

A report by Budge (1997) on a study carried out at the Institute of Education revealed that junior school boys were two-and-a-half times more likely to receive SEN support than girls (eight times as many in one school). 'Boys were also given more help – in terms of time, and the prestige and expense of the form of support. Cheaper forms of help were more evenly spread and girls actually got more help from volunteers – the help which didn't cost anything at all.'

The study acknowledges that the greater teacher dependency and the stronger anti-learning behaviours of boys had a strong impact on the provision of support. The 'acting out' behaviours of boys were more likely to be recognized as emotional and behavioural difficulties, whereas many forms of girls' 'acting out' behaviours (withdrawal, anorexia, flirtatiousness or overcompliance following sexual abuse) may go unrecognized (Duffield, 2000). In addition girls' greater tendency to support each other may keep them out of SEN provision. Other research (Duffield, 2000: 165) suggests that lower-achieving girls were less likely to be called upon when they were ready to answer, and less likely to receive individual attention.

Hey and colleagues (1999) warn that because boys are already receiving the bulk of SEN resources in schools, 'we should resist simplistic arguments that (all) boys now need more money spent on them at the expense of (all) girls' (1999: 140). They conclude that we should prevent boys from commandeering all SEN support by separating behavioural from academic needs.

## Attitudes to boys' underachievement

When Stephen Byers, Minister for Schools, announced in 1998 that all schools should acknowledge the gender gap in performance, he asked for action strategies to tackle the new 'laddish anti-school culture' (Arnot, David and Weiner, 1999: 8).

Few would disagree that boys take up a disproportionate amount of teacher-time in the classroom, but this is being interpreted as a possible factor in boys' lack of success. Much of the classroom attention focuses on behavioural matters rather than learning. Teachers are said to be more likely to 'pick on' boys and reprimand them for misdemeanours that may be overlooked when perpetrated by girls (La France, 1987). Girls are more likely to be nudged and cajoled into working whereas boys are more likely to be publicly rebuked. It has also been observed that it is usually a small proportion of the boys that dominates classroom time.

Pickering (1997) warns of the stereotyping of male as well as female pupils, for example in the assumption that male pupils are uniformly subject to peer-group pressure and recommends that schools find out from higher-achieving males the secret of their success. His advice to teachers is to talk more *to* boys to find out their own perceptions rather than *about* them. The Ofsted 'Boys and English' (1993) report also indicates that boys' performance improved when they had a clear understanding of the progress they needed to make in order to achieve well.

Such approaches should apply equally to girls. However, the reorganization of teaching styles to take into account boys' supposed preference for competition, shorter attention spans and desire for quick feedback (Channel 4, 1998) can have repercussions on girls. For example, Raphael Reed (1998: 62) takes a recent report that girls are not seen to be benefiting as much as boys from the introduction of the numeracy strategy and links it with the findings of Boaler (1997), showing how girls are disadvantaged in mathematics when it is delivered in a procedural way, and become anxious in fast-paced, competitive settings.[2]

## Literacy

A particular emphasis has been placed on boys' attitudes to literacy. Jordan (1995) suggests that boys are less willing readers due (partly) to prevalent definitions of masculinity that prioritize action and daring over reflection and empathy. This may go some way to explaining why boys regard English as a 'female' subject, according to the Ofsted Review of Research (Arnot *et al*, 1998). According to researchers at Cambridge University, three-quarters of mothers read with their children between the ages of five and seven, but only half of fathers (the National Literacy Trust, 2000).

Murphy and Elwood (1998) suggest that reading schemes based on stories about people may be harder to access for boys due to their pre-school reading preferences for books about machines (1998: 165). There are early indications that the more varied reading requirements of the National Literacy Strategy may be having an effect, although texts should not be chosen to appeal exclusively to boys and boys need to be encouraged to extend their reading repertoires.

Literacy is not, however, an autonomous entity (Street, 1984). Failure to read undoubtedly leads to various forms of disadvantage in later life, but Fairclough (1989) points out that functional literacy without a political critical focus will not necessarily lead to greater empowerment. Traditional definitions of literacy are being challenged by the development of computer technology. Girls' responses to information technology (IT) are more polarized than those of boys (Littleton, 1996: 82). They participate less in computer clubs and computer rooms are often regarded as male territory. Studies have shown that the use of IT can be a powerful tool for motivating boys even in subjects (like modern languages) perceived by boys as female (Johnston, 1999), yet without vigilance towards girls' access to and progress in IT, women may once again suffer disadvantage in the electronic medium (Spender, 1995).

## Social change

Chris Woodhead (as Chief Inspector of Schools) reported that it is white working-class boys in the inner city schools who are achieving least well. This is not a new phenomenon but part of the ongoing and disproportionate impact of the restructuring of capitalism on working-class communities. The decline in manufacturing industry and increased globalization, for example, create a context in which international companies can rationalize, without any loyalty to the local workforce. Employment in unskilled manual labouring is lost while the service sector grows, and with it more part-time and short-term jobs. One effect is that by 2000 only 40 per cent of the workforce enjoyed full-time tenured employment or secure self-employment, with 30 per cent of the population idle or working for poverty wages.

Many observe among working-class boys a failure to deal with reality. Grant (1996), in a classic case of blame the victim, finds this the fault of the boys themselves – 'The jobs their fathers got do not exist any more, yet their strategy for dealing with the world of work has not altered'. Fine *et al* (1997) also report that in the United States males are constructing their identities 'as if they were wholly independent of corroding economic and social relationships', as if they are 'outside history' (1997, in Lingard and Douglas, 1999).

However, the study of Parnell School by Mac An Ghaill (1994) shows that male working-class attitudes to the changing economic and educational climate are not uniform, finding different constructions of masculinity by different groups of boys, which are echoed by Sewell (1998) in his study of African-Caribbean teenagers. Within the developing entrepreneurial culture of the school, Mac An Ghaill identifies three broad groups among male working-class pupils. Of these, the 'academic achievers' adopt an individualistic 'hard-work' ethic, while the 'new enterprisers' follow an entrepreneurial agenda, using the new vocationalist courses in business studies and IT as an alternative route for upward mobility (and, in the process, colonize the computer club originally set up to encourage girls). However, the third group of 'macho lads' constitute a 'hyper-masculine' male-bonding subculture opposed to the academic values of the school and are the potential source of a new male 'underclass' (Bleach, 1998).

Various studies on adolescent boys in secondary schools (Willis, 1977; Corrigan, 1979; Connell, 1989; Mac an Ghaill, 1994) have shown how schools have helped to construct male working-class identities through streaming (bottom sets made up of the 'macho lads') and definitions of knowledge that accord lower status to vocational subjects than to academic subjects. The new emphasis on performance puts increased emphasis on streaming and ability setting (for example setting in the numeracy and literacy hours) and may well be a factor in a continuing search for alternative sources of self-esteem for boys who are continuously placed in bottom sets. In a competitive environment, not everyone will win prizes.

In contrast, more females – including working-class females – have responded to changing social and economic circumstances by redefining the gender role. A generational shift in values is identified by Demos (Arnot et al, 1999) in which young working-class women increasingly appear to want 'the outer directed values of male working-class lives' with young, black girls in particular expressing resentment of the domestic division of work experienced in their families and communities (1999: 116). It may be argued that male unemployment has necessitated this shift, but there is no concomitant shift of males in relation to the domestic sphere. Numerous studies, in North America (Weis, 1990) and Australia (Connell, 1989) as well as Britain (Riddell, 1992 cited in Pickering, 1997) show that working-class attitudes towards the division of labour within the household have not changed greatly, but girls are more prepared to challenge the status quo than boys.

## Masculinities

Despite the attention that boys have received over the past 300 years, Jackson (1998) finds little questioning of what it really means to be male. Dominant hierarchical masculinity has been naturalized as the norm for everyone, against which females are seen as 'the other' and gay men and boys are demonized. Boys who do not match up to the dominant values – for example those who are not good at team games – are viewed as deficient in all-male public school cultures and are often the victims of verbal and physical bullying, which is tacitly condoned by staff.

For restorative 'masculinists' the underachievement of boys in schools is seen as symptom of a general 'crisis in masculinity' and provides a convenient focus for 'backlash' campaigns, against feminism in particular and equal opportunities in general. This position often links with a nostalgia for dominant forms of English nationality where 'boys knew their place' and England ruled an Empire (Mac An Ghaill, 1994: 25). Jackson warns that we should not overlook the potential of the Right to exploit the feelings of inadequacy of some disadvantaged males in the present economic climate. In the United States, the anger of white males is becoming a focus for Right-wing nationalist exploitation (see Lingard and Douglas, 1999). For Jackson (1999), the scrutiny of masculinities is necessary (rather than indulgent) because males do not benefit equally from patriarchal privilege, and gender 'absolutism' does not account for the range of male positions within the hierarchy of dominant masculinity. Lingard and Douglas (1999) point out that examination performance is part of wider problems for boys, indicated by the rise in suicide rates among males in the 14–25 age group.

## The feminization of schools argument

Pro-feminist projects (by both males and females) to help deconstruct dominant masculinities, such as *Boys Talk* in Australia (Masa, 1996), have been rejected by some 'masculinists' as yet more attempts to make boys confused by or ashamed of their 'real natures'. For these masculinists, schools are hostile places for boys, dominated by women who do not understand and cannot cope with their style of learning.

Leo McKinstry (1997) exemplifies this argument in an article for the *Daily Mail*. A supposed increase in juvenile delinquency and indiscipline in schools is laid at the door of social workers, single mothers and the inadequate supply of male role models in the classroom. In primary schools, he claims, only 12 per cent of teachers are male, excluding heads and deputies, whereas in secondary schools there are less than 50 per cent,[3] and 'The TTA has warned that there may be no male teachers in primary classrooms by 2010'.[4] According to McKinstry, women dominate schools physically and, in addition, the curriculum boys are subjected to is feminized:

> We have hastened the abandonment of concepts such as order, toughness and self reliance – what might be termed traditional 'masculine' values [for] ideas about self expression, understanding and compassion – what could be termed traditional 'feminine' values – which are all too often exploited by young men intent on causing trouble.

Educational and other public discourses are increasingly characterized by a tough, macho rhetoric – 'tough on crime; tough on the causes of crime', 'zero tolerance of failure', 'targets', 'action zones', 'hit squads' and the like. These accord with a general 'regendering' of state apparatuses away from policies of social care to 'old-style economist economic values', where efficiency predominates over equality and increased attention is paid to quantifiable results (testing, grading of lessons in Ofsted reports) and accountability (performance-related pay) (Lingard and Douglas, 1999: 61).

This is an educational climate in which winners and losers, between schools and within them, are integral to the system. At the same time, Davies (cited in Mac An Ghaill, 1994) notes that collegial and collaborative management styles in schools have been replaced by a version of masculinity that is 'competitive, point-scoring, over-confident, sporting and career and status conscious' and 'lends itself to divide and rule. . . the breeding ground for the fragmentation of the teaching staff which is necessary if teachers are not to become a political force' (1992, in Mac an Ghaill, 1994: 23).

However, there is an increasing circularity about the feminization of schools arguments. Failure to deal with dominant views of masculinity means that fewer males than females take up the more 'people-related' professions. As teachers and social workers, women bear the brunt of policing male anti-social behaviour and are blamed for its occurrence. Women who make up the greater part of the teaching profession are therefore subjected to the increasing pressure of accountability, inspection, monitoring of performance, completing the 'emotional labour' for the distant policy-makers while having to implement 'more efficient', whole class teaching methods that may be at odds with child-centred philosophy.

At the same time, women provide cheap labour in a variety of support services in schools – not only as lunchtime care assistants and secretaries but, increasingly, as classroom support workers. Marr (2000) reports the increasing ratio of support staff to teachers between 1992 and 1998, when the number of support staff rose by 60 per cent while the number of teachers rose by 2 per cent. A classroom assistant costs a school about one-third as much as an experienced teacher, so the support staff of mainly women, without permanent contracts or full employment rights, contribute significantly to the drive for efficiency in schools.

## Beyond the classroom: gender in society

In the world of work, women still have a long way to go to achieve equality. They may now hold more than 50 per cent of the available jobs, but 43 per cent of women (as opposed to 7 per cent of men) were working part time in 1998, and of these just over half were working in three major occupational groups – clerical/secretarial, personal and protective services, and sales (as opposed to 3.4 per cent of men). The proportion of women in managerial positions in industry is slowly increasing (to an estimated 41 per cent of managers and administrators by 2006) but women are still underrepresented in the highest positions in the judiciary, the police force, the law, the Church and financial institutions. Successful women in public life provide excellent role models for girls but they are still the exception rather than the rule. Women constitute less than 5 per cent of senior management in the UK and US; only 5 per cent of the Institute of Directors are women and less than 1 per cent of chief executives. Most women operate as state professionals in teaching, nursing and social work and are less likely to occupy senior posts in 'hard-nosed' departments such as the Treasury or Defence (see Connell, 1987, 1989). They are also less likely to take up highly paid jobs in computer-related industries.

After the 1997 election, more women work in the House of Commons, but comparative figures across Europe indicate that Britain has nothing to be complacent about. With 18.4 per cent of women MPs, the UK ranks twenty-seventh in a world league table of 70 countries compiled by the European Commission (2000), one place above Turkmenistan but considerably below France and Italy. The Greater Manchester Low Pay Unit (2000) records that despite equal pay legislation and increased participation in the labour market, women still earn less than three-quarters of men's weekly earnings in Great Britain, while the difference between women's and men's earnings remains the widest in Europe.

As part-time workers, women are also disadvantaged in terms of training, pensions and other benefits. Women tend to live longer than men, so a substantial number of today's labour force are preparing for at least 20 years of poverty, a significant but less vocal underclass than 'young men bent on trouble'. The long and unsocial hours expected in many areas of occupation (including the House of Commons) prevent women from competing equally with men when, in addition, many of these women will be occupied in unpaid domestic and care work in the home, their 'second shift'.

This is so both for single mothers and those in partnerships. Even when men express beliefs in the equal sharing of domestic work, around 70 per cent of domestic work is carried out by women. Bittman and Pixley (1997) refer to this as 'pseudomutuality'. Unequal divisions of labour in the home are not a trivial matter. For Martin (1996) male 'domephobia' (fear of things domestic) symbolizes the public/private divide, which schools have done nothing to address and which must be broken down before true gender equality is reached. Reproduction and its consequences are still, it seems, the province of the female. Women on the whole have greater control of their own fertility, through the greater availability of contraception, but this does not account for the pressures experienced by many young women. Britain has the highest rate of teenage pregnancies in Western Europe (7,700 conceptions by females under 16).

Statistics indicate that the gap between male and female criminality closed rapidly in the late 20th century, from one female offender for every 11 males in the late 1950s to one woman to 3.6 men by 1995, but with women less likely to be involved in crimes of violence. New research indicates that more than 75 per cent of 11- and 12-year-old boys believe women deserve to be hit if they make men angry, and that boys aged 13 to 14 also show a tendency to blame the victims of violence (Campbell, 2000).

## Conclusion

School systems serve in many ways to reproduce the inequalities between the sexes and between social classes. These can be resisted but gender equity programmes that ignore the ways in which schools reproduce the values of the wider capitalist society are doomed to failure. Encouragement of boys to 'be more caring', to 'engage with their emotions' is unlikely to meet with acceptance when they see that, in the world outside, the movement of capital is rewarded more highly than the care of people and that social relationships are increasingly commodified.

At the same time, we have a dilemma in the education of girls. Does gender equality really mean the occupation of a higher position in an exploitative system, the acceptance of a hard-edged approach to knowledge and learning, in which certain forms of knowledge and pedagogy are legitimized by the state and other forms precluded, where what is worthwhile is that which can be easily quantified and monitored?

Discussions of gender inequality cannot take place out of the context of social class and neither should discussions of social class ignore the particular gendered manifestations of class oppression. The divide-and-rule policy of recent educational initiatives has militated against (admittedly complex) opportunities for boys and girls, men and women to fight together for social justice. Such policies emphasize the gender divide at the expense of considering the more complex relationship between class, ethnicity and gender, while attention to economic constructions of masculinity may endanger the 'girl-centred' anti-sexist approaches that have contributed so significantly to the raising of girls' self-confidence and expectations.

A social justice programme that includes gender, therefore, must consider how males and females are both engaged in a wider project of resistance to inequality.

## Notes

1.  Mead found that both sexes of the Arapesh of the South Pacific displayed the qualities of our traditional stereotype of 'femininity', whereas both sexes of the Mundugumour conformed to the 'masculine' stereotypes (Meade, 1935).
2.  Regarding the mentoring of 'at risk' boys by male teachers, a pilot study undertaken with Kingsthorpe Upper School and University College, Northampton, showed that a number of boys indicated their preference for a female mentor (Foreman-Peck et al, 2000).
3.  The latest figures from the Department for Education and Employment, at the time of writing, reveal that the proportion of female head teachers has increased in the last 10 years. Women now make up 51 per cent of all head teachers, 57 per cent in primary schools but only 27 per cent in secondary schools. The number of female deputies has also increased. However, in proportion to the makeup of the workforce, women are still under-represented at the highest levels.

4.  However, it is claimed by the Teacher Training Agency that the proposed training salary of £6,000 for PGCE students has led to an 18 per cent increase in enquiries from men interested in primary teaching.

# References

Abrams, J (1995) *Divide And School,* Falmer, London

Amos, V and Parmar, P (1984) Challenging imperial feminism, *Feminist Review* **17,** pp 3–19

Arnot, M and Weiner, G (1987) *Gender and the Politics of Schooling*, Hutchinson, London

Arnot, M, Gray, J, James, M, Rudduck, J with Duveen, G (1998) *Recent Research on Gender and Educational Performance*, Ofsted, London

Arnot, M, David, M and Weiner, G (1999) *Closing the Gender Gap*, Polity Press, London

Ball, S J and Gewirtz, S (1997) Girls in the market: choice, competition and complexity, *Gender and Education,* **19** (2), pp 207–22

Barber, M (1994) *Young People and Their Attitudes to School* (Interim report of research project in the Centre for Successful Schools), Keele University, Keele, Staffs

Barrett, M (1980) *Women's Oppression Today: Problems in Marxist feminist analysis,* New Left Books, London

Benn, C and Chitty, C (1986) *Thirty Years On: Is comprehensive education alive and well or struggling to survive?,* David Fulton, London

Bhavanani, K and Coulson, M (1986) Transforming socialist-feminism: the challenge of racism, *Feminist Review,* **23,** pp 81–92

Bittman, M and Pixley, J (1997) *The Double Life of the Family: Myth, hope and experience,* Allen & Unwin, Sydney

Bleach, ed (1998) *Raising Boys' Achievement In Schools,* Trentham Books, Stoke-on-Trent

Boaler, J (1997) *Experiencing School Mathematics: Teaching styles, sex and setting,* Open University Press, Buckingham

Bourdieu, P (1991) *Language and Symbolic Power,* Polity Press, London

Brah, A and Minhas, R (1988) Structural racism and cultural difference: schooling for Asian girls, in *Family, School and Society,* eds M Woodhead and A Mcgrath, Hodder & Stoughton, London

Budge, D (1997) Huge gender gap revealed in special needs, *TES,* 24 January

Budge, D (1998) Girls may not be so superior, *TES,* 18 September

Butler, J (1990) *Gender Trouble: Gender and the subversion of identity,* Routledge, London

Campbell, E (2000) Boys back domestic violence, *TES,* 9 June

Carby, H (1982) White woman listen! Black feminism and the boundaries to sisterhood in *Gender and the Politics of Schooling,* eds M Arnot and G Weiner, Hutchinson, London

Centre for Successful Schools (1994) *Young People and their Attitudes to School*, Keele University, Keele

Channel 4 (1998) *Why Men Don't Iron*, Quality Time Television, 23 June, 30 June, 7 July

Chodorow, N (1978) *The Reproduction of Mothering*, University of California Press, California

Cohen, M (1999) 'A habit of healthy idleness': boys' underachievement in historical perspective, in *Failing Boys*, eds D Epstein *et al*, Open University Press, Buckingham

Cole, M (1997) Equality and primary education: what are the conceptual issues? *Promoting Equality in Primary Schools*, eds M Cole, D Hill and S Shan, Cassell, London

Cole, M and Hill, D (1995) Games of despair and rhetorics of resistance: postmodernism, education and reaction, in *British Journal of Sociology of Education* **16** (2), pp 165–82

Cole, M and Hill, D (1996) Postmodernism, education and contemporary capitalism: a materialist critique, in *Values and Education*, eds O Valente *et al*, University of Lisbon, Lisbon

Cole, M and Hill, D (1997) New labour, old policies: Tony Blair's 'vision' for education in Britain, *Education Australia*

Cole, M, Hill, D and Shan, S (1999) *Promoting Equality in Secondary Schools*, Cassell, London

Cole, M, Maguire, P and Bosowski, J (1997) Radio 1 in the 80s: Day-time DJs and the cult of masculinity, in *Gender, Sport and Leisures Continuities and Challenges*, ed A Tomlinson, Meyer and Meyer Verlag, Aachen

Connell, R W (1987) *Gender and Power: Society, the person and sexual politics*, Allen and Unwin, Sydney

Connell, R (1989) Cool guys, swots and wimps: the interplay of masculinity and education, *Oxford Review of Education*, **15** (3), pp 291–303

Corrigan (1979) *Schooling The Smash Street Kids*, Macmillan, London

Croxford, L (2000) Gender and national curricula, in *Gender, Policy and Educational Change: Shifting agendas in the UK and Europe*, eds J Salisbury and S Riddell, Routledge, London

David and Weiner, (1997) *Guardian*, 23 May

Davis, J (1998), quoted in Budge, D, Girls may not be so superior, *TES*, 18 September

Department for Education and Employment (DfEE) (1999) *Preparing Young People for Adult Life*, DfEE

DfEE (2000) *Key Stage 4*, www.standards.dfee.gov.uk/performance/html

Duffield J (2000) Gender in the classrooms of more or less effective schools, in *Gender, Policy and Social Change*, eds J Salisbury and S Riddell, Routledge, London

Eisenstein, Z (1981) *The Radical Future of Liberal Feminism*, Longman, New York

Elwood and Coomber (1995) Gender difference in A-Level examinations: the reinforcements of stereotypes, Paper presented to ECER Conference, Bath

European Commission (2000) *Women of Europe*, Newsletter

Fairclough, N (1989) *Language and Power*, Longman, London

Fine, M *et al* (1997) (In)secure times: constructing white working class masculinities in the late 20th century. *Gender and Society*, **11** (1), pp 52–68

Firestone, S (1972*)* *The Dialectic of Sex*, Paladin, London

Foreman-Peck, L *et al* (2000) Paper presented to BERA Conference, 7 September

Fuller, M (1980) Black girls in a London comprehensive school, in *Co-education Reconsidered*, ed R Deem, Open University Press, Milton Keynes

George, R (1993) *A Handbook on Equal Opportunities in Schools: Principles, policy and practice*, Longman, Harlow

Grant, L (1996) Under pressure, *Guardian*, 11 March

Greater Manchester Low Pay Unit (2000) *The Gender Pay Gap – A report for the Equal Pay Task Force*, 36, October

Hannan, G (1996) *Improving Boys' Performance*, Private publication

Harris, S, Nixon, J and Rudduck, J (1993) School work, homework and gender, *Gender and Education* **5**, pp 3–15

Hey V *et al* (1999) Boys' underachievement, special needs and questions of equity, in *Failing Boys*, eds D Epstein *et al*, Open University Press, Buckingham

Holland, J (1989) What is gender? Gender in Britain today, in *Contexts of Schooling. The Social*, ed M Cole, Falmer Press, London

Jackson, D (1998) Breaking out of the binary trap, in *Failing Boys*, eds D Epstein *et al*, Open University Press, Buckingham

Johnston, C (1999) New boys' network, *TES*, 8 October

Jones, A (1993) Becoming a 'girl': post-structuralist suggestions for educational research, *Gender and Education*, **5** (2), pp 157–66

Jordan, E (1995) Fighting boys and fantasy play, *Gender and Education*, **7** (1), pp 69–86

Kelly, J (1992) Postmodernism and Feminism, *International Marxist Review* **14**, Winter

Kelly, J (1994) Feminism and Postmodernism: a productive tension or an incompatible collusion? Paper given to the British Educational Research Annual Conference, Oxford

Kelly, J (1998) Reworking gender and education, in *Postmodern Excess in Educational Theory: Education and the politics of human resistance*, eds D Hill, M Cole and G Rikowski, Tufnell Press, London

King R (1978) *All Things Bright And Beautiful? A sociological study of an infants' classroom*, Wiley, Chichester

Labour Market Trends (2000), *The Pay Gap*, April

Lacan, J (1973) *The Four Fundamentals of Psychology*, Penguin, Harmondsworth

La Fontaine, J (1978*)* *Sex and Age as Principles of Social Differentiation*, Academic Press, London

La France, M (1987) School for scandal: differential experiences for females and males, *Gender and Education*, **13** (1), pp 3–15

Lather, P (1991) *Feminist Research and Pedagogy Within the Post Modern*, Routledge, London

Lingard, B and Douglas, P (1999) *Men Engaging Feminisms*, Open University Press, Buckingham

Littleton, K (1996) Girls and information technology, in *Equity in the Classroom*, eds P Murphy and C Gipps, Falmer, London

Lodge, C and Pickering, J (1996) Boys' underachievement: challenging some assumptions, Paper presented to BERA Conference, Lancaster

Lloyd, G (2000) Gender and exclusion from school, in *Gender, Policy and Educational Change*, eds J Salisbury and S Riddell, Routledge, London

Lorde, A (1984) *A Sister Outsider*, Crossing Press, New York

Mac An Ghaill (1994) *The Making of Men*, Open University Press, Buckingham

Mahony (1985) *Schools for the Boys?* Hutchinson, London

Marr, A (2000) A very visible means of support, *TES*, 28 April

Martin, (1996) A Girls' Pedagogy, in *Equity in the Classroom*, eds P Murphy and C Gipps, Falmer Press, London.

Matthews, B (1996), Drawing Scientists, *Gender and Education*, **8** (2), pp 231–43

McKinstry, L (1997) *Daily Mail*, 15 October

Mead, M (1935) *Sex and Temperament in Three Primitive Societies*, Routledge & Kegan Paul, London

Mead, M (1950) *Male and Female*, Pelican, London

Measor, L and Sikes, (1992) *Gender and Schools*, Cassell, London

Merrett, F, and Wheldall, K (1992) Teachers' use of praise and reprimands to boys and girls, in *Educational Review*, **44** (1), pp 73–79

Men Against Sexual Assault (Masa) (1996) *Talking About Men: Understanding men and masculinities*, Masa, Melbourne

Millet, K (1970) *Sexual Politics*, Doubleday, London

Mitchell, J (1971) *Women's Estate*, Penguin, London

Mitchell, J (1974) *Psychoanalysis and Feminism*, Pelican, Harmondsworth

Mohanty, C (1988) Under Western eyes: feminist scholarship and colonialist discourses, *Feminist Review*, **30**, pp 61–88

Murphy, P and Elwood, J (1998) Gendered learning outside and inside school, in *Failing Boys*, eds D Epstein, J Elwood, V Hey and J Haw, Open University Press, Buckingham

Murphy, P and Gipps, C (1996) *Equity in the Classroom*, Falmer, London

Myers, K (2000) *Whatever Happened to Equal Opportunities in Schools?* Open University Press, Milton Keynes

National Literacy Trust (2000), www.literacytrust.org.uk

Nicholson, L J (ed) (1990) *Feminism/Postmodernism*, Routledge, London

Oakley, A (1972) *Sex, Gender and Society*, Temple Smith, London

Office for Standards in Education (Ofsted) (1993) *Boys and English*, Ofsted, London

Office of Her Majesty's Chief Inspector of Schools and the Equal Opportunities Commission (1996), HMSO, London

Parsons, C (1995) *Final Report to the Department of Education: National survey of LEAs' policies, and procedures for the identification of, and provision for, children who are out of school by reason of exclusion or otherwise*, DfEE, London

Pickering, J (1997) *Raising Boys' Achievement,* Network Educational Press, Stafford

Raphael Reed, L (1999) Zero tolerance: gender performance and school failure, in *Failing Boys,* eds D Epstein *et al,* Open University Press, Buckingham

Regan, C (1998) Boys' underachievement is not the real question, *Socialist Teacher,* **65,** Spring

Riddell, S (1992) *Politics and the Gender of the Curriculum,* Routledge, London

Rowbotham, S (1973) *Hidden From History: 300 years of women's oppression and the fight against,* Pluto Press, London

Rudduck, J, Chaplain, R and Wallace, G (1995) *School Improvement: What can pupils tell us?* David Fulton, London

School Curriculum and Assessment Authority (SCAA) (1996) *A/AS level Results Analysis,* SCAA Publications, London

School Curriculum and Assessment Authority (1996) *GCSE Results Analysis,* SCAA Publications, London

Sewell, T (1998) Loose canons: exploding the myth of the 'black macho' lad, in *Failing Boys,* eds D Epstein *et al,* Open University Press, Buckingham

Skelton, C (ed) (1989) Whatever happens to little women? in *Gender and Primary Schooling,* Open University Press, Milton Keynes

Skelton, C (1993) Women and education, in *Introducing Women's Studies,* eds D Richardson and V Robinson, Macmillan, London

Smith, A (1996) *Accelerated Learning,* Network Educational Press, Stafford

Spender, D (1978) The facts of life: sex differentiated knowledge, *English in Education,* **12** (3), pp 1–9

Spender, D (1980) *Man Made Language,* Routledge & Kegan Paul, London

Spender, D (1982) *Invisible Woman: The schooling scandal,* Writers and Readers Press, London

Spender, D (1987) *The Education Papers: Women's quest for equality in Britain, 1850–1912,* Routledge and Kegan Paul, London

Spender, D (1988) *Learning to Lose: Sexism and Education,* Women's Press, London

Spender, D (1995) *Nattering on the Net: Women, power and cyberspace,* Spinifex, Melbourne

Stanworth, M (1983) *Gender and Schooling,* Hutchinson, London

Street, B (1984) *Literacy in Theory and Practice,* Cambridge University Press, Cambridge

Tiger, L and Fox, R (1972) *The Imperial Animal,* Secker & Warburg, London

Tomlinson, A (ed) (1997) *Gender, Sport and Leisure: Continuities and challenges,* Meyer & Meyer Verlag, Aachen

Walden, R and Walkerdine, V (1982) Girls and mathematics. the early years, in *Bedford Way Papers* 8, Heinemann, London

Walkerdine, V (1981) Sex, power and pedagogy, in *Screen Education,* **38,** Spring, pp 14–24

Walkerdine, V (1989) *Counting Girls Out,* Virago, London

Weis, L (1990) *Working Class Without Work,* Routledge, London

Willis, P (1977) *Learning to Labour,* Saxon House, London

Wragg, T (1997) Oh Boy, *TES,* 16 May

Wragg, T (1999) *TES,* 12 November

# 10

# Sexuality

## Iain Williamson

### Editors' introduction

*Iain Williamson defines how sexual equality within schooling is the least developed of all social justice strategies within education. In society, the nature of sexual prejudice is shown to differ according to social context yet the various advances in gay, lesbian, transsexual and bisexual visibility still contend with two dominant factors: aggressive homophobia and the absence of legislation to compel equality for all sexualities. In education under Section 28 of the Local Government Act 1988, the problems of visibility without support are traced to specific instances of sexual harassment, abuse and violence within schooling, and illustrated by reference to major research in the United States and England. Practical measures are then proposed to enable pupils and teachers to deal with heterosexist abuse and to promote sexual equality through the curriculum, staff training, teaching unions and access to appropriate information about different sexualities.*

### Introduction

Sexuality is an important issue within British schools. Significant numbers of teachers, student teachers and other workers in schools are lesbian, gay or bisexual. Guardians and parents of secondary school students may be lesbian, gay or bisexual. It is estimated that at least 10 per cent of gay men and 20 per cent of lesbians are parents (Patterson, 1996). Many secondary school students identify themselves as gay or lesbian and disclose this to friends or teachers (Savin-Williams, 1998). Indeed, there is evidence that some children may identify as gay or lesbian in the primary years (Epstein, 1994).

Most primary age children and virtually all secondary school students encounter gay and lesbian, transsexual and bisexual issues from various media (TV, newspapers and so forth). A number of British soap operas feature, or have featured, lesbian and/or gay characters and stories.

Lesbians, gay men and bisexuals are here to stay and are making significant progress towards acceptance of their inalienable right to their sexuality. The issue is firmly on political, cultural, social and academic agendas. Politically, campaigns for greater lesbian and gay rights assume a high profile. In the 1980s, British 'municipal socialism' (particularly in cities like London and Manchester) took a number of lesbian and gay issues on board and local authorities retain varying degrees of commitment to lesbian and gay equality. As Cole (1997) observes, homosexuality is now firmly on the agenda. Each year a number of festivals and parades – such as Manchester's Gay Fest, the Brighton Pride and London's Mardi Gras – increase in participation and colour. The Labour government elected in 1997 presented a 'gay-friendly' image plus proposals for significant legislation.

A vibrant and diverse lesbian and gay scene forms a significant part of the social and economic infrastructure of many large towns and cities, with numerous gay and lesbian venues. There are also lesbian and gay film festivals, theatre groups and a wide range of publications, music and video targeted explicitly at 'pink consumers', and 'after three decades of campaigning in Britain, gay men have never had it so good' (Marks, 1997). Other issues of sexual diversity, such as transsexualism and transvestism, are being more openly discussed. An expanding range of academic publications in the area of gay and lesbian studies and a number of degree and diploma courses at British universities offer significant opportunities to study in these areas.

Yet this phenomenon is markedly less in evidence within compulsory education. While (generally anti-) lesbian and gay discourse is a marked feature of peer communication within secondary schools, homosexuality as a topic is often noticeably absent from the school curriculum, with relatively few opportunities for young people to learn about lesbian and gay lifestyles and discuss their feelings. Young people are often faced with a marked contrast between increasing coverage of lesbian and gay issues and images outside of school and a continuing unease and silence within the school walls.

At the same time, it is evident that levels of anti-gay and lesbian prejudice in society are still worryingly high, a serious concern for all of us involved with promoting equality in British society and institutions. This chapter aims to deconstruct the nature of anti-lesbian and gay prejudice, and suggest strategies for empowering lesbian, gay and bisexual staff and students in British schools.

# Sexual prejudice and society

## The nature of anti-gay and lesbian prejudice

In common with other attitudes, anti-gay and lesbian prejudice has three components. The *affective* component comprises the negative feelings that some heterosexuals have about gays and lesbians – for example, fear, dislike, revulsion, hatred. The *cognitive* component refers to the derogatory beliefs that may be held – stereotyping is important here, but there may also be a tendency to pathologize homosexuality and juxtapose gay (male) sexuality with paedophilia (sex with minors). The *behavioural* component comprises all negative actions towards lesbians and gay men, ranging from avoidance to discrimination to 'queer bashing' (physical and/or verbal harassment.)

There is some debate within the social sciences about how best to label the prejudice experienced by lesbians and gay men. The most commonly used term is 'homophobia', defined by Sprecher and McKinney (1993) as 'negative and/or fearful attitudes about homosexuals or homosexuality'. This is the term typically used by lesbians and gay men themselves[1] but many lesbian and gay theorists dislike the heavy concentration on the affective component at the expense of other aspects, and because in many cases it can be inaccurate: homophobia has little in common with other clinical phobias and prejudiced individuals may feel contempt and hostility towards lesbians and gay men rather than fearing them. In an influential paper Hudson and Ricketts (1980) devised the term 'homonegativism' as a multidimensional construct that places far more emphasis on people's intellectual attitudes towards issues around homosexuality such as equal rights and the moral acceptability (or not) of same-sex relationships.

An important related concept is 'heterosexism', and its underlying belief that heterosexuality is the only natural/normal/acceptable form of sexuality, and that being gay or lesbian is either sick or at least inferior. Heterosexism involves the expectation that everyone is 'straight' unless told otherwise or unless the individual conforms to cardboard stereotypes. There is less research into other dimensions of sexuality, such as transsexualism or bisexuality, despite the finding by Eliason (1997) that levels of prejudice towards bisexuals by heterosexuals may be even greater than towards gay men and lesbians.

## Lesbian and gay self-definition

When dealing with (homo)sexuality, nomenclature is important. Many gay men and lesbians understandably dislike the term 'homosexual', which has been used as a negative label for discrimination in legal, medical and psychiatric contexts. It also emphasizes sexual orientation as opposed to other aspects of gay and lesbian lifestyles. 'Gay' appears to be the term preferred by most men, and 'lesbian' by most females – although gay is often used as a generic term (felt by some to increase lesbian invisibility as most people's image of a gay person tends to be male).

Former terms of abuse such as 'queer', 'dyke' and 'bent' have been reclaimed as positive and assertive by some lesbian and gay activists, artists and academics (just as some black rap artists reclaim terms like 'nigger' in the United States). It is important to be aware of the variety of self-definitions and the disagreements and different preferences of individuals. Self-definition can change over time and context: the term 'queer' used by heterosexuals is unlikely to be well received by gay men and lesbians, particularly in 'straight' cultural settings.[2]

The definition of a lesbian and gay community is similarly complex and sensitive.[3] The visible gay 'scene' is often a male-dominated space, which many lesbians find alienating. Nationwide, there are only a small number of lesbian bars and clubs. Gay men may also be sexist or misogynist, and members of minority groups (such as ethnic minorities and people with disabilities) report negative experiences or a general feeling of not fitting in at gay venues populated almost entirely by white, often body-conscious males. Many lesbians and gay men feel that as venues become 'trendy' and more welcoming of (gay-friendly) heterosexuals, they cease to be safe spaces for all members of the gay community. This is an ongoing debate in the gay communities of large urban centres such as Manchester. The gay community is heterogeneous and many of its members choose (for a variety of reasons) to participate minimally, if at all, on the commercial scene.

There is, however, significant growth in the range of services available for lesbians and gay men, often within the voluntary sector. These usually offer telephone counselling, social groups and specialist support, particularly for HIV+ people, or young people 'coming out'. Such organizations are of central importance in campaigning for civil rights, lobbying on political issues and providing valuable networks for local (and sometimes regional) lesbian and gay communities.

## Coming out and social identity

For any lesbian or gay man, coming out is an integral part of accepting and developing a social identity. The degree and timing of disclosure has to be a personal decision although on occasions people are 'outed' by others for a variety of motives. Coming out involves infinite scope for rejection by others and is almost invariably a time of anxiety and vulnerability for the individual. Most gay men and lesbians spend a considerable amount of time coming to terms with their own sexuality before confiding in anyone else. It can be difficult for heterosexuals to fully appreciate the centrality of the issue for the individual, but the potential for harm through negative coming out experiences must not be underestimated.

In such a traditionally homophobic environment as most of British society, these are not uncommon. Importantly, many men and women who have a predominantly or exclusively gay orientation choose not to disclose this to others, and are often unkindly referred to, by 'straights'[4] and gays alike, as 'closeted'. For many people, sexuality is a personal, sometimes taboo issue, and their choices in this respect should be accepted and supported even if not always agreed with. Most gay men and lesbians see 'outing' as acceptable only if an individual is in some way doing harm to lesbian and gay communities. People who choose not to come out, or who take a fluid rather than fixed perspective on their sexual identity (a lot of outreach work is done with men who have sex with other men but do not define themselves as gay or bisexual), are unlikely to participate in an organized gay community as such. Consequently, it is impossible to know how many people in Britain are predominantly or exclusively lesbian or gay. There are no 'official' statistics – as there are for gender, ethnicity and special educational needs (SEN) – and estimates vary widely (often according to different political agendas), but between 5 per cent and 10 per cent is probably a reasonable approximation.

## Economics and gay or lesbian visibility

One effect of gay culture and visibility is commercial, with businesses vying for 'the pink pound'. Moneyed gay men may form the most visible part of the gay community but are only a minority of that community. Marks (1997) argues that lesbians have been left behind and it is primarily gay men who have benefited from 'pink consumerism', which is marketed at and consumed by gay men who are usually childless and can take advantage of an increasing range of consumer products and services. Despite the coming out of a number of women in the public eye (Ellen de Generes, kd lang, Amelie Mauresmo), lesbian chic does not share status with gay male sexuality. Gay men, it seems, are perceived as stylish, androgynous and fashionable whereas lesbians are more likely to be associated with rough masculinity.

The lesbian community remains largely invisible and not as widely integrated into popular consumerism as its gay male counterpart. The commercial value of lesbianism may be less secure because society continues to be guarded about overt evidence of female sexuality. Conversely, the disparity may be due to the increasingly compassionate publicity the gay male community has received due to HIV and AIDS – the AIDS red ribbon has become the almost archetypal symbol of 'political correctness'. Some research suggests that coming out may typically be more difficult for women, which may explain why significant numbers of women acknowledge their sexuality later in life, often when married and financially dependent. For the estimated 15 per cent of lesbians with children, there may also be the fear of losing out in a custody battle. Marks (1997) argues that lesbians may be perceived as especially threatening to the most (socially) powerful group within society – heterosexual males – because they operate independently of them. The higher levels of confidence evident within the gay community may not reflect the experience of many women, or indeed subgroups of the gay male community, such as disabled, working-class, or minority ethnic groups.

## Homophobia and homonegativism: a closer look

Research into anti-gay and lesbian prejudice typically addresses the attitudes of individuals where high levels of prejudice are found. The most common method is a survey, collecting small amounts of standardized information from a large sample of people. This generally relies on either a questionnaire or attitude scale. The results are reliably depressing, with homophobic responses the norm and not the exception. Data from the General Social Surveys in the United States collated by Davis and Smith (1997), for example, show that in 1994, from respondents who had completed high school education, 81 per cent of those over 60 believed homosexuality to be 'always wrong', and only 11 per cent believed it to be 'not wrong at all'. Among those under 30, the figures were somewhat more encouraging, with figures of 56 per cent and 36 per cent respectively. On the assumption that between 5 and 10 per cent of the population is lesbian or gay, this suggests only a minority of non-prejudiced heterosexuals.

However, there is a significant degree of variation regarding lesbian and gay rights. A report in *The Economist* (1995) on a British survey by Social and Community Planning Research (SPCR), for example, shows that attitudes vary in relation to different aspects: many people believing homosexuality to be sinful or morally wrong might still argue that lesbians and gays should have equal rights in employment, education and housing. The SCPR found a clear minority of individuals believing that anti-gay discrimination to be acceptable. Equally, although 14 per cent of individuals wanted to recriminalize gay sex acts and 26 per cent wanted the age of consent to be changed back to 21, a larger 33 per cent supported the age of 18, and 19 per cent wanted it lowered to 16 to be equal with heterosexuals (suggesting a growing 'live and let live' approach). This egalitarianism does not, however, extend in the SPCR survey to the rights of (particularly) gay men with children, with 46 per cent opposing gay men as teachers in primary schools and 75 per cent opposed to gay men adopting children. Similar trends are reported for the United States by Strand (1998).

In addition to significant ambiguities and variations in different aspects of prejudice, some people are generally more homophobic than others. There are established variables here, which have been found with reliability across most studies. The SCPR study shows that age and level of education are powerful predictors of degree of prejudice with the older and less educated being more prejudiced. Research in the United States suggests that a lack of contact with lesbians and gay men, a belief in traditional gender roles and living in rural areas may also be related. Herek (1998) indicates a positive correlation between homophobia and racism.

In the past, research from the United States has suggested that men are more homophobic than women generally, but recent findings question this. The SCPR survey finds men a little more liberal in attitudes than women, and research by Herek (1988) relates the degree of prejudice to the gender of the (gay) individual in question, with women likely to be more prejudiced against lesbians than gay men and the reverse true for men. This finding seems particularly true for male heterosexuals, but in both cases shows the tenacity of the stereotype of gay men and lesbians as predatory and in some way a sexual threat to the vulnerable heterosexual.

Asking people directly about prejudice is filled with difficulties because many play down their prejudiced attitudes to appear socially acceptable. Psychologists have therefore devised other more covert ways of assessing prejudice in real-life situations. Gray, Russell and Blockley (1991) used two confederates (one male, one female) to approach shoppers on a busy high street in Aberdeen and ask them to change a pound. For one half of the time the confederates wore plain T-shirts, for the other T-shirts with a pro-gay slogan. A clear difference emerges after approaching 120 people in each condition: wearing the plain T-shirt the confederate is helped 58 per cent of the time, but this drops to only 41 per cent when the confederate wears the 'pro-gay' T-shirt.

Other social scientists look at anti-gay and lesbian prejudice from the institutional or cultural (rather than individual) perspective. This shows homophobia to be an integral part of social relationships, from anti-gay jokes to the frequency and way that lesbians and gays are represented in the media. The partners of lesbians and gay men rarely enjoy equal rights with spouses or common-law heterosexual partners and cannot enjoy a legal partnership in this country. In the criminal justice system, gay men do not have a range of rights enjoyed by heterosexuals in terms of sexual activity. In cases where gays have been murdered, their attackers often receive a significantly reduced sentence if they plead 'homosexual panic' in defence (Toolis, 1997). The argument here is that their victim made sexual advances to them, filling them with such rage and revulsion that a vicious, indeed fatal assault is (at least partially) justified. Another obvious example is the extent of homophobic attitudes among the police. A study in New Zealand of the discourse used by police officers to express their reservations about working alongside gay (male) officers (Praat and Tuffin, 1996) shows beliefs in the inevitable effeminacy of gay men, the drive towards deviant acts (such as cross-dressing) and that if gay officers are 'open' about their sexuality it will tarnish the image of the force and reduce public confidence. Given that such attitudes undoubtedly exist in Britain too, it is not surprising that despite the efforts of forces like South Yorkshire (by advertising vacancies in the gay press) relatively few lesbians or gay men choose to become police officers. Another area of concern is Mental Health. A report by MIND (Golding, 1997) shows that many gay men and lesbians confirm negative experiences at the hands of nurses, GPs and psychiatrists, which at times creates a reluctance to participate in all aspects of healthcare provision.

Anti-gay and lesbian prejudice often manifests itself in violence against lesbians and gay men. In 1994, the lesbian and gay lobbying group Stonewall undertook a major survey of experiences of harassment and violence against gay men and lesbians recruited through their own publication database and the pink press. The subsequent report, *Queer Bashing*, is based on over 4,200 replies and shows that 73 per cent of respondents had been verbally abused, 63 per cent reported multiple experiences of name calling, 34 per cent of men and 24 per cent of women had experienced physical violence because of their sexuality and 32 per cent reported harassment such as threats or blackmail. As a result, most of them engaged in strategies to avoid violence: 88 per cent always or sometimes avoided demonstrating affection with partners or friends, for example, and 65 per cent of those surveyed always or sometimes avoid telling others they are gay (Mason and Palmer, 1995).

Franklin (1998) analyses the accounts of young men who disclose engaging in anti-gay violence with their friends. Here, singular psychological explanations such as repressed homoerotic urges have less explanatory power than a combination of various social forces, which Franklin refers to as 'the mutually reinforcing melding of hierarchical gender norms, peer dynamics, youthful thrill-seeking and economic and social disempowerment' (1998: 19). For a discussion of homophobic violence see Herek and Berrill, 1992; for the psychology of homonegativism see Herek, 1998). In extreme cases, hatred of lesbian and gay people by an individual or group leads to murder. In April 1999 a nail bomb was planted in *The Admiral Duncan*, a gay pub in the Soho area of London, by David Copeland. Three people were killed and more than 60 people were injured in this attack, one in a series of hate attacks which had previously targeted the African-Caribbean and Bangladeshi communities (Hopkins *et al*, 1999).

### Anti-gay and lesbian prejudice and the law: social injustice

Members of minority ethnic communities, women and people with disabilities are afforded (admittedly limited) protection under a range of Acts, yet there is no Act of Parliament specifically to protect the rights of lesbians and gay men. Equalization of the age of consent laws has finally been achieved (although the gay community also urges other, more radical, demands such as legal recognition of partnership rights).

There is a common problem with government and other socio-political institutions 'over-sexualizing' lesbians and gay men and thereby paying relatively little attention to any rights other than sexual rights. Many gay men and lesbians feel highly alienated from the political system, although the 1997 election did produce a record of three 'out' gay MPs, and Angela Eagle, the junior Environment Minister, announced her lesbian sexuality in the press later that year. Four MPs followed and Michael Portillo disclosed a same-sex relationship as a young man. Nonetheless, gay men and lesbians are denied the multiple rights assumed by heterosexuals, and although many lesbians and gay men fight discrimination through the European Court of Justice, it is not always with successful results.

## Education and Section 28

The most significant aspect of the 1988 Local Government Act for schooling is Section 28, which defines how local education authority (LEA) schools should handle the topic of homosexuality. The LEAs themselves are prohibited from 'intentionally promoting homosexuality' or promoting 'the teaching in any maintained school of the acceptability of homosexuality as a pretended family relationship'. Following some confusion on the accountability of individual schools and teachers, circular 11/87 acknowledged that the Act 'does not impose any direct responsibilities' on schools. To fully understand the situation that most teachers work in, it is necessary to be aware of the 1986 Education Act (No 2) which gives to school governors the duty of defining sex education policies.

In response to these pieces of legislation, the Ofsted handbook states categorically that 'promoting homosexuality through resources or teaching is prohibited' (see Epstein, 1994). Meanwhile, the National Union of Teachers advised that Section 28

> should not be interpreted as a prohibition on objective factual teaching about homosexuality, and teachers should feel confident that if they follow Union advice and their school governors' policy on sex education, the process of educating against prejudice and discrimination is clearly within the law.
>
> (Cole, 1997: 57–58).

Although not a single LEA has been prosecuted under Section 28, it undoubtedly inhibits gay-affirmative policy and practice in British schools. Media coverage of this issue is widespread and typically divided (although the *Daily Mail* launched a campaign urging readers to write to their MPs to prevent recent attempts to repeal Section 28). The general difficulty of making progress with these pieces of legislation does not augur well for more radical reform, even if the political will is present.

## Gay and lesbian rights in schools

Although most schools and colleges have equal opportunity policies, usually produced by a committee of the teaching staff, they often exclude sexual orientation. Equality across sexualities is often perceived as a political issue rather than a humanitarian principle, and senior staff and governors may feel that its inclusion would attract negative attention from (homophobic) parents, or may lead to difficulties under Section 28.

There is no legislation compelling schools to address the issue and many choose to avoid potential conflict by non-inclusion. In real terms, this means that lesbian and gay students have no official rights regarding their sexuality within the institution and implies that their concerns are not felt to be valid. For Walters and Hayes (1998), this is 'the culturally sanctioned dismissal of gay students and colleagues' (1998: 9). In response to the large growth in literature on bullying, many schools writing and implementing policies so that harassment on the grounds of ethnicity, disability, religion and gender are likely to be explicitly addressed. In contrast, only 6 per cent of school bullying policies make any mention of homophobic harassment (Hulme, 1998: 1). The message for lesbian and gay students is that the school sanctions any physical or verbal abuse that they might receive and does not regard such behaviour as bullying.

## The anti-gay and lesbian environment in schools

The attitudes of schools reflect those of the communities and societies they exist in. Given that anti-gay and lesbian prejudice is the norm rather than the exception in British society, schools will reflect this. It may be compounded by the lack of recognition of lesbian and gay rights in schools, the drive towards conformity that many adolescents adopt as they resolve issues of identity, and the particular sensitivity of sexuality for adolescents.

It should not be surprising that harassment of lesbian and gay students is widespread. A study by the Terrence Higgins Trust finds 82 per cent of teachers are aware of homophobic bullying in their schools (Hulme, 1998). Young heterosexual males are socialized into adopting anti-gay nicknames as normative insults during conflicts. Any observation of classroom or playground interaction will note the terms 'queer', 'bender' or 'poof' widely used. The message is clear – to be gay is to be denigrated as inferior, deviant and maladjusted.

Most of the literature on homophobic harassment in schools is produced in the United States (for example, Telljohann and Price, 1993; Besner and Spungin, 1995; Walters and Hayes, 1998; Smith, 1998), although there have been a number of significant British contributions. In *Young, Gay and Bullied* (1996), Rivers presents part of ongoing research into this issue. This finds that lesbian and gay youngsters are much more likely to be bullied at school and that this bullying is likely to be especially prolonged and severe, with long-term effects upon their social development and psychological health. Of the sample, 40 per cent had attempted suicide more than once and many reported high levels of depression and anxiety. In the 1980s, Trenchard and Warren carried out considerable research with the London Gay Teenage Group which resulted in *Something To Tell You* (1984a) and *Talking About School* (1984b), two publications defining the anti-lesbian and gay environment experienced by most (lesbian and gay) students. The participants were interviewed in discussion groups, and 164 young gay and lesbian teenagers volunteered past or present problems at school, as outlined in Table 10.1.

The total figure of 154 in Table 10.1 is smaller than the total number of people who said that they had problems because 10 respondents did not specify the sort of problems they experienced.

The interviews about harassment and its effects on the young person include the following comments:

> They called me 'queer' because I never played football and hung around with girls. I got beaten up and had my face slashed. The teachers didn't know how to deal with it. I had to leave school because of the threats. (male)

**Table 10.1** *Problems at school*

| Problem | Female frequency (percentage) | Male frequency (percentage) | Overall frequency (percentage) |
| --- | --- | --- | --- |
| Isolation | 10 (27) | 28 (24) | 38 (25) |
| Verbal abuse | 3 (7.7) | 29 (25) | 32 (21) |
| Teasing | 5 (13) | 15 (13) | 20 (13) |
| Beaten up | 1 (2.6) | 18 (16) | 19 (12) |
| Ostracizing | 4 (10) | 7 (6.1) | 11 (7.1) |
| Pressure to conform | 6 (15) | 5 (4.3) | 11 (7.1) |
| Other | 10 (26) | 13 (11) | 23 (15) |
| Total | 39 (100) | 115 (100) | 154 (100) |

From Trenchard and Warren (1984b)

No-one talked to me for a year, I nearly got beaten up and all the girls thought I'd jump them. (female)

People, especially the boys, kept saying 'Poof, gay black bastard.' The usual uneducated names. (male)

(in Trenchard and Warren, 1984b: 16–17)

Research in the United States produces similar results. Savin-Williams (1995) reviews a series of studies carried out across a number of US cities and finds 'a significant number of sexual minority youths report that they have been physically assaulted, robbed, raped and sexually abused' (1995: 175). Almost all had experienced negative attitudes and most feared harassment, especially if they had come out at high school. Less than 10 per cent identify a peer group supportive of lesbian and gay people. The Stonewall study, *Queer Bashing* (Mason and Palmer, 1995) also found that young people were particularly vulnerable to abuse and its effect, with 50 per cent of violent attacks being carried out by fellow students and 40 per cent of these occurring on school premises.

Such prejudice affects the school performance as well as the social development of young gays and lesbians. According to Savin-Williams (1995), poor performance, dropping a grade, truancy and school phobia and sometimes dropping out of school altogether are common. Research by Remafedi et al (1991) finds gay youth significantly more likely to engage in substance abuse and suicide attempts, whereas Williamson (2000) documents potential health consequences for those lesbians and gay men who internalize the prejudice they experience, including vulnerability to disordered eating behaviours and irregular safer sex behaviours. Aware of the homophobic climate of most schools, many youngsters understandably prefer not to disclose their lesbian or gay orientation. A study in Chicago through the 'Horizons' youth project (Herdt and Boxer, 1996)

**Table 10.2** *Hiding sexuality*

|  | Males (%) | Females (%) |
|---|---|---|
| Very much hidden | 33 | 29 |
| Mostly hidden | 20 | 29 |
| Open to some, not others | 13 | 8 |
| Open to most people | 13 | 13 |
| Very open to everyone | 22 | 19 |

From Herdt and Boxer (1996)

gives the degrees to which young people feel they must hide being gay or lesbian at school as shown in Table 10.2.

This sample is not likely to be representative of all the lesbian and gay students in a school. The participants had taken the step of affiliating with a lesbian and gay youth organization, but many lesbian and gay teenagers prefer not to do so, or not to do so within their local area, and these young people are even less likely to disclose and discuss their sexuality at school.

There are some signs of improvement. The Telljohann and Price (1993) study in Toledo finds a majority of 'out' gay and lesbian adolescents reporting positive responses from teachers and school counsellors. Nevertheless, it is increasingly clear that the environment of most secondary schools is far from lesbian and gay-affirmative. There is both covert and overt pressure on young people not to explore or disclose their (lesbian or gay) sexualities, and there is an explicitly homophobic environment that typically goes unchecked, affecting the academic performance and psychological adjustment of many teenagers.

The process of understanding and developing a lesbian or gay identity may be difficult even in a supportive environment. Gay youngsters typically feel vulnerable and may have a great need to disclose to others. As educationalists, we are failing them by not protecting them from homophobic harassment while in school, and by not allowing them access to a safe space where they can meet and discuss these issues. There are a number of initiatives around the country (a homework club for lesbian and gay youth was recently established in Manchester, for example) but many young people, particularly those outside the large centres of population, do not have access to such resources.

For those young people who continue to higher education, the situation may be somewhat better. Most universities and colleges have 'gay and lesbian' societies and many have policies for gay equality and against homophobic harassment. Nonetheless, a number of studies in Britain and the United States (such as Slater, 1993) show that homophobic violence is still a major issue for gay and lesbian students on campus (for strategies to deal with prejudice and harassment, see Rothblum and Bond, 1996; Epstein, 1994).

## What about bisexual youth?

It is important at this point to consider the position of another significant sexual minority – young bisexual adolescents. Unfortunately research into bisexuality is rare, particularly in Britain and especially about the experiences of young people, rather than adults. As Eliason (1997) points out, 'Until recently, bisexual people have been a largely invisible segment of the population. . . Little scientific attention has been paid to bisexuality or to societal attitudes about bisexual people' (1997: 317). Ironically, given the influential nature of Kinsey's work conceptualizing sexuality as a continuum rather than a 'hetero/homo' dichotomy, most people continue to see sexuality in these black and white terms and have regarded sexual attraction as fixed rather than fluid.

However, it is increasingly being recognized that significant numbers of people do have sexual relationships with both genders and perceive themselves as bisexual, including some young people. The term typically used for prejudice against bisexuals is 'biphobia', which presents the same semantic difficulties as 'homophobia' but occurs frequently in common and academic reference. It may seem logical to see biphobia and homophobia as aspects of the same prejudice, and indeed there is typically a high correlation, yet research by Eliason (1997) finds that in some respects prejudice against bisexuals is stronger than against lesbians and gay men. Eliason's sample of 229 heterosexual students at the University of Iowa were asked to select which of six statements best expressed their attitude towards lesbians, gay men, male bisexuals and female bisexuals. From positive to negative, these statements can be summarized as celebration, acceptance, tolerance, disapproval, disgust and hatred (see Table 10.3).

Significantly, this survey of US undergraduates finds that 76 per cent of the sample had no bisexual friends, 64 per cent knew no one who was bisexual and 59 per cent indicated that they had little knowledge about bisexuality. Some young people identifying themselves as bisexual in British schools may later adopt a lesbian, gay or heterosexual sexual identity, but many will continue to self-identify as bisexual. There are very limited resources available for young bisexuals and most of these come under the umbrella of lesbian and gay

**Table 10.3** *Attitudes to sexual minorities*

| Category: | Bisexual men % | Bisexual Women % | Gay Men % | Lesbians % |
|---|---|---|---|---|
| Celebration | 6 | 7 | 6 | 6 |
| Acceptance | 44 | 46 | 53 | 53 |
| Tolerance | 26 | 27 | 24 | 25 |
| Disapproval | 21 | 18 | 15 | 14 |
| Disgust | 2 | 2 | 1 | 1 |
| Hatred | 0.5 | 0 | 0.5 | 1 |

Percentage endorsing each category (N = 229)

organizations. This may inhibit participation, either because bisexual adolescents are reluctant to identify with lesbian and gay services or because of the prejudice from lesbians and gay men identified by some bisexuals. The latter may arise from a misguided belief by some members of the gay community that bisexuals do not want to fully come out and are merely more closeted gays and lesbians, who do not wish to take a politico-sexual stance. There is a need for more research in this area but it is important for youth workers and teachers to be aware of and sensitive to the needs of bisexual students and in particular the lack of resources for them (see Fox, 2000, for a contemporary and detailed account of bisexual issues).

## Lesbian and gay teachers

If we are to try and promote equality in primary and secondary schools, we need to ensure equal rights and the full participation of lesbian and gay staff. This is important for a number of reasons. It is essential that lesbian and gay teachers are supported and feel able to disclose their sexuality should they want to.

Openly 'out' teachers are a benefit to a school, providing positive images to heterosexual students and potential role models for lesbian and gay students. Lesbian and gay teachers are in a unique position to appreciate and empathize with a range of difficulties related to sexuality that may face their pupils. Unfortunately, many lesbian and gay teachers chose either to pass as heterosexual or to come out only to close colleagues.

The decision about how much to disclose is a dilemma for many gay and lesbian teachers who wish to maintain a degree of privacy but also to have the freedom to express their sexuality with colleagues and students. Many teachers in schools do not come out because there is no legislation guarding their rights and because schools are often conservative environments (not aided by perceptions of Section 28). There may also be increased levels of resistance from senior staff, governors and parents of primary-age children.

The experiences of some lesbians and gay teachers are documented in *Outlaws in the Classroom: Lesbians and gays in the school system*, produced by the Lesbian and Gay Working Party of the City of Leicester Teacher's Association (1987). During her PGCE year, one teacher was strongly advised by a union representative not to participate in demonstrations or marches concerning lesbian or gay rights, so that:

> During my probationary year. . . I made every attempt to suppress, hide and deny my lesbianism. . . I was determined that workmates should be colleagues, not friends, and to make my lesbianism a secret for fear of misunderstanding, rejection, even dismissal. . . School life is riddled with heterosexist attitudes, assumptions and conversation.
>
> (1987: 87–88)

This teacher, over a period of five years, felt able to come out to some colleagues and take her partner to staff functions. However, although there is a genuine anxiety for the potential effects on teaching position or career progress, few gay and lesbian teachers want to come out to all members of a school community. Trenchard and Warren (1984) reports, 'my co-worker and I spoke with many lesbian teachers, yet we could not find one who had the support and confidence to be open to her pupils about her lesbianism' (1984: 34).

Research by Clarke in the 1990s among PE teachers and students indicates that lesbian games teachers are forced to conceal their sexuality for fear of being labelled deviant and a danger to children. Particular concerns involve the supervision of showering and bodily contact in sport. Strategies used by lesbian teachers to avoid trouble include steering staffroom conversations away from risky topics and sometimes deliberately using 'Mrs' as a screen. Despite this, many of the interviewees on the study define verbal or physical harassment from pupils and moral blackmail by colleagues.

Hulme (1998) describes various forms of homophobic harassment experienced by a gay teacher in Cardiff, who 'was having to face the taunts in school, the cocks drawn on blackboards, sarcastic comments from homophobic colleagues, no promotion prospects and being lumbered with poor classes' (1998: 11). A number of gay and lesbian teachers consider their unions to have been slow to take a proactive role in supporting their rights and trying to dismantle the cultural heterosexism of most schools, although the situation appears to be improving. Both the National Union of Teachers (NUT) and the National Association of Teachers in Further and Higher Education produce gay and lesbian-affirmative documentation, and a number of groups – such as the NUT Lesbian and Gay Task Group and Schools Out group – support and advise lesbian, gay and bisexual teachers. More support not only from unions but also local authorities and senior management within their own schools is needed before many teachers are able to come out.

## Promoting lesbian and gay equality in schools

There are two central and related aims for promoting lesbian and gay equality in British schools. Firstly, to establish policies and procedures designed to support gay and lesbian members of the school community, be they students or staff. Secondly, to create a climate to encourage and value diversity, re-educate prejudiced heterosexuals and support freedom of expression for all (except those who would take away rights from others).

Heterosexism can be tackled through the curriculum, through staff training and the pastoral system. A first step, though, has to be the inclusion of anti-gay and lesbian prejudice in equal opportunities policies, complete with procedures and policies for monitoring how effectively issues are addressed. Similarly, anti-bullying and harassment policies need to include homophobic abuse. A recent European Commission ruling will force schools to confront homophobic bullying and put sexuality more clearly on the agenda in secondary schools, so clear statements of intent are required to manage these issues rather than avoid them. Changing the attitudes of the prejudiced is a painstaking, time-consuming process but protecting the rights of lesbians and gays within schools is more easily achievable given the will. Trade unions have a duty here to campaign on behalf of their members and heterosexual teachers need to support their lesbian and gay colleagues to achieve these changes within schools.

## Curriculum issues

Ignorance is a major part of prejudice, and if schools avoid discussion on these sensitive issues, that ignorance will be nurtured. Young people increasingly see images of gay and lesbian sexuality in the media but if these issues are not openly discussed at school homosexuality will be seen as taboo and stigmatized. Trenchard and Warren (1984) record how 416 young lesbians and gay men were asked to recall whether homosexuality had been mentioned in lessons and in what context and manner. A clear majority of students (60 per cent) could not recall homosexuality ever being mentioned in any lesson, whereas 80 per cent of those who could recall the topic coming felt it was discussed in a negative or unhelpful way. Subjects in which homosexuality was most likely to be discussed were English (11 per cent), religious education (10 per cent), biology (9 per cent) and sociology (5 per cent). In terms of library provision, only 11 per cent could find any books on the topic in their school libraries, and less than half of these could find a book that they deemed at all helpful to them.

Teachers are clearly constrained to some extent by exam board syllabuses and the National Curriculum, but there is little reason for school libraries not to include some stock of gay and lesbian literature or factual books written especially for lesbian and gay youth. There are a range of novels of literary merit such as Jeanette Winterson's *Oranges are not the Only Fruit* (1985), Michael Cunningham's *Flesh and Blood* (1995) and Edmund White's *A Boy's Own Story* (1982). The inclusion of such books on school reading lists should reduce feelings of isolation in gay and lesbian youth and encourage greater understanding in heterosexual students.

There is an almost total absence of resources featuring lesbian and gay people within the primary school. Glaister (1997) notes that the moral panic generated around *Jenny lives with Eric and Martin* – the book removed from London school libraries in the 1980s because it concerned a young girl being brought up by a gay couple – still lingers on. Indeed, it is revived in media discussions about Section 28. Glaister also reports how youth-oriented educational anthologies published to great acclaim in Australia, New Zealand and Canada were turned down by a leading British publishing house on the grounds that some of the lesbian and gay encounters described in some of the stories would not be suitable for the more 'traditional' British market.

There is even greater potential in tutorial or PSE time for gay issues to be discussed; sex education comprises another opportunity. Unfortunately, the only reference often made to bisexuality and homosexuality is in association with HIV and AIDS, which tends to reinforce stereotypes of gay men and bisexuals as diseased, promiscuous and helpless. Furthermore, research by the British

Medical Association, the Sex Education Forum and the National Campaign for Arts (NCA) shows ample evidence that teachers have wrongly used Section 28 as an excuse not to teach about homosexuality (Spencer 1997), and how the section had been 'positively harmful' to sex education in schools.

It is also important that, whatever the subject, examples are not used that are heterosexist and homophobic. Periodic reviews of resources are helpful here, as offensive and prejudiced items can be removed and examples of good practice shared. When teachers produce new resources, it is useful if examples used are not universally heterosexist, just as in the same way, examples should not be racist or anglocentric. There is understandable concern about tokenism here, although it may be argued that one or two examples of positive lesbian and gay imagery are better than none at all.

Gross (1991) refers to the under-representation and misrepresentation of lesbians and gay men by the media as 'symbolic annihilation'. The use of lesbian and gay examples promotes comments from students that can lead to discussion of the issues. Indeed, according to research by an AIDS-awareness charity AVERT (Forrest, Biddle and Clift, 1997), all pupils benefit when homosexuality is discussed in schools. Discussion challenges playground myths and stereotypes, reduces bullying and intolerance and prepares students for adult life.

## Staff training

It is unrealistic to expect all heterosexuals to feel comfortable discussing issues of sex and sexuality without training. Many heterosexual members of staff will be prejudiced themselves and may pass these prejudices on to their students. As Walters and Hayes (1998) observe, 'it can be a daunting experience for a teacher-trainer to attempt to move reluctant individuals beyond a history of discomfort with sexuality toward becoming competent teachers who are comfortable discussing sexuality' (1998: 10).

In line with other areas of equality promotion, schools must commit to anti-heterosexism training programmes, which are often available within LEAs or through courses advertised in the teaching press. Many gay and lesbian organizations will provide training if approached, or supply materials. There are also a number of useful texts in this area that staff could read privately, such as *Lesbian and Gay Youth* by Ryan and Futterman (1998). Staff need an opportunity to address their own prejudices and practices and to access information for the delivery of good-quality gay and lesbian-affirmative education. This may involve considerable work in developing skills, including how to deal with homophobic incidents or to answer sensitive questions.

At present, very few teachers experience such training either through their initial training or through in-service provision. Issues of lesbian and gay equality are usually dealt with briefly among general equal opportunities INSET, if at all. It is especially important for those with pastoral responsibilities, who are perhaps the most likely to be approached by vulnerable young people, to experience good-quality training. For example, heads of years could participate in detailed training outside of school, then provide some in-house development work for all the personal tutors in their year.

Gay and lesbian teenagers may prefer to explore issues and find support outside of school in a more anonymous, lesbian and gay-affirmative setting and it is important that teachers can provide them with contact numbers and addresses for organizations and services able to help them. It is vital that such information is delivered in a supportive and non-judgemental manner. Equally, however, many teenagers who have good relationships with particular members of staff may seek support from those they feel they know and trust. This can only be delivered when those members of staff are confident with the subject. Greater availability of counsellors in schools (who are not teachers) would be another step forward, as students may find it easier to disclose to someone with whom they do not have regular interaction or see in a particular role.

## Conclusions

The promotion of gay and lesbian equality in both primary and secondary schools has arguably made the least progress of all issues of social justice within education. British society remains strongly prejudiced and members of gay and lesbian communities are offered few rights and little protection within schools and in wider societies. Homophobic harassment is common in schools, mostly from peers but occasionally from members of staff. For these reasons many lesbian and gay students and staff chose not to disclose their sexuality. Those who do often face abuse or isolation and typically feel alienated, depressed and anxious. The implications for self-esteem, mental health and social development can be severe. Many gays and lesbians within the school system access resources within the wider gay community, but these are not always available within their locality.

If we are concerned with social justice, it is not acceptable to simply refer young gay men and lesbians to outside agencies. Changes have to be implemented within the school itself. As Forrest (2000) argues:

> Currently young people are being denied a right to an education that equips them for adult life. . . For young gay people, their enforced invisibility and the denial of basic access to basic relevant sex education is a breach of a human right. The prospect of the equalization of the ages of sexual consent and repeal of Section 28 is welcome, but until schools take up the issues in the classroom, changes in the law are unlikely to have any impact on knowledge or attitudes.
>
> (2000: 115)

A number of suggestions for anti-heterosexist practice include a review of the curriculum and materials, training for staff and the broadening of equality opportunity and anti-bullying/harassment policies to include clauses protecting the rights of gays and lesbians. It would also be beneficial for there to be more

British research into which strategies and initiatives are more successful in reducing anti-gay and lesbian prejudice in schools.

## Notes

1. For this reason the term will be used on occasion in this chapter.
2. With this in mind, the term has been avoided here.
3. The 'gay community' is a conceptually imprecise term. As this chapter illustrates, gay, lesbian and bisexual communities may be diverse yet enjoy a degree of commonality with each other.
4. Although widely used by lesbians and gay men as an alternative to 'heterosexual', 'straight' implies the opposite of 'bent' and is therefore another problematic term.

## References

Besner, H and Spungin, C (1995) *Gay and Lesbian Students: Understanding their needs*, Taylor & Francis, Bristol

Cole, M (1997) Equality and primary education – what are the conceptual issues? in *Promoting Equality in Primary Schools*, eds M Cole, D Hill and S Shan, Cassell, London

Cunningham, M (1995) *Flesh and Blood,* Penguin, Harmondsworth

Davis, J and Smith, T (1997) *General Social Surveys 1972–1996,* National Opinion Research Centre, Chicago, IL

Eliason, M (1997) The prevalence and nature of biphobia in heterosexual undergraduate students, *Archives of Sexual Behaviour,* **26** (3), pp 317–26

Epstein, D (ed) (1994), *Challenging Lesbian and Gay Inequalities in Education,* Open University Press, Buckingham

Forrest, S (2000) Difficult loves: learning about sexuality and homophobia in schools, in *Education, Equality and Human Rights*, ed M Cole, Routledge-Falmer, London

Forrest, S, Biddle, G and Clift, S (1997) *Talking About Homosexuality in Secondary Schools*, AVERT, Horsham

Fox, R (2000) Bisexuality in perspective, in *Education, Research and Practice in Lesbian, Gay, Bisexual and Transgendered Psychology*, eds B Greene and G Croom, Sage, Thousand Oaks, CA

Franklin, K (1998) Unassuming motivations: contextualising the narratives of antigay assailants, in *Stigma And Sexual Orientation*, ed G Herek, Sage, Thousand Oaks, CA

Glaister, J (1997) No gay teen sex please, we're British! *The Guardian,* 4 Jun

Golding, J (1997) *WithOut Prejudice: MIND lesbian, gay and bisexual mental health awareness research*, MIND Publications, London

Gray, C, Russell, P and Blockley, S (1991) The effects upon helping behaviour of wearing pro-gay identification, *British Journal of Social Psychology*, **30**, pp 171–78

Gross, L (1991) Out of the mainstream, *Journal of Homosexuality*, **21** (1/2), pp 19–46

Herdt, G and Boxer, A (1996) *Children of Horizons*, Beacon Press, Boston, MA

Herek, G (1988) Heterosexuals' attitudes towards lesbians and gay men: correlates and gender differences, *Journal of Sex Research*, **25**, pp 451–77

Herek, G (ed) (1998) *Stigma and Sexual Orientation*, Sage, Thousand Oaks, CA

Herek, G and Berrill, K (1992) *Hate Crimes: Confronting violence against lesbians and gay men*, Sage, Thousand Oaks, CA

Hopkins, N *et al* (1999) Nail bomber strikes in Soho, in *Guardian*, 1 May

Hudson, W and Ricketts, W (1980) A strategy for the measurement of homophobia, *Journal of Homosexuality*, **5**, pp 356–71

Hulme, J (1998) Gay couple live in fear, *The Teacher*, January–February, p 38

Lesbian and Gay Working Party of City of Leicester Teachers' Association (1987), *Outlaws in the Classroom: Lesbians and gays in the school system*, City of Leicester Teachers' Association, Leicester

Marks, J (1997) US lesbians come out to party, UK ones don't even come out, *The Independent*, 11 November

Mason, A and Palmer, A (1995) *Queer Bashing: A national survey of hate crimes against lesbians and gay men*, Stonewall, London

Patterson, C (1996) Lesbian and gay parents and their children, in *The Lives of Lesbians, Gays and Bisexuals*, eds R Savin-Williams and K Cohen, Harcourt Brace, Fort Worth, TX

Praat, A and Tuffin, K (1996) Police discourses of homosexual men in New Zealand, *Journal of Homosexuality* **31** (4), pp 57–73

Remafedi, G, Farrow, J and Deisher, R (1991) Risk factors for attempted suicide in gay and bisexual youth, *Paediatrics*, **87** (6), pp 869–75

Rivers, I (1996) Young, gay and bullied, *Young People Now*, January, pp 18–19

Rothblum, E and Bond, L (1996) *Preventing Heterosexism and Homophobia*, Sage, Thousand Oaks, CA

Ryan, C and Futterman, D (1998) *Lesbian and Gay Youth*, Columbia University Press, New York

Savin-Williams, R (1995), Lesbian, gay and bisexual adolescents, in *Lesbian, Gay and Bisexual Identities over the Lifespan*, eds A D'Augelli, and C Patterson, Oxford University Press, Oxford

Savin-Williams, R (1998) *And Then I Became Gay*, Routledge, New York

Smith, G (1998) The ideology of fag: the school experience of gay students, *The Sociological Quarterly* **39** (2), pp 309–34

Slater, B (1993) Violence against lesbians and gay male college students, *Journal of College Student Psychotherapy*, **8** (112), pp 177–202

Spencer, D (1997) Call to scrap gay clause, *TES*, 22 August, p 9

Strand, D (1998) Civil liberties, civil rights and stigma, in *Stigma and Sexual Orientation*, ed G Herek, Sage, Thousand Oaks, CA

Sprecher, S and McKinney, K (1993) *Sexuality*, Sage, Thousand Oaks, CA

Telljohann, S and Price, J (1993) A qualitative examination of adolescent homosexuals' life experience: ramifications for secondary school personnel, *Journal of Homosexuality*, **26** (1), pp 41–58

The Economist (1997) Gay times, *The Economist*, 11 January

Toolis, K (1997) Licence to hate, *The Guardian*, 30 August

Trenchard, L and Warren, H (1984a) *Something to Tell You: The experience and needs of young lesbians and gay men in London*, Central Books, London

Trenchard, L and Warren, H (1984b) *Talking About School*, Central Books, London

Walters, A and Hayes, D (1998) Homophobia within schools: challenging the culturally sanctioned dismissal of gay students and colleagues, *Journal of Homosexuality* **35** (2), pp 1–21

White, E (1982) *A Boy's Own Story*, Picador, London

Williamson, I (2000) Internalised homophobia and health issues affecting lesbians and gay men: a critical review, *Health Education Research: Theory and practice*, **15** (1), pp 97–107

Winterson, J (1985) *Oranges Are Not the Only Fruit*, Pandora Books, London

Young, S (1996) Lesbian teachers fear for their jobs, *TES*, 17 October, p 8

# I I

# Special educational needs

*Richard Rose*

## Editors' introduction

*Attempts to ensure equality of opportunity and outcome for students with special educational needs are seriously undermined, Richard Rose argues, by negative categorizations. These are shown to be rooted (like other prejudice) in the lack of knowledge brought to the subject of different abilities. This is evident in the names, attitudes, concepts and medical taxonomy applied in the past, through to the inappropriate standards of assessment deployed within modern education. The chapter defines the major impact of the Education Act 1970 and the Warnock report (1978) on the improvement of teaching provision, and on subsequent debate about the integration, inclusion and rights of students with special educational needs. Persistent confusions and obstructions are also identified. These are ultimately offset by proposals to ensure the proper, informed definition of equality in specific relation to disability.*

## Introduction

The history of attitudes towards people with disabilities, or indeed towards any individuals regarded as 'different', is far from honourable.

As late as 1815, if a report presented to the House of Commons is to be believed, the hospital of Bethlehem exhibited lunatics for a penny, every Sunday. The annual revenue from these exhibitions amounted to almost £400; which suggests the astonishingly high number of 96,000 visits a year. In France, the excursion to Bicêtre and the display of the insane remained until the Revolution one of the Sunday distractions of the Left Bank bourgeoisie. Mirabeau reports in his *Observations d'un voyageur anglais* that the madmen of Bicêtre were shown 'like curious animals, to the first simpleton willing to pay a coin' (Foucault, 1997: 68).

Social historians such as Foucault (1977, 1997), Porter (1987), Barham (1997) and Thane (1998) have demonstrated how an obsession with social order and control has targeted minority groups, particularly those who have abilities or 'afflictions' that are not easily understood. Anything beyond our comprehension engenders fear, and with this comes a reluctance to accept the incomprehensible into our daily lives.

Collective societal perceptions of disability and special educational needs have shifted over time, yet they still occupy an area fraught with confusion and misunderstandings.

Progress towards a more tolerant and equitable society is clearly evident in the legislation and actions of the late-20th century, yet there remains much to be done in education before people with special needs can gain a status that comes anywhere near equal to that enjoyed by the majority of the population.

## What's in a name? The impact of labelling and the promotion of equality

In *Madness and Civilization*, Foucault (1997) recognizes the confusion of the language and terminology associated with mental illness and disability. The lack of understanding of the causes of disability and the inadequacies of knowledge with regards to treatment, care and habilitation have led to approaches to managing people that, viewed in terms of present day *mores*, are often unacceptable and debilitating. Nowhere has this confusion been more evident than through the inability of society to discover a language of disability devoid of a connotation or derivation that is either demeaning or insulting. Early terminology includes 'cretin', derived from *chrétien*, the French word for a 'Christian', signifying someone who even in adulthood retained innocence; also 'handicap', derived from the hand-in-the-cap action, placing alms in the caps of the needy. These terms have their origin in false notions of benevolence from a society wishing to be perceived as caring, but demonstrating an inability to come to terms with a section of population challenging notions of 'normality'.

Even in the second half of the 20th century and within educational provision, this inability to determine an acceptable language of disability persisted. Within the UK education system, the progression of labels from mentally handicapped through to severely subnormal and educationally subnormal marks our inability to provide an understanding of the people upon whom such titles are bestowed. The very use of the prefix 'sub', meaning beneath, indicates the level of regard with which individuals labelled as 'sub-normal' are held. Since 1978 and the Warnock era, educationalists seem to have settled upon notions of special educational needs and learning difficulties, but this still indicates a need to label individual children who challenge our concept of the 'ordinary'.

Sandow (1994) provides a comprehensive picture of the ways in which models of special educational needs have developed, and in so doing she assists us in our understanding of why an obsession with labels has become established when addressing issues of special needs. The care and management of people with disabilities has, throughout most of history, remained within the medical domain. Medical sciences, with a focus upon taxonomy and categorization, need to apply descriptors to all aspects of the human condition. Often, these labels have taken little account of human sensitivities or the rights of the individuals to whom they are applied.

A clear example of this is the early use of the term 'mongol' when referring to a person now described as having Down syndrome (named after John Langdon Down who, in 1866, first applied the term 'mongolism' to describe a specific, genetically determined human condition). The label was applied with little concern for the individuals thus named, or for the race of Asian peoples deriving the name from their geographical location. The term 'mongol' is now regarded as unacceptable. Taxonomy as an important science that supports the medical profession in the provision of treatment and care. However, there is a clear danger when its terms are applied that stereotyping also occurs and assumptions are made about the people clustered together beneath them. From the example of Down syndrome, it is possible to trace the stereotyping involved back to Langdon Down's original research (1866), where he describes this group of people as having 'a strong sense of the ridiculous, obstinacy and mimicry' (1866: 259). The writings of people who themselves have a disability show that such a perception remains in the mind of the general public to this day, despite the fact that we know that people with Down syndrome run the whole gamut of emotions, behaviours and abilities. Such stereotyping leads almost inevitably to low expectations of individuals and to a tendency, albeit well meaning, to patronize.

Disabled writers who have recorded their experiences of both schooling and attitudes in all aspects of society, describe the many obstacles placed in the way of becoming accepted and valued. Often, these writers define the negative attitudes and stereotyped views that pervade society and prevent them from contributing fully to its further development (Nolan, 1987; Mason, 1990; Hegarty, Pocklington and Lucas, 2000).

Even within the teaching profession, which should display a more enlightened set of attitudes and should be promoting equal opportunities, there are examples of teachers with disabilities who have been forced to navigate a path through bureaucratic and attitudinal barriers in order to pursue a career for which they are eminently qualified (Morris, 1990; Watson, 1990). Simply having the label 'disabled' is often enough to prevent individuals being accepted or making progress within their chosen profession. In Table 11.1, the challenges faced by people with disabilities in gaining employment can be gauged by comparison with non-disabled unemployment figures.

People with disabilities who do obtain employment are likely to be paid a wage that is significantly beneath the remuneration gained by their able-bodied peers (see, for example, Martin and White, 1988).

**Table 11.1** *Unemployment rates for disabled and non-disabled people in Britain, 1995–96*

| People with disabilities | | People without disabilities |
| --- | --- | --- |
| | Unemployed (%) | Unemployed (%) |
| Females (age in years) | | |
| 16–19 | Unavailable★ | Unavailable★ |
| 20–24 | 15.9 | 8.5 |
| 25–34 | 16.3 | 6.5 |
| 35–49 | 11.8 | 4.6 |
| 50–64 | 12.6 | 3.4 |
| ALL | 14.8 | 6.0 |
| | | |
| Males (age in years) | | |
| 16–19 | Unavailable★ | Unavailable★ |
| 20–24 | 24.6 | 15.0 |
| 25–34 | 31.8 | 8.8 |
| 35–49 | 20.5 | 6.4 |
| 50–64 | 22.6 | 7.2 |
| ALL | 25.2 | 8.9 |

★ Unemployment rates calculated for 16–24 years only
Adapted from Sly (1996)

The labels associated with disability inevitably focus upon 'conditions' rather than individuals, and may inhibit the provision of opportunity to recognize individual talent, ability or personality. Contrast, for example, the two labels *motor neurone disease* and *astrophysicist*. The first brings to mind an image of someone probably in a wheelchair, highly dependent and with possible difficulties of communication; the second is likely to summon a more positive picture of someone highly intelligent and learned. Both labels can be applied to Professor Stephen Hawking, one of the world's leading scientists. A failure to look beyond his 'condition' could have denied the world an opportunity to benefit from the scientific wisdom of one of the world's leading intellects.

Similar contrasting labels can be found within many aspects of public life. Contrast the labels 'blind' with 'Secretary of State' in describing David Blunkett or 'deaf' with 'concert percussionist' for Evelyn Glennie and the detrimental impact of condition on personal image is quickly evident. A national survey conducted in Britain in the mid-1980s estimates that more than 6 million individuals had some degree of disability, approximately 14.2 per cent of the population. This is a highly significant number of people being devalued through the labels of reference being deployed within this society.

In education, Wood and Shears (1986) suggest that the provision of labels does little more than emphasize those characteristics that single a child out as being different, while Sebba, Byers and Rose (1993) warn that low expectations of students result from the application of negative labels. The relatively recent term 'special educational need' implies a likelihood that a child will not be successful in learning and may provide a justification for his or her failure to make academic or social progress. This theme is further developed by Slee (1993) who claims that the debate about educational provision for students perceived as having special educational needs has often failed to move beyond a concern for lack of resources, and that this emanates largely from a concentration upon labels that home in on the difficulties presented by the child, rather than addressing issues of pedagogy or school organization. For Slee (1993), 'One consequence of labelling is the creation in teachers of a belief that they are unable to address the needs of children with disabilities without the provision of adequate resources. The debate then becomes "technocratic" rather than educational' (1993: 357).

Of course, teachers do still need to consider the resources they require for work with children with special educational needs, and many argue that labels do serve as a starting point for teachers genuinely concerned to discover teaching approaches of benefit to students who are seen as having particular learning characteristics. Yet labelling is a difficult area when addressing issues of special educational needs, as well as an important one if genuine moves are to be made towards establishing equality within education. Sandow (1994) is far from being an apologist for labels imposed through medical models, yet she recognizes that some form of categorization may be essential and acceptable so long as it is motivated by the improvement of the living conditions of the individual.

## The 'moral' model

Of greater concern is the approach described by Sandow (1994) as the 'moral' model, which involves a belief that humanity is in some way perfectible and that individuals can be measured against ideal models. Within this theory, comparisons are made between idealized models and the individual, allowing for measurement and assessment to be made. The standards that society holds to be good and of high value provide a target towards which individuals should aspire. The pressures to conform come from many sources.

For example, the fashion industry along with advertising and the media establish icons against which individuals may measure themselves. Thus, the desirable look of the day – as exhibited by supermodels on catwalks or the covers of popular magazines, or the advertising of luxury and desirable goods – is to be sylph-like and, some might argue, to the point of appearing meagre. Some girls measure themselves against these models and may believe themselves to fall short of the mark, and in finding themselves inadequate take to drastic levels of dieting, which in turn lead to psychological and physiological disorders.

The influence of the moral model can be seen within the education system. The ideal value of success is often unobtainable for a significant proportion of the population. An education system that continually reports that successful schools are those that achieve high academic results, and that categorizes students according to 'end of key stage' levels, has established ideals to which many will aspire but will leave significant numbers floundering and feeling inadequate. The values expressed by the images of success in the media, and reinforced in government policy and the statements made by ministers, may well be perpetuated through the systems operating within schools and inevitably send a message to students and parents that to fall short of the ideal means failure and inadequacy.

This is not to say that the majority of schools are not aware of the potential dangers: in many instances measures are taken to counteract the detrimental effects of restrictive values and narrow views of success. However, the perpetuation of beliefs that the achievements of individual students can be recognized only through quantitative means is a key factor in denying the human rights and the equality of students with special educational needs (an issue to be discussed later in this chapter).

## Four main perceptions of special educational needs

Labelling is also an issue at the heart of equal opportunities in relation to special education. Norwich (1996) discusses this matter as a potential inhibitor of quality education for students with special educational needs, and expresses concerns regarding the whole concept of special education. He finds that medical and social models of our perceptions of special educational needs are:

- relative to the educational context, as opposed to being a stable child characteristic;
- along a continuum in order that no categoric distinction can be made between those *with* and those *without* SEN;
- about what education provision is needed as opposed to focusing on deficiencies;
- about individual needs and not about treating children in terms of general categories in stereotyped ways.

(Norwich, 1996: 101)

Norwich suggests that while these separate ways of viewing special educational needs may have been helpful in the past – for example, as a means of gaining additional resources and training – they have established fixed dichotomies that are unhelpful if we are to move towards an education system that no longer focuses upon segregating one group of children from another. The greatest limitation of these four types of perception resides in the perpetuation of beliefs that one child may be different and in some ways inferior to her or his peers, thus requiring different 'treatment' and provision. Yet Norwich also considers that the focus on the individual needs of students labelled as 'special' may provide a helpful starting point when attempting to overcome the negative aspects of labelling. He proposes that, rather than labelling individual students in terms of their special educational needs, we could apply a more positive approach if we view *all* students as having three types of learning needs. These he describes as:

- Individual needs – arising from characteristics different from all others.
- Exceptional needs – arising from characteristics shared by some, such as visual impairment, high musical abilities.
- Common needs – arising from characteristics shared by all.

(Norwich, 1996: 103)

Viewing all students in this way can address the stereotyping that characterizes the denial of rights to individuals with special educational needs. If, as Norwich suggests, the labels are dispensed with but the positive elements of learning characteristic identification are retained, then students who are regarded as vulnerable can be protected without emphasis on their perceived deficiencies. Such an approach would provide a significant move away from the negative aspects of labelling while retaining an identification of characteristics, which would be valued by many teachers.

Labelling has been convenient for the categorization of children with special educational needs, and has been influential in defining the locations in which they have been educated. Special schools for those students exhibiting the most challenging learning needs came to be regarded as the most realistic places in which to teach. However, the idea of special schools providing a segregated learning environment for students with special educational needs away from their 'more able' peers is now being challenged. This constitutes one of the most complex areas for debate within education.

## Moving towards inclusive schooling: recognizing individuality within an equal opportunities context

Proportionately, a special educational need is a significant issue within education as a whole. In 1998, around 242,300 students in all schools had a statement of special educational needs, which identified them as needing facilities, resources or approaches that were over and above those normally provided for the majority of students. This figure represents 2.93 per cent of the overall population of students in schools. The major significance of these figures is illustrated by comparison with the increase of 3.3 per cent in one year from 1997 and a 36 per cent overall increase over a five-year period from 1993 (DfEE, 1997). Together, these statistics are even more significant when considering the emphasis placed by consecutive governments on lowering the number of statements issued and moving more students into mainstream schools.

# The Warnock report, 1978

The publication of the Warnock report in 1978 was recognized immediately as one of the most significant events in the history of special education in the UK. Indeed, its influence spread to provide a focus for debate and development in the education of children and young people with special educational needs across Europe and Australasia (Jenkinson, 1997).

Warnock influenced many facets of the education system, not least the introduction of procedures for the identification of students with special educational needs and the protection of their rights through statementing procedures. The Warnock Committee confronted concerns that some students with learning difficulties or disabilities were not receiving their entitlement to resources or the support necessary to enable them to learn. They recommended the introduction of legislation and procedures designed to ensure that the rights of students with special education needs were recognized and protected through a new emphasis upon local education authority administration of systems to support children, young people, parents and schools.

Historically, the Warnock report appeared in a decade of dramatic change in special needs education, initiated by the Education Act of 1970. This Act was particularly significant in that it recognized the right of *every* child of school age, regardless of need or ability, to receive an education within the state system. Prior to April 1971, when the 1970 Act took effect, there was no obligation upon local education authorities (LEAs) to provide an education for children and young people described as 'educationally subnormal' within their schools.

This new legislation led to the opening of special schools across the country, to new initiatives in teacher education, and to an acceleration of research into the effective teaching of children and young people with special educational needs. This was indeed a landmark year in terms of the rights of children with special educational needs. Yet its greatest significance is only just being realized. The 1970 Act fostered the beginnings of the current debates surrounding inclusion, by recognizing the fact that no individual is uneducable – a term still in common use in the 1960s. This promoted far greater attention to the ways in which students with special educational needs might be encouraged to learn.

Building upon the momentum of special needs developments through the 1970s, Warnock recognized an opportunity to expand the debate beyond the narrow confines of how children and young people might learn to one that focused upon where they might best be educated. The Warnock report was significant for opening discussions related to how mainstream schools might become better equipped to provide for students with a range of special needs.

In particular, the ensuing debate focused upon the movement of children and young people with special educational needs from *segregated* special schools into *integrated* mainstream schools. Writers in the immediate post-Warnock era (Hegarty, Pocklington and Lucas, 1981; Swann, 1981) began to develop the theme of integration and spawned an argument that was largely based around the premise that the education of students with special educational needs alongside their mainstream peers would be an important stride towards ensuring that equal opportunities were provided.

## Warnock's three phases of integration

Warnock saw the move towards integration as having three distinct phases, describing them as the locational, social and functional phases.

*Locational integration*, seen as the easiest form to achieve, refers simply to the location of provision for students with special educational needs on the same site as that provided for their peers. It does not suggest that these students would be in any way educated alongside their peers, or indeed that there would necessarily be any social contact. The term integration may in fact be a misnomer in this respect. However, Warnock recognizes that it may be a necessary precursor to any more radical moves towards integration.

*Social integration* was thought to be more difficult to achieve, demanding the development of positive attitudes on the part of teachers, students and parents. Within this stage of integration, Warnock perceives that students will engage in social activity, possibly on the playground, and consort with their peers in a variety of non-academic settings. This, she stressed, would fall short of an ideal situation but would place new demands upon all involved and require a higher level of training and support than simple locational integration.

*Functional integration* was viewed by Warnock as the ultimate goal. At this level, students work together throughout the school day, engaged in all social and academic activities. It is acknowledged by Warnock that functional integration can only be achieved with time and after provision of a wide programme of re-education for teachers and the public at large. However, this is seen as a target towards which all concerned for the welfare of children and young people should strive.

The Warnock report has many critics (Booth, 1981; Kirp, 1982) not least because of the compromise it was seen to make in terms of grasping the equal opportunities nettle. Hornby, Atkinson and Howard (1997) claim that by imposing a series of four conditions, Warnock sidestepped the most important issues that could have ensured integration. The four statements within the report causing them the greatest difficulty are those indicating that integration should take place when:

- this is in accordance with parental wishes;
- there is a guarantee that all the student's needs can be met in the mainstream school;
- it is consistent with efficient use of resources;
- it will not detract from the education of other students in the class.

These four criteria, the authors claim, provide an easy escape clause for schools opposed to integration and may be responsible in part for the slow progress in this area.

Whatever the debate about the Warnock report and its influences, it must be recognized for its significance in opening up debate. Advocates of moves towards greater integration largely see the issue in humanistic and equal opportunities terms, yet as the debate progresses it is apparent that this is too simplistic a view. The term *integration* has been replaced by that of *inclusion*, though it is an error to suppose that the terms are interchangeable. The integration debate was flawed by concentration on education as a resource and location issue, and at times those advocating the transfer of students from special to mainstream schools have done so on the basis of a limited argument which takes little account of pedagogical factors.

## Integration, inclusion and equal opportunity

Florian (1998) expresses the view that the term *integration* is too much associated with the physical environment in which education takes place, without regard for the quality of that placement or for the teaching that the student receives within it. She suggests that the term *inclusion* is most appropriate for those who wish to see the education of students with special educational needs considered in terms of the quality of the learning experience. Inclusion, she stresses, acknowledges a history of exclusion, and emphasizes a commitment to ensuring that students previously denied educational opportunities will in future receive the same treatment as their non-disabled peers.

Thomas (1997) supports this view, recognizing that the inclusion of students with special educational needs from special schools alongside those educated in the mainstream may require significant modifications to the ways in which schools operates. He observes that the education climate emphasizes an increasingly academic outcome, and that a lack of flexibility within pastoral systems may well be a significant factor in determining the speed with which inclusion can be achieved. Unless the requirements for effective inclusion are adequately defined, there is a real danger that students with special educational needs may find themselves alongside their peers in mainstream settings before those requirements have been met. Some schools are already struggling to meet the needs of their existing population of students with special educational needs, and unless additional support in terms of training and resources is provided for staff, they will be unable to provide adequately for a population of increasing complexity.

The simple move towards the greater placement of students in mainstream school (which might comply with Warnock's concept of *locational integration*) will not guarantee that equal opportunities will be provided. Elsewhere, I have argued that there already exists a population of children with special educational needs who, in the name of inclusion, attend mainstream classes but remain isolated from the learning expected of their peers (Rose, 1998a). Successful inclusion must be built around the promotion of positive attitudes on the parts of teachers, students and administrators, and understanding of appropriate and flexible teaching methodologies, the revision of curricular restrictions that inhibit access for students with special educational needs and the creation of sympathetic learning environments. Tilstone and Rose (2000) argue that much remains to be learnt about effective teaching that will enable students to be included, and that until such time as this is achieved some will have their learning opportunities better addressed within special schools.

## Rights and efficacy

The inclusion of all students with special educational needs into mainstream schools must remain a goal, but must do so within an equal opportunities context. This will only be achieved by giving recognition to the individuality of students and by acknowledging that not all children and young people learn in the same way or that they all need the same curriculum diet.

Dyson (1999) describes inclusion as being process marked by two discourses. The first of these, and in most respects the one that has received the greatest attention, he describes as *a discourse of ethics and rights*, concerned to gain an understanding of students' rights and how these may best be addressed within the education system. The second he refers to as *the efficacy discourse*, concerned with the educational order that will enable a school to be inclusive. This second discourse he believes to be far less well developed. The two must be intrinsically linked if we are to protect the best interest of students with special educational needs.

The belief that we should endeavour to provide educational opportunities for all children and young people alongside their peers, irrespective of ability or special educational need, is far from universal. As a human rights issue, many teachers believe that the achievement of this state must remain our ultimate goal. However, there is an danger that in our anxiety to address the first of Dyson's discourses, and to be seen to be doing that which is generally accepted as morally and politically correct, we may advance ahead of the proper preparation of schools, which is necessary if inclusion is to succeed.

## Empirical research

There is a clear need for a more substantial empirical basis upon which to identify the procedures that work to positive effect in inclusive practice. Hornby (1999) argues that the acceleration of inclusive practice is founded on well-meaning but ill-researched principles of more equitable provision, and could lead to a backlash.

In calling for an extended research base, which might provide evidence about the efficacy of inclusion, Hornby suggests that to move students from special schools into the mainstream may actually deny them the opportunity of having equal access to appropriate learning and teaching methods. There is a danger that teachers who are ill-prepared for teaching a broader range of needs and abilities, and who fear that additional students with special educational needs may disrupt their classes or challenge their ability to achieve successful results, may resent inclusion that is enforced upon them. Far from supporting the rights of students with special educational needs, this situation could lead, ultimately, to their greater isolation.

The debate surrounding inclusion is fraught with contradictions and difficulties of interpretation, yet this single area is possibly the one where equal opportunities issues will need to be most closely defined, and where changes to procedures and practices will be essential before progress can be guaranteed. Calls for further research and the development of a research base of empirical evidence in relation to changes in educational provision (Croll and Moses, 2000; Rose, 2000) recognize that the dilemma Dyson discusses in terms of two separate discourses of inclusion remains as a central issue in special education.

The first decade of the 21st century may be one in which the intentions to improve the rights of students with special educational needs is supported by a greater understanding of how this might be achieved through effective classroom practice. In order to advance from an idealistic view of what might be achieved towards the reality of improved educational provision and practice, there needs to be a cogent and consensual approach to the implementation of legislation to promote change.

## Procedures and policies: supporting equality or an impediment to progress?

Since the 1970s, legislation in the area of special education, such as the introduction of a Code of Practice on the Identification and Assessment of Special Educational Needs (DfE, 1994), has aimed to improve the provision for all students. Yet it may be argued that while such legislation has been put into place, there remains much to be achieved before equal opportunities can be guaranteed. Indeed it is suggested (Booth, Ainscow and Dyson, 1997; Rose, 1998b; Booth,

2000) that some systems and legislative procedures are impacting on schools in ways that may inhibit the experience of equal opportunities for students with special educational needs.

In 1997, the Labour government set out its vision for special education in a Green Paper entitled *Excellence for All Children* (DfEE, 1997). In his introduction, the Secretary of State David Blunkett describes this document as a 'fundamental reappraisal of the way we meet special educational needs', and asserts that the government has the objective of 'sustaining high quality provision for children with special educational needs well into the twenty first century' (1997: 6).

This paper, largely welcomed by the teaching profession, provided an opportunity for wide consultation and placed a focus upon issues related to special educational needs. However, certain contradictions in the Green Paper, and some of the actions following its publication, have done little more than add to the confusion surrounding ways forward for improving provision for students with special educational needs. In an early response to *Excellence for All Children* (DfEE, 1997), Farrell (1998) is critical of the narrow definition of inclusion adopted within the document. He states that an emphasis is placed upon the view that the term inclusion applies only to children and young people placed in mainstream schools. This is a regressive definition, confusing notions of integration that emphasize location with the more progressive view of inclusion that relates to learning processes and teaching approaches (as discussed earlier in this chapter).

Farrell argues that placement in a special school, where a child's special educational needs may be fully met, can lead to greater inclusion in society. By contrast, a student may be placed in a mainstream school in which his or her needs are not addressed and may therefore underachieve and become isolated from society. The equal opportunities of children will only be addressed when the focus of attention shifts towards the provision of an education that is appropriate to the individual. Corporate approaches may make for easier control, but will invariably result in the exclusion of some students who have difficulties in complying with systems that are too narrow to meet diverse needs. This is the argument taken up by Booth and his colleagues (1997), who see the drive towards uniformity within the UK education system as too focused upon false notions of a mythical average student, who may be addressed as the common denominator, and therefore failing to address students at either end of the needs and ability continuum.

## Universal standards and individual progress

If equal opportunity means including all children within the current mode of educational provision, there remains much to be achieved. In particular, there is a need to address some of the divisive approaches to assessing and reporting student progress.

The success of schools is now largely measured according to criteria of academic achievements. Those schools producing good 'end of key stage' assessments or high percentages of students achieving GCSE grades A to C are seen as successful, whereas those that do not gain these results are regarded as less effective. This view is reinforced through the publication of league tables that provide statistical information and little analysis of school populations or performance trends. Teachers and parents of children and young people with special educational needs, who are working at levels different from national expectation, find themselves frustrated by a system unable to recognize the endeavours of teachers and the progress that their students are making.

Many schools have put into place approaches to baseline assessment that provide a detailed picture of where a child is at the beginning of a teaching process. Such procedures enable them to keep detailed records, and to indicate the progress that students make during the course of a school year. However, even in situations where students with special educational needs can be seen to make progress that is commensurate with, or even exceeding, the progress of their peers, their successes remain undervalued by the national approach to assessment of standards if they do not meet nationally expected levels of achievement.

The 'end of key stage' assessment procedures have become the major instrument for determining the success of schools, yet these procedures do little to recognize the excellent work undertaken by teachers who achieve considerable success with students with special educational needs, and may in fact deter movement towards more inclusive schooling. Rouse and Agbenu (1998), in a survey of teacher beliefs about 'end of key stage' assessments in relation to students with special educational needs, find many considering them to offer no useful information or purpose. Here, teacher perceptions include the notion that 'end of key stage' assessments are more about how well schools are performing than about providing indicators of how well the needs of specific students are being addressed. Rouse and Agbenu conclude that while the introduction of national systems of assessment was said, by the Conservative government that introduced them, to have the purpose of raising standards, the extent to which this has been achieved is questionable.

Indeed, it may well be the case that the most significant impact of these assessment procedures is to create a competitive ethos in which schools become increasingly reluctant to accept children who might have an adverse impact upon the school's overall assessment performance. This point is taken up by Lunt and Norwich (1999), who express concerns that the quasi-marketplace culture established within the UK education system in the 1990s means that in some schools students with special educational needs are not a welcome section of the population. The demand for increasing inclusiveness, they suggest, sits uneasily with the call for higher standards and increased effectiveness when the main focus of measurement is test and examination results.

Writers and researchers working in the area of special education attempt to provide positive alternatives to curriculum planning and assessment so as to protect the individuality of the student with special educational needs. Some have produced guidelines and materials that enable those with the most severe learning difficulties to participate within the National Curriculum framework (Carpenter, Ashdown and Bovair, 1996; Byers and Rose, 1996; Byers, 1999). The term 'entitlement', which was said to be at the heart of the National Curriculum when it was introduced, is still precious to teachers who are concerned for students with special needs. Entitlement demands that the needs of every student are addressed, and that procedures put into place recognize every individual within the education system.

Curriculum 2000 recognizes the importance of key skills as a target for student development and makes important strides towards enabling teachers to provide a more balanced curriculum, focused upon individual needs. The series of schemes of work from the Qualifications and Curriculum Authority provide useful keys to access for students with special educational needs, and recognizes the need for wider and more effective forms of differentiation. These changes, brought about largely in response to pressure from teachers who are experienced in working in special education, are to be welcomed. However, these alone will not ensure that the needs of all students are addressed.

## Looking to the future

Much progress has been made in the effort to ensure that the rights of students described as having special educational needs are met, but there is no room for complacency. The battle for equal opportunities has been fought around changing attitudes, increasing understanding and the development of efficient and manageable educational provision. These three areas will remain at the core of matters to be addressed in the 21st century.

Stereotyped images of students with disabilities and some negative attitudes towards children and young people with special educational needs remain. A particular challenge before all teachers must be the one of acceptance of the principle that everyone, regardless of their needs or abilities, can learn. Not all will learn at the same pace, neither will they all need to learn the same things. Positive attitudes only become a reality when students with special educational needs are valued for their abilities and individuality, rather than being measured against preconceived ideas of what the ideal child should be, or should achieve.

Increased understanding must be based upon familiarity, and this will not be gained until greater opportunities are provided for students with special educational needs to have access to their mainstream peers. However, before this can happen teachers need to be supported in developing an understanding of what works in the classroom, and need to be provided with the training and resources that will enable them to be confident and effective in addressing the needs of all students. Teachers must also be provided with systems able to recognize their successes and those of all the students for whom they have responsibility, and which enable them to address the individual, exceptional and common needs of every child in their class.

Changes in the ways in which we manage students with special educational needs in the future must be based upon sound empirical research. Furthermore, a duty must be placed upon the makers of policy to avoid the narrow concentration on raising academic standards, and to establish processes that involve all students rather than addressing only the perceived needs of the majority.

The progress made so far in addressing the equal opportunities of students with special educational needs in the 20th century can be applauded. There does, however, remain much to be done before theses students feel they that have at last taken their rightful place in the education system.

# References

Barham, P (1997) *Closing the Asylum*, 2nd edn, Penguin, Harmondsworth

Booth, T (1981) Demystifying integration, in *The Practice of Special Education*, ed W Swann, Open University Press, Buckingham

Booth, T, Ainscow, M and Dyson, A (1997) Understanding inclusion and exclusion in the English competitive education system, *International Journal of Inclusive Education*, **1** (4), pp 337–55

Booth, T (2000) Inclusion and exclusion policy in England: who controls the agenda? in *Inclusive Education: Policy, contexts and comparative perspectives*, F Armstrong, D Armstrong and L Barton, David Fulton, London

Byers, R (1999) Experience and achievement: initiatives in curriculum development for students with severe and profound and multiple learning difficulties, *British Journal of Special Education*, **26** (4), pp 184–88

Byers, R and Rose, R (1996) *Planning the Curriculum for Students with Special Educational Needs*, David Fulton, London

Carpenter, B, Ashdown, R and Bovair, K (1996) *Enabling Access*, David Fulton, London

Croll, P and Moses, D (2000) Ideologies and utopias: education professionals' views of inclusion, *European Journal of Special Needs Education*, **15** (1), pp 1–12

Department for Education (DFE) (1994) *The Code of Practice on the Identification and Assessment of Special Educational Needs*, DFE, London

Department for Education and Employment (DfEE) (1997) *Excellence for all Children*, The Stationery Office, London

Down, J (1866) Observations on an ethnic classification of idiots, *Clinical Lectures and Reports*, **3**, p 259

Dyson, A (1999) Inclusion and inclusions: theories and discourses in inclusive education, in *World Yearbook of Education: Inclusive education*, eds H Daniels and P Garner, Kogan Page, London

Farrell, M (1998) Notes on the Green Paper: an initial response, *British Journal of Special Education*, **25** (1), pp 13–15

Florian, L (1998) Inclusive practice: what, why and how? in *Promoting Inclusive Practice*, eds C Tilstone, L Florian and R Rose, Routledge, London

Foucault, M (1977) *Discipline and Punish*, Penguin, Harmondsworth

Foucault, M (1997) *Madness and Civilization*, Routledge, London

Hegarty, K *et al* (2000)'I didn't ask to have this': first person accounts of young people, in *The Education of Children with Medical Conditions*, ed A Closs, David Fulton, London

Hegarty, S, Pocklington, K and Lucas, D (1981) *Educating Students with Special Needs in the Ordinary School*, NFER-Nelson, London

Hornby, G (1999) Inclusion or delusion: can one size fit all? *Support for Learning*, **14** (4), pp 152–57

Hornby, G, Atkinson, M and Howard, J (1997) Integration of children with special educational needs into mainstream schools – inclusion or delusion?, in *Controversial Issues in Special Education*, eds G Hornby, M Atkinson and J Howard, David Fulton, London

Jenkinson, J (1997) *Mainstream or Special?* Routledge, London

Kirp, D (1982) Professionalism as a policy choice: British special education in comparative perspective, *World Politics*, **34** (2), pp 137–74

Lunt, I and Norwich, B (1999) *Can Effective Schools be Inclusive Schools?* London Institute of Education, London

Martin, J and White, A (1988) *OPCS Surveys of Disability in Great Britain, Part 1: The prevalence of disability among adults*, HMSO, London

Mason, M (1990) Internalised oppression, in *Disability Equality in the Classroom: A human rights issue*, eds R Rieser and M Mason, ILEA, London

Morris, J (1990) Progress with Humanity? in *Disability Equality in the Classroom: A human rights issue*, eds R Rieser and M Mason, ILEA, London

Nolan, C (1987) *Under the Eye of the Clock*, Weidenfeld & Nicolson, London

Norwich, B (1996) Special needs education or education for all? Connective specialisation and ideological impurity, *British Journal of Special Education*, **23** (3), pp 100–04

Porter, R (1987) *A Social History of Madness*, Phoenix, London

Rose, R (1998a) Including students: developing a partnership in learning, in *Promoting Inclusive Practice*, eds C Tilstone, L Florian and R Rose, Routledge, London

Rose, R (1998b) The curriculum: a vehicle for inclusion or a lever for exclusion?, in *Promoting Inclusive Practice*, eds C Tilstone, L Florian and R Rose, Routledge, London

Rose, R (2000) An evaluation of inclusion programmes: is there an empirical base which can inform inclusive practice? Paper presented at Inclusion of Students with Special Needs in General Education, Greek National Conference, Athens, 15–16 April

Rouse, M and Agbenu, R (1998) Assessment and special educational needs: teachers' dilemmas, *British Journal of Special Education*, **25** (2), pp 81–87

Sandow, S (1994) *Whose Special Need?* Paul Chapman, London

Sebba, J, Byers, R and Rose, R (1993) *Redefining The Curriculum For Students With Learning Difficulties*, David Fulton, London

Slee, R (1993) The politics of integration – new sites for old practices? *Disability, Handicap And Society*, **8** (4), pp 351–60

Sly, F (1996) Disability and the labour market, in *Labour Market Trends*, September, pp 413–24

Swann, W (1981) *The Practice of Special Education*, Open University Press, Buckingham

Thane, P (1998) Histories of the welfare state, in *Historical Controversies and Historians*, ed W Lamont, UCL Press, London

Thomas, G (1997) Inclusive schools for an inclusive society, *British Journal of Special Education*, **24** (3), pp 103–07

Tilstone, C and Rose, R (2000) Policy to practice: inclusion through education in the UK, in *Educational Policy and Practice in Relation to Disability*, eds A Zaniou-Sideri and A Vlachou, Elinika Gramata Press, Athens

Warnock, M (1978) *Report of the Committee of Enquiry into the Education of Handicapped Children and Young People*, HMSO, London

Watson, J (1990) My story, in *Disability Equality in the Classroom: A human rights issue*, eds R Rieser and M Mason, ILEA, London

Wood, S and Shears, B (1986) *Teaching Children with Severe Learning Difficulties*, Croom Helm, London

# Policy, equality and inequality: from the past to the future

*Kevin Myers and Ian Grosvenor*

## Editors' introduction

*This chapter looks beyond the fact of prejudice against ostracized groups, and the forms it takes in attitudes and types of behaviour, to address the crucial question of why it still exists in our society. Insisting on the historical perspective as the proper basis of critical understanding, Kevin Myers and Ian Grosvenor chart a 'chronology of exclusion' in the political rhetoric, education policy and practical treatment of 'outsider' children and their communities in Britain, throughout the 20th century. This chronology shows the consistent basis upon which the inequality of various children within the UK education system has been assumed – for Jewish children in the 1930s through to the children of refugees and asylum seekers in 2000. It also reveals the tradition of resistance to social, political and cultural alienation, most notably in the development of positive and progressive education systems.*

## Introduction

*England 1939:*
To my recently acquired title of 'the refugee' was now added another: 'the evacuee'.
I hated both heartily, wishing only to be a normal member of the class. To add to

my embarrassment, my long German name of Immerdauer often caused a crisis at registration-time. . . Hearing this strange name, some of my classmates decided I must be a German spy. They reckoned that the proper treatment for spies was to make their life as uncomfortable as possible. So three of them, of varying sizes and degrees of threat used to waylay me after school, chase me on the way home and if they caught me, trip me up and punch me.

(in Blend, 1995: 72)

*England 1998:*
I was so enthusiastic about starting school and learning English. I had been away from school for two years because we were travelling and did not have a permanent place to live. . . Nobody wanted to sit next to me in lessons and no-one wanted me as their partner in PE. I was all alone. . . Once I even got beaten up by a group of students who used to bully everyone. They beat me up one evening when I was walking home alone. They said they couldn't stand me because I was a refugee who lived on the Government's money.

(in Jones and Rutter, 1998: 1)

These reflections on school life are divided by over 50 years and yet, taken together, they indicate that discrimination against young refugees in schools has a long history in Britain. In these two cases, the basis of the discrimination is the refugee identity of the children. It is the ascription of refugee identities that precedes or seems to justify (at least in the minds of its proponents) the verbal and physical abuse experienced by some children at school. Yet while the extracts suggest that all those identified as outsiders may be susceptible to bullying and persecution, they do not explain why.

This chapter seeks to explain why those children identified as outsiders at school have been subjected to discrimination and persecution. It seeks to demonstrate why, despite the rhetoric of equality that has surrounded education policy for many years, a significant proportion of young people in Britain's schools continue to feel outcast, alienated or, in the words of one gay former pupil, 'irreparably second-rate human beings' (*Observer*, 2000). So while this analysis focuses on explaining the unequal position of refugee pupils, it is important to note at the outset that other groups of children who have been identified as different to the norm have also experienced discriminatory treatment in schools. Indeed, when such a list of outsiders is contemplated – those with specific class, gender and cultural identities and those with a different sexual orientation or disability – it is quickly apparent that discrimination against outsider children is one of the more consistent features of schooling in Britain (Copeland, 1999).

In explaining how and why this discrimination occurs, this chapter also makes a wider argument about the importance of historical study for understanding contemporary education systems, for any convincing explanation of the persistent discrimination against refugee or other 'outsider' pupils in schools must necessarily involve engaging with and interpreting the past. Indeed, the broad argument of this chapter is that any research that accounts for patterns of equality and inequality in education must, if it is to be plausible, include an analysis and an understanding of history.

In arguing for the centrality of history in education, this chapter challenges a dominant model of research, planning and policy-making in the field of education that relegates the place of history to a set of background remarks or simply ignores it altogether. This model of policy-making can be broadly termed managerial and has its immediate origins in the application of market principles to education throughout the 1980s and 1990s by the Conservative Party. In practice, the development of the managerial ethos has meant that education policy is increasingly based around national targets, modes of assessment and league tables that, it is claimed, objectively assess educational progress.

However, one problematic element in the rise of this managerialism has been that 'historical policy research has been largely neglected territory or somewhat superficial' (Silver, 1990: 6). The blame for this neglect may, argues Harold Silver (1990), rest with historians who have been wary about or unwilling to engage in politically controversial research. Alternatively, it may be that history has been marginalized – mistakenly – by the persistent calls for social research that is relevant and applicable and, more broadly, by the kind of ahistorical thinking informing the New Labour programme of 'modernization' (Finlayson, 1998; Cole, 1998: 321–22). Whatever the reasons for the neglect of history in educational research, this chapter aims to demonstrate why such neglect is problematic. Using contemporary and controversial debates surrounding the position of refugees in British society it attempts to show that history can bring new insight and understanding to current policy formulation. It offers an analysis of why refugee pupils continue to experience verbal and physical abuse at school and why, despite a long-standing formal commitment to equal opportunities, the education system in Britain continues to produce unequal educational experiences for some children.

In the first part of this chapter the development of current policies to deal with refugees are examined in historical perspective. The aim here is to create what might be termed a chronology of exclusion. This chronology is a critical historical narrative that documents how discriminatory educational policies have been developed around specific and exclusionary notions of the refugee. It examines how both prominent political actors and key political ideas have shaped the development of this discriminatory policy. The second part of this chapter then offers a set of reflections on this discourse of exclusion. These reflections assess the importance of historical study for both understanding and transforming the current relationship between education policy, equality and inequality.

## Refugees and the exclusion from equality

In 1998, a report by the Refugee Council showed that many refugees and asylum seekers were being denied 'access to education' because their assumed examination results and their patterns of attendance were expected to lower the schools' position in national league tables (*Times Educational Supplement*, 1998). Subsequent research confirms this pattern of exclusion and estimates that, as a result, 2,500 asylum-seeking children are absent from school (*TES*, 2000). Of those children who do attend schools the majority are, as a result of their exclusion from those deemed to be successful, concentrated in 'unpopular and under-subscribed schools', frequently located in inner city areas, where they 'come into contact with the educational system at its most under-resourced and stretched'. Moreover, though refugee children may be physically admitted to such schools, their experiences once there continue to be those of outsiders who are alienated or excluded by the routine practices of schooling (*TES*, 2000).

One important area of schooling that contributes to the feelings of exclusion reported by refugee students is the curriculum. As part of the 1988 Education Reform Act a centrally prescribed 'national curriculum' was introduced in schools across Britain. This National Curriculum laid down a number of 'core' or 'foundation' subjects for all children to study whose selection was problematic-ally underpinned by static notions of culture, community and national dentity. David Gillborn (1990), for example, argues that the National Curriculum was 'a nationalist curriculum, stressing "English" language, history and "culture"' with little relevance to pupils from ethnic minority backgrounds' (Gillborn, 1990: 206). Moreover, changes made to the National Curriculum consistently fail to address the myth of cultural homogeneity that underpinned the original version (John, 1999: 10).

There is also evidence to show that the 'hidden curriculum' of a school – in rules, practices and general ethos – also helps to shape the unequal educational opportunities offered to refugee children. To take just one example, a study in 1998 of the experiences of refugee students finds that 'Among the many obstacles that they [refugee students] have to overcome are the negative attitudes of some teaching staff, attitudes which include ignorance from lack of awareness, and which range through low expectations to "deficit model" assumptions about the learning capacities of bilingual students' (McDonald, 1998: 161).

As well as highlighting the low expectations that teachers extend to refugee pupils, the study also finds that the attainment of refugee students is adversely affected by a lack of advice and guidance about pedagogical methods, educational opportunities and by inappropriate or inadequate initial assessment. It should also be recognized that for many refugee students verbal and physical abuse are facts of daily life. The independent Glidewell Inquiry heard, for example, submissions from community workers who reported that children in playgrounds referred to refugees as 'bogus, scroungers, beggars, dirty and disgusting' (in Alibhai-Brown, 1999: 76).

The challenge for educationalists lies in understanding why, despite the formal commitment of successive governments to equal opportunities, refugee students continue to experience such discrimination. In highlighting league tables and the National Curriculum as factors that help explain refugees' unequal access to and experience of education, the report by the Refugee Council indicates implicitly that the rise of a particular educational ideology in the 1980s and 1990s had a deleterious effect on refugee children. League tables that purport to measure the performance and progress of schools according to a number of narrowly defined criteria are one of the more obvious signs of the implementation of free market principles to education. Behind the introduction of league tables lies a whole series of less visible but important changes in the funding, management and administration of schools. The cumulative effect of these sweeping reforms has been to undermine commitment to principles of social justice and equal opportunity (Gillborn and Youdell, 2000; Grosvenor, 1999c; Griffiths and Troyna, 1995). To some degree, then, the unequal experiences of refugee children in schools can be explained by the introduction of market ideology in education.

A number of important studies have documented the negative effect that free market ideology in education has had on refugee children (Rutter, 1994; Jones and Rutter, 1998). Changes in the funding, management and administration of schooling that are linked to the introduction of the free market can explain a number of important points about the educational experiences of refugee students. For example, they help explain the difficulties of refugee students in gaining access to certain schools, the increasing scarcity of support services for those pupils and the harmful effect that this scarcity can have on their educational attainment. Yet such studies rarely argue that the experiences of refugees in education are shaped purely and simply by educational policy. Educational policy alone does not, for example, explain why some teachers may have low expectations of their refugee students and why such a large number of these pupils are subjected to verbal and physical abuse. For a detailed and convincing explanation as to these experiences it is necessary to examine the wider social and political context in which schools exist.

Schools do not exist in a social and political vacuum. Rather, what happens in schools – the subjects studied, the way children are taught, the relationships both 'between pupils' and 'between pupils and their teachers' – are all related in complex ways to wider politics, culture and society. Indeed, the idea that schools are a microcosm of wider society is a point that, implicitly at least, most studies of refugee children in education accept. Jill Rutter (1998), for example, argues that 'legal and policy changes' regarding the entry, recognition and settlement of refugees in Britain have 'multiple effects on refugee children' and, like other commentators, she identifies an 'increase in racism, xenophobia and nationalism in Europe' as a causal factor in the development of increasingly restrictive policies in respect of refugees at both a European and a national level (1998: 26). As the result of these policies the right of asylum becomes ever more elusive and the freedom of asylum seekers ever more restricted throughout the European Union.

In Britain, the regime of surveillance and control to which asylum seekers are subjected was introduced through a series of Asylum and Immigration Acts – in 1993, 1995 and 1999 – each of which was preceded by prolonged political debate on the problems of 'bogus' or 'illegal' refugees. Yasmin Alibhai-Brown (1999) argues that the language of such debates served to 'dehumanise the refugees and the immigration policies that result from these debates may have increased public hostility towards immigrants and ethnic minorities' (1999: 72, 75; see also Joly, Kelly and Nettleton, 1997: 118–19). Little wonder, then, that in the playgrounds and classrooms of Britain this language of hostility towards refugees is evident. For children in the playground are simply reproducing the range of negative and dehumanizing images of refugees that they have learnt from wider society. The debates and discourses of wider society similarly influence teachers who may unconsciously have low expectations of their refugee students and advise them against 'unrealistic expectations'. In other words, the popular and political debates that identified asylum seekers as a problem, the legislation that made their arrival more difficult and the policies that subjected them to popular suspicion, institutionalized a level of hostility towards refugees that was reproduced in schools. This helps explain why refugee students are discriminated against in schools and why, as Jones and Rutter (1998) argue, 'anti-refugee sentiment in schools. . . is alive, active and well' (Jones and Rutter, 1998: 9).

Placing the educational experiences of refugee children in a broad social and political context can clearly aid a descriptive account of why young refugees are discriminated against in schools. In the brief account given above, the development of anti-refugee sentiment and the low expectations that some teachers have of refugee students link with a wider discourse, about the problems allegedly posed by those who seek asylum in Britain. Yet it is possible to go one step further than this descriptive account and ask exactly *why* refugees began to be seen as so problematic in the 1980s and 1990s?

It is important to note in passing that this is not, as it appears in so much political debate, a question about the numbers of refugees since there has been no research that proves either the economy or 'race' relations benefit from restricting immigration (Alibhai-Brown, 1999: 72; Dale and Cole (eds), 1999; Holmes, 1988: 306–07). Rather, the question of why refugees have been subjected to such a degree of popular and official antipathy is one that requires both a rather more detailed account of political ideology and an engagement with the past.

The Conservative government, which introduced both the market reforms of education and the immigration and asylum legislation, based its political programme on a New Right ideology that aimed for nothing less than the political, economic and moral regeneration of Britain. For the purposes of this chapter, it is not the aspects of that regeneration (the market, the family, individualism, law and order) that are of interest, but rather its perceived necessity. The position of the New Right that was embraced by Margaret Thatcher in particular was that the story of post-war Britain was one of decline. This held that the foundation of the welfare state had encouraged dependency, nationalized industries had promoted inefficiency and a liberal consensus had attempted to excuse the problems caused by immigration, the collapse of standards in education and the growth of sexual 'deviancy'. The self-appointed task of the New Right in the 1980s and 1990s was the restoration of a sense of national vigour, decency and purpose. Central to the whole political philosophy of the

New Right and the Thatcher project was a specific sense of national identity that, Phillip Dodd (1995) argues, depended 'upon a sustained process of purification and exclusion. In her British story enemies were here, there and everywhere' (1995: 26–27).

In the vision of the New Right, among the more prominent of these enemies were both actual and potential immigrants and asylum seekers, liberal or left-wing teachers and permissive local authorities that encouraged homosexuality. As a result, the legislative programme of the Conservative government in the 1980s and 1990s eroded the professional freedom of teachers, attacked local democracy and, as has already been indicated, restricted (non-white) immigration and the right to asylum. These diverse areas of legislative reform share the determination to protect and promote specific notions of morality and decency that were encapsulated in a deliberately constructed and exclusionary sense of Britishness.

However, it is crucial to note that the Conservative Party was hardly pioneering in using a sense of national identity as a strategy for government. Eric Hobsbawm (1983) notes that in the early years of New Right political dominance, 'the "nation", with its associated phenomena: nationalism, the nation state, national symbols, histories and the rest' are 'exercises in social engineering which are often deliberate and always innovative' (Hobsbawm, 1983: 13). The idea of the nation has, in other words, always been used as an instrument of government to identify those who belong, those who are like 'us', and those who are different, a threat and who therefore must be excluded. An important part of this simultaneous process of inclusion and exclusion is the attention to historical perspective. This means constructing a narrative of the past, or promoting an authentic version of the national story, that makes sense of present social, political and economic circumstances. In recent years, that authentic version of national history has marginalized the long history of refugee settlement in Britain and, in doing so, helped to stigmatize the contemporaneous arrival of refugees.

The construction of the historical narrative of the nation has developed towards placing refugees decisively outside of the national community, by suppressing their histories and denying the centrality of their experiences in the development of British history. It is significant to note, for example, that not until 1999 was there a social history of refugee settlement in Britain. Tony Kushner and Katherine Knox (1999), the authors of that pioneering study, point out that although the presence of unprecedented numbers of refugees in exile was one of the 'hallmarks of our time' there remained a 'general silence on refugee questions' in historical research (1999: 3–4). It is important to note that historians of education have, for the most part, helped maintain this silence by resolutely ignoring the presence of refugees in Britain.

This ignorance surrounding the historical experiences of refugees is not just a matter of factual accuracy that should only concern academics. For the absence of refugee history has important consequences for the way in which refugees are perceived and treated in exile today. Indeed, the current political inability to understand, or even openly recognize, issues relating to refugee children's experiences at school can be ultimately linked to popular understandings of national history. Kushner and Knox (1999) argue, for example, that one of the reasons for the general silence on refugee questions in history is that it 'challenges assumptions of mono-culturalism at both national and regional level' (1999: 4). In other words, the marginal status of refugee (and other minority) history originates in the belief that Britain is, has been in the past, or should be, an ethnically, socially and culturally homogeneous place.

Although nationalism and national identity have become subjects of fierce academic and popular debate, historians, politicians, policy makers and the general public all still speak and write about Britain in common-sense and self-evident terms. In 1999, the rhetoric of the Conservative Party led by William Hague championed 'the British Way', while for the Labour Party under Tony Blair the programme for government was based on a thousand years of British history (*Guardian*, 1999a; Grosvenor, 1999a: 249). Moreover, this conviction that the British people and British national life are essentially homogeneous remains at the centre of beliefs about national identity and can be traced in complaints against the process of refugee settlement in Britain. The words typically assigned to refugees raise questions about their integrity – 'bogus', 'illegal' and 'scroungers' for example. When objections to refugee settlement are articulated in more detail they reveal that such hostility is clearly underpinned by a specific, and historically inaccurate, sense of the nation.

In protests against the arrivals of refugees in Dover in 1999, the leader of Kent County Council argued that the local population felt 'swamped' and 'resentful' at the arrival of 1,000 refugees from Kosovo (*Daily Mail*, 1999). Similar sentiments are expressed by the *Daily Telegraph* newspaper, in suggestions that public concern about refugee settlement was stimulated by a 'huge population influx' that had occurred over a period of five years and was 'changing the character of South-east England' (*Daily Telegraph*, 2000). Yet the numbers of asylum seekers in Dover, a centre of anti-refugee hostility, was defined by Kent Social Services as just 790 in 1997, or 0.06 per cent of the local population (cited in Mahamdallie, 1999: 9).

The Refugee Council (2000) reports a more sinister but nonetheless enlightening complaint against its own lobbying activities, which argues that 'you people do not care about your own country at all. You only care about foreigners. Blood will flow' (*iNexile*, 2000). The articulation of such protests is significant because the metaphors used to describe the arrival of the refugees all relate, more or less directly, to preserving or maintaining a specific and static sense of national identity. At the same time as describing fears about the arrival of the refugees in terms of being 'swamped' and predicting inevitable violence that results from a sense of 'frustration', these protests also convey a sense of British culture as static, and somehow tainted or damaged by contact with refugees. Indeed, what is interesting about these complaints is that they all recall, in varying degrees of detail, the sense of Britishness used by Enoch Powell to mobilize opposition to the settlement of black immigrants in the 1960s (Grosvenor, 1997).

Alan Phillips (1997) argues that, whereas in the past black immigration was the area in which ideas about national identity were articulated, 'many of the themes of ethnicity, belonging, nationality and xenophobia are now increasingly debated in the arena of refugees' (1997: 3). In other words, over a period of approximately 15 years the discourse of nationality shifted away from the focus on black immigration and on to the problems posed by asylum seekers and refugees. It is important to note that this is a change in context, language and the arena of debate, rather than content. For many of the assumptions that underpin the current debate on refugees have also been made about Irish, Jewish and black immigration in the past.

In the middle of the 19th century, for example, immigrant Irish communities in Britain – simultaneously feared and despised as feckless Fenians with an alien religion – were subjected to 'psychological terror, small-scale brawls, attacks on individuals and a routine diet of discrimination' (O'Day, 1996: 26). For the first half of the 20th century it was arguably the Jews – both immigrant and British – who were popularly thought to constitute the biggest danger to the British nation (Kushner, 1989, 1994). After 1945, argues Shyllon (1992), Britain 'was disfigured by the naked and undisguised racism of the British authorities and the British people towards the Black communities' (1992: 214–15). Seen in this historical perspective, contemporary complaints against refugee settlement are simply aimed at the latest targets in a discourse of exclusion that has been central to the development of British society, politics and culture over the past century or more.

Uncovering the history of refugee settlement in Britain, and placing the study of minority groups at the very centre of historical research, may help to develop a more accurate view of the national past. Such a view would reclaim, popularize and publicly celebrate the history of refugee settlement in Britain. It would recount refugee movements, experiences and struggles. It would openly recognize domestic traditions of intolerance to outsiders, document moments of resistance to that intolerance and, in doing so, offer alternative narratives of the past that also offer the possibility of understanding the present and changing the future.

Such a change in historical perspective may help to change the current climate of suspicion and hostility that surrounds conversations regarding the number and character of refugees now settling in Britain. As the journalist Isabel Fonseca (2000) has written, in the context of a press campaign against Roma asylum-seekers in Britain, history is an important antidote to myth and 'the only meaningful basis for intelligent discussion about their [Roma] future' (2000). Indeed, as has already been suggested, the obvious reluctance to recognize and celebrate refugee settlement in Britain is a politically important strategy of forgetting, one that helps the general public, politicians and policy makers to rationalize the increasingly punitive system of surveillance and control to which all refugees are now subjected (Haynes, 1999: 33–37).

However, if this emergent history of refugee settlement is to be successful it must not be confined either to academic study, or to the public celebrations of the national past. Rather, if rational attitudes to refugees are to be established in Britain, then more affirmative action is required. In particular, recognition of the way in which the development of social policy in general, and education in particular, has historically promoted racism and helped secure the wider exclusion of refugees, is a necessary prelude to making that policy more democratic, equal and liberating.

Formal systems of schooling are widely recognized as crucial to the development of Western capitalist societies. In such societies, formal schooling has a disciplinary function that seeks not only to impart useful knowledge to pupils but also to shape their behaviour, beliefs and conduct (Rousmaniere, Dehli and de Connick-Smith, 1997). Since the introduction of mass compulsory schooling in late-19th-century Britain, one important method of disciplining the minds and bodies of children was to teach them how to be British. This attempt at instilling a sense of national identity was pervasive, influencing every part of the school experience and shaping the grammar and the choreography, the routines and rituals and the symbolic events of everyday schooling for successive generations of children in Britain. This symbiotic relationship between mass education and national identity is important because it means that, as well as developing policies, practices and processes aimed at promoting a sense of Britishness, schools also played a key role in constructing problematic identities for various minority groups. Put slightly differently, the aims of compulsory schooling in Britain – teaching all children how to be good subjects – meant that school was a key site in both promoting the idea that those children who are not white, Anglican or Anglo-Saxon are somehow a problem (Blair and Cole, 2000: 63–72). Indeed, one of the reasons for increasing state expenditure on schooling in the early 20th century was their assumed ability to assimilate and civilize the alien 'Other'.

While late Victorian and early Edwardian elementary school pupils were encouraged to regard 'white skin and "Anglo-Saxon" civilization' as the 'culmination of the evolutionary process', they simultaneously learnt to see outsiders – however defined – in stereotypical and frequently xenophobic terms (Fryer quoted in Davin, 1996: 202; see also Blair and Cole, 2000: 58–63). In other words, the majority of schools promoted the wider prejudices of society. Anna Davin argues, for example, that 'the supposition that all Irish were stupid impeded progress at school for some Irish children' and the widespread belief in the intelligence or 'sharpness' of Jewish children – some of them refugees – was either 'resented or mocked'. Similarly, 'children of African, Caribbean, Indian or Chinese origin. . . had to contend with images which. . . denigrated them as savage, dirty, uncivilised and childlike, or devious, cunning and artful' (Davin, 1996: 204–06; see also Blair and Cole, 2000: 61–63). Paradoxically, while schools helped promote stereotypical ideas about outsider communities, they also took on responsibility for assimilating the children of such communities. The pedagogical tools that teachers employed in order to encourage assimilation were varied. So while all migrant children were taught English and were simultaneously prohibited from using a first language, some also had their names changed or anglicized and all were taught to show reverence to the Union Flag.

The experiences of refugee children arriving in Britain from Nazi Germany in the 1930s provide a concrete example of how the process of assimilation was understood to work. Between December 1938 and September 1939 almost 10,000 refugee children, most of them Jewish, arrived in Britain from Central Europe. Despite official sanction for their arrival, argues Mary Ford (1983), the Home Office 'made it a condition of entry that the refugee children should be dispersed widely throughout the country' (1983: 143). The widespread anti-Semitism characteristic of British society for many decades helps explain this policy of dispersal and also the many cases of encouraging refugee children to anglicize their names and drop or forget their Judaism in favour of Christianity. Elsewhere, absolute priority was given to lessons in English language, culture and elocution. As one head teacher in the 1930s saw it, the teacher's responsibility was not only to ensure that refugee pupils could 'speak and write English well' but also to ensure that they 'assimilated English ways and ideas' (Myers, 2000: 249).

By the middle of the 20th century, the education system in Britain had developed and established a pattern for understanding and responding to the arrival of refugee and migrant children in schools. This consisted of the teaching of English language and, at the same time, of cultural values that served to denigrate the home language and culture of migrant children. In the post-war period, the educational policy of assimilation that had characterized the response to German refugee children in the 1930s became increasingly targeted at the children of black and Asian migrants arriving in Britain. In 1966, for example, Section 11 of the Local Government Act made additional funds available to schools for providing lessons in English as a second language (ESL). The purpose of ESL teaching was not, however, 'limited to the transmission of skills, it also acted as a means of cultural indoctrination' (Carter and Grosvenor, 1992: 16). In those lessons, black children learnt, or were encouraged to think, that they were in need of intervention, a people, culture and language that was, in comparison with the white norm, 'abnormal, in need of correction and whitetization' (Mukherjee in Carter and Grosvenor, 1992: 16).

In addition to ESL teaching, the dispersal of black children around some local authority schools in the 1960s both confirmed and helped develop a problematic view of black children in British society. This policy of dispersal was based on the idea that the process of assimilation stood a greater chance of success if schools avoided what the Department of Education and Science regarded as 'undue concentrations of immigrant children'. The resulting forcible removal of black children from their local schools to other parts of an LEA was designed to reassure non-immigrant parents that the educational progress of their children would not be adversely affected by the presence of 'excessive numbers' of black pupils. Once again, however, the 'policy of dispersal illustrates both the perception of black children as a problem and the racist attitudes embedded within the education system' (Grosvenor, 1997: 65). Throughout the 1980s and 1990s the application of market ideology to education served only to exacerbate these racist attitudes because it also effectively ended a policy commitment to anti-racism and wider principles of social justice. Indeed, the Office for Standards in Education reported in 1999 that many schools in Britain remain institutionally racist and so continue to regard outsiders – and refugee pupils in particular – as a problem (*Guardian*, 1999b).

## From the past to the future

This brief history of refugee settlement and education in Britain can help promote understanding of the contemporary experiences of refugee children in a number of ways. First, recognizing and appreciating the long history of refugee settlement in Britain makes it much more difficult to regard refugees as a threat, either to the British way of life or to the economic prospects of British citizens. The historical reality is that refugees have been a characteristic feature in the development of British society for centuries. Rather than threatening Britain, history illustrates how refugees are an integral part of the national story.

Second, however, the dearth of historical research into refugee experiences has important implications for educational policy making. Coulby and Jones (1995) argue, for example, that the recent public and educational attention being given to refugee children only demonstrates the propensity in much of the education system to learn little of its own history (1995: 122). They argue that states across Europe continue to regard refugee children as a temporary phenomenon and a new one, equally mistaken views that facilitate the introduction of policies and practices that either ignore or marginalize the needs of refugee children in school. As in wider society, the perception that refugees are somehow a transient and problematic feature of modern societies undermines attempts to give young refugees equal access to, and opportunities in, the experience of education. In other words, recovering the history of refugee schooling in the past is an integral and necessary part of any attempt to understand and improve the educational experiences of refugee children in the present.

Third, one consistent and prominent strand in the complex set of historical reactions to both refugee and migrant settlement in Britain has been a discourse of exclusion. The fact that Irish, Jewish and Asian, black and other migrants, as well as contemporary refugees, have all been subjected to varying levels of discrimination, prejudice and violence indicates that racist attitudes are consistently present in British society. These attitudes and actions are not natural reactions to outsiders or justified responses to unacceptable behaviour, two of the more popular explanations for the continuing and widespread hysteria against refugees in Britain. Rather, such hysteria is another specific example of the discourse of exclusion in operation and more concrete evidence of the central role that this discourse plays in British society and politics. However, it is only with the long-term perspectives provided by historical study that the discourse of exclusion can be identified and that current expressions of intolerance and racism against refugees can be critically understood.

Fourth, the critical historical narrative offered here shows that the development of education policy over a period of more than 100 years has helped promote the discourse of exclusion. Even from the brief historical analysis offered here, it is clear that there has been a consistent set of educational responses to the presence of refugee and migrant children in the classroom. So while the language of educational policy may change – from assimilation, to integration, to multiculturalism and then to anti-racist education – historical study illustrates how, beyond the level of policy rhetoric, there is a deeply embedded culture of racism and intolerance in British schools. The term 'institutional racism' focuses attention on the subtle and unintentional ways that schools discriminate against people from certain cultural backgrounds (see Chapter 4 for a discussion of the concept of racism). Such indirect racism is often manifested in modes of practice and ways of working that are underpinned by racist assumptions inherited from the past. One ESL teacher states:

> I have honestly worked in schools where it's like a sort of condescending attitude, a sort of missionary attitude – basically they [some teachers] equate lack of English with lack of intelligence. . .There are still some people who have that sort of attitude that they [bilingual children] are second-class citizens.

> (in Stead, Closs and Arshad, 1999: 4)

The reference here to a missionary attitude is, like the earlier example of deficit models of learning, another important reminder that the everyday activities of education institutions are far more difficult to change than policy rhetoric. It suggests that, unless direct action is taken to identify and attack racism, it will, through a process of institutional stasis, remain a feature of the educational experiences of a significant number of young people. This anticipates the final reflection on the discourse of exclusion. For history offers not only a method for critically understanding contemporary education policy, it also offers concrete examples of how such policy can be resisted.

The fifth and final reason for studying history in connection with education policy is for the instances and examples of resistance to intolerance and racism that it brings to light. Despite the consistently important role played by anti-alienism and racism in British society and culture during the 20th century, a critical study of history also reveals regular moments of resistance to British traditions of intolerance. These moments of resistance have taken place in different periods, have been organized by different movements and have taken place across a range of social and political sites but they all have shared the determination to counter the effect of racism in the lives of migrants and refugees (Virdee, 1999; Virdee and Cole, 2000: 43–53). Moreover, as the following two examples indicate, independent educational activity has been crucial to historic attempts to counter intolerance.

As already shown, the strand of intolerance that has concentrated on the alleged problematic identities of immigrant groups in British society has, it was suggested earlier, led to consistent educational attempts to assimilate first and second generation 'alien' children. Yet both the construction of problematic identities and the related attempts to anglicize children have long been resisted. David

Feldman (1989) completed a study of Jews in London between 1880 and 1914, for example, which shows how the immigrant *chedarim* and *talmud torah* schools reproduced and sustained East European Jewish culture in the face of hostility from both the Anglo-Jewish and non-Jewish communities in England. Partly as a result of the ability of such schools to resist the imposition of an anglicized Judaism, 'a more forceful assertion of Jewish identity in England was apparent' in the inter-war period (1989: 224).

Similarly, the inequalities directed against Asian, black and other minority ethnic pupils under the policy of assimilation in the 1960s were challenged by a range of local initiatives that sought to counter a racist educational discourse. One such initiative was undertaken by the Sikh community of Birmingham and established a notable system of supplementary education based around the Guru Nanak Gurdwara in Smethwick. Arising partly out of community dissatisfaction with state schooling, the Gurdwara offered lessons in Punjabi, English, history, music and world religions. In addition, the Gurdwara was explicitly committed to 'combating anti-social, racial and Fascist activities in Smethwick' and actively engaged in 'a politics of opposition' where 'the issue of equality in education was invoked, racism was challenged and equality was pursued' (Grosvenor, 1999b: 291–93).

Therefore, both the pre-war Jewish and post-war black instances demonstrate independent political and educational activity designed to combat different forms of intolerance towards immigrant groups in British society. In short, a critical reading of history offers not just a means of understanding the past but concrete examples of how to organize in the present to change the future.

# References

Alibhai-Brown, Y (1999) *True Colours: Public attitudes to multiculturalism and the role of government*, Institute for Public Policy Research, London

Blair, M and Cole, M (2000) Racism and education: the imperial legacy, in *Education, Equality And Human Rights: Issues of gender, 'race', sexuality, special needs and social class*, ed M Cole, RoutledgeFalmer, London

Blend, A (1995) *A Child Alone*, Vallentine Mitchell, London

Carter, B and Grosvenor, I (1992) *The Apostles of Purity: Black immigration and education policy in post-war Britain*, AFFOR, Birmingham

Cole, M (1998) Globalisation, modernisation and competitiveness: a critique of the New Labour project in education, *International Studies in Sociology of Education*, 8 (13), pp 315–32

Cole, M (ed) (2000) *Education, Equality and Human Rights: Issues of gender, 'race', sexuality, special needs and social class*, RoutledgeFalmer, London

Copeland, I (1999) *The Making of the Backward Pupil in Education in England 1870–1914*, Woburn Press, London

Coulby, D and Jones, C (1995) *Postmodernity and European Education Systems: Cultural diversity and centralist knowledge*, Trentham Books, Stoke-on-Trent

Dale, G and Cole, M (eds) (1999) *The European Union and Migrant Labour*, Berg, Oxford

*Daily Mail* (1999), 16 August

*Daily Telegraph* (2000), 10 March

Davin, A (1996) *Growing up Poor: Home, school and street in London 1870–1914*, Rivers Oram Press, London

Dodd, P (1995) *The Battle Over Britain*, Demos, London

Feldman, D (1989) Jews in London, 1880–1914, in *Patriotism: The making and unmaking of British national identity* ed R Samuel, **2**, pp 207–29

Finlayson, A (1998) Tony Blair and the jargon of modernisation, *Soundings*, **3**, pp 11–27

Fonseca, I (2000) The truth about Gypsies, *Guardian*, 24 March

Ford, M (1983) The arrival of Jewish refugee children in England, 1938–1939, *Immigrants And Minorities*, **2**, pp 135–51

Gillborn, D (1990) *Race, Ethnicity and Education: Teaching and learning in multi-ethnic schools*, Unwin Hyman, London

Gillborn, D and Youdell, D (2000) *Rationing Education: Policy, practice, reform and equity*, Open University Press, Buckingham

Griffiths, M and Troyna, B (eds) (1995) *Anti-racism, Culture and Social Justice in Education*, Trentham Books, Stoke-on-Trent

Grosvenor, I (1997) *Assimilating Identities: Racism and education policy in post 1945 Britain*, Lawrence & Wishart, London

Grosvenor, I (1999a) There's no place like home: education and the making of national identity, in *History of Education*, **23** (3), pp 235–50

Grosvenor, I (1999b) 'Faith in the city': religion, racism and education in 1960s Britain, in *Faiths and Education: Historical and comparative perspectives*, eds J Coolahan, R Aldrich, and F Simon, CSHP, Ghent

Grosvenor, I (1999c) 'Race' and education, in *An Introduction to the Study of Education*, ed D Matheson and I Grosvenor, David Fulton, London

*Guardian* (1999a), 20 January

*Guardian* (1999b), 11 March

Haynes, M (1999) Setting the limits to Europe as an 'imagined community', in *The European Union and Migrant Labour*, eds G Dale and M Cole, Berg, Oxford

Hobsbawm, E (1983) Inventing traditions, in *The Invention of Tradition*, eds E Hobsbawm and T Ranger, Cambridge University Press, Cambridge

Holmes, C (1988) *John Bull's Island: Immigration and British Society 1871–1971*, Macmillan, Basingstoke

*iNexile* (2000) The Refugee Council, London, January

John, G (1999) Paved with good intentions, *Runnymede Trust Bulletin*, September, pp 9–10.

Joly, D, Kelly, L and Nettleton, C (eds) (1997) *Refugees in Europe: The hostile new agenda*, Minority Rights Group International, London

Jones, C and Rutter J (1998) Mapping the field: current issues in refugee education, in *Refugee Education: Mapping the field*, eds J Rutter and C Jones, Trentham Books, Stoke-on-Trent

Kushner, T (1989) *The Persistence of Prejudice: Anti-Semitism in British Society during the Second World War*, Manchester University Press, Manchester

Kushner, T (1994) *The Holocaust and the Liberal Imagination: A social and cultural history*, Blackwell, Oxford

Kushner, T and Knox, K (1999) *Refugees in an Age of Genocide: Global, national and local perspectives during the twentieth century*, Frank Cass, London

McDonald, J (1998) Refugee students' experiences of the UK education system, in *Refugee Education: Mapping the field*, eds J Rutter and C Jones, Trentham Books, Stoke-on-Trent, pp 149–70

Mahamdallie, H (1999) *Refugees are Not to Blame: No to scapegoating, no to immigration controls*, Socialist Workers Party

Myers, K (2000) Englishness, Identity and Refugee Children in Britain, 1937–1945, unpublished PhD thesis, University of Coventry

O'Day, A (1996) Varieties of anti-Irish behaviour in Britain, 1846–1922, in *Racial Violence in Britain in the 19th and 20th Centuries*, ed P Panayi, Leicester University Press, Leicester, pp 26–43

Phillips, A (1997) Preface, in *Refugees in Europe: The hostile new agenda*, ed D Joly, L Kelly and C Nettleton, Minority Rights Group International, London

Rousmaniere, K, Dehli, K, and de Connick-Smith, N, (1997) *Discipline, Moral Regulation and Schooling: A social history*, Garland, New York

Rutter, J (1998) Refugees in today's world, in *Refugee Education: Mapping the field* eds J Rutter and C Jones, Trentham Books, Stoke-on-Trent

Shyllon, F (1992) The black presence and experience in Britain: an analytical overview, in *Essays on the History of Blacks in Britain*, eds J S Gundara and I Duffield, Avebury, Aldershot

Silver, H (1990) *Education, change and the policy process*, Falmer, London

Stead, J, Closs, A, and Arshad, R (1999) *Refugee Pupils in Scottish Schools*, Scottish Council for Research in Education, Edinburgh

*Observer* (2000), 13 February

*Times Educational Supplement* (1998), 10 April

*TES* (2000), 7 April

Virdee, S (1999) Racism and resistance in British trade unions: 1948–79, in *Labour and Difference in the USA, Africa and Britain*, eds P Alexander and R Halpern, Macmillan, London

Virdee, S and Cole, M (2000) 'Race', racism and resistance, in *Education, Equality and Human Rights: Issues of gender, 'race', sexuality, special needs and social class*, ed M Cole, RoutledgeFalmer, London

# Conclusion

## Mike Cole

The school is not a neutral objective arena; it is an institution which has the goal of changing people's values, skills, and knowledge bases.

(Shirley Brice Heath, 1983)

Education is a meaningless process unless it is concerned with the struggle against all forms of tyranny, whether based on ignorance, oppression, inequality or exploitation.

(Chris Mullard, 1988)

## The role of education: lessons from the past

While it is neither possible nor desirable to return to the past per se, there have been situations and eras in the past from which we can learn as we envision and plan for the future. In a classic essay *Really useful knowledge*, published in 1979, a year of great significance in Britain – the election of the Thatcher government – Richard Johnson addressed himself to the rediscovery of popular educational traditions in the period, 1790—1848. Johnson identified four aspects of popular 'radical education': a critique of the existing system, alternative educational goals, education to change the world and education for all (1979: 76–77). Each of these still have considerable relevance today. To conclude the book we revisit Johnson's analysis to review and indicate how they might inform education for equality in the 21st century.

### Critique of the existing system
First, radicals conducted a running critique of all forms of 'provided' education, which, in later phases of the period, involved a practical grasp and a theoretical understanding of cultural and ideological struggle in a more general sense (Johnson, 1979: 76).

Essential to this process is a conception of the teacher as transformative intellectual and the notion of critical reflection. A transformative intellectual is

one who exercises forms of intellectual and pedagogical practice which attempt to insert teaching and learning directly into the political sphere by arguing that schooling represents both a struggle for meaning and a struggle over power relations. Teachers who assume the role of transformative intellectuals treat students as critical agents, question how knowledge is produced and distributed, use dialogue, and make knowledge meaningful, critical, and ultimately emancipatory.

(Giroux and McLaren, 1989)

A central feature of the role of transformative intellectual is the fostering of critical reflection, which helps pupils/students 'develop a deep and abiding faith in the struggle to overcome economic, political and social injustices, and to further humanise themselves as part of this struggle' (Giroux, 1988: 127–8; see also Hill, 1994, 1997). Earlier, Giroux set out in more concrete terms what pupils/students actually need to learn. This embraces the active nature of their participation in the learning process. Pupils/students need to be taught to think critically, enabling them to 'appropriate their own histories, to delve into their own biographies and systems of meaning. . . to authenticate their own experiences' (1983: 203). Drawing on Gleeson and Whitty (1976) Giroux stresses the need for pupils/students 'to learn about the structural and ideological forces that influence and restrict their lives' (1983: 203). Inherent in Whitty's suggestion is that pupils/students 'must be taught to act collectively to build political structures that can challenge the status quo' (Giroux, 1983: 203).

Schools and other educational institutions could be, and sometimes have been and are, centres of critical debate, involving the local trade unions, institutions, teaching and non-teaching staff, parents and pupils/students (relative to age).

### Alternative educational goals: really useful knowledge

Second, radicals were involved in the development of alternative educational goals: this entailed notions of how educational utopias could actually be achieved and a definition of 'really useful knowledge', incorporating a radical content – a sense of what it was really important to know (Johnson, 1979: 76).

What knowledge is 'really useful' in the promotion of equality? The school curriculum has for too long been structured to exclude, repress and prevent certain issues being addressed (Young, 1984: 236; Carrington and Troyna, 1988: 208; Cole, 1997: 68–69). It is time to open it up. It is time to liberate the mind (Cole, 2000).

Prior to the ascendancy of the radical Right in the 1980s, the dominant educational paradigm, the liberal progressive one, determined what happened in many, though not all, British primary schools and in some secondary schools.

Debbie Epstein (1993) has offered a trenchant critique of what liberal progressivism often meant in practice (see also Sarup, 1983 and Brehony, 1992), in the context of the real critical potential of primary age children. The Plowden report's (CACE, 1967) conceptualization of children as individuals rather than as members of groups (and the fact that social groups tended to be pathologized when they were mentioned) made it difficult to raise issues of power relations in primary schools. In addition, Plowden's deficit model of working-class children meant that efforts to promote equal opportunity focused on repairing the deficiencies of individual children rather than concentrating on structures and on curriculum (Epstein 1993: 92). Underpinning the report is the work of Piaget, who has suggested that children cannot 'decentre' (empathize with others) until they reach a 'mental age' of 10 or 11. In practice, this meant that teachers found it difficult to accept (or easy to reject) the idea that primary age children can handle concepts of 'race' and gender (Epstein, 1993: 91) or indeed, we would add, issues of sexuality, disability, social class as well as the running of economies (actual and potential).

The Plowden report contains two contradictory views about the relationship between children and society. Society is treated both as something from which children must be protected, and as an entity that they will enter at some future date, and for which they therefore need to be moulded. It is worth quoting Epstein at length:

> Both these views were aspects of Plowden discourse which diminished the likelihood that primary teachers working within their framework would try to consider and challenge social inequalities with the children they teach – for if the school is regarded as a safe haven from the ills of society, why allow disruptive ideas about inequality to enter the classroom? Furthermore, while 'preparing' children to take their place in society (at some specified future date) might involve some ideas of liberal tolerance. . . it also carries the implicit assumption that the 'nature' of society is fixed and that we can predict what kind of society children should be prepared for. Again, there is no compelling logic which says that predictions about a future society will not involve recognition of a need to combat inequalities but the notion does preclude the idea that children should be involved, in the here and now, in deconstruction of dominant ideologies. (1993: 92–3)

In place of the Plowden/Piaget learning process set of perspectives, Epstein advocates a cooperative, democratic learning process, but in the mode of critical reflection, rather than Plowdenesque liberalism (see also Giroux 1988; Hill 1991, 1994, 1997). Judy Dunn, has shown that children are aware of the feelings of others as early as their second year of life and can therefore 'decentre' and are thus amenable to understanding issues of equality. 'Child-centred' education per se is not the problem, she argues, and it is possible to reappropriate it and make it more 'political and oppositional' (Epstein, 1993: 98). Drawing on the work of Vygotsky and Bruner, and Walkerdine, Tizard and Hughes, Epstein stresses how culture and the social context form the basis for learning. From this perspective, children are seen as social beings, active in the construction of their own realities and subjectivities and therefore potentially active in the deconstruction of ideologies. They are thus able to develop notions of power relationships. Anything can be taught honestly at any age. It is not the content that matters most, but rather the way in which the teaching is framed. To understand new concepts, children need simpler explanations and more scaffolding. As their understanding increases, they become more independent in their handling of concepts (Epstein, 1993: 104). The implications for the possibilities for education to challenge all inequalities at a very early age are obvious. In Epstein's words, '[i]t is essential to view every school as a site of struggle, where the negotiations taking place can either strengthen or weaken possibilities for developing education for equality' (Epstein, 1993: 57).

Elsewhere in this book the various authors have provided detailed practical analysis of, and advice on, education for equality, with respect to issues of social class, 'race', gender, sexuality and disability. In the longer term, it may be that a new Education Act is required to fully address the complex and sometimes conflicting issues of equality in education, that would give children from an early age the right to alternative explanations of what is going on in the world.

### Education to change the world

Third, radicalism incorporated an important internal debate about education as a political strategy, that is as a means of changing the world (Johnson, 1979: 76).

The pre-Thatcherite debates about whether education is political or not have not surprisingly subsided. As detailed in Chapters 1 and 5 of this volume, not only is education in Britain political (small 'p'), it is also quite clearly Political (large 'P'). Hatcher (1995) argues that three developments can help in this context of popular self-activity. First, information technology can allow the pupil much greater choice and undermine the role of the teacher as gatekeeper of knowledge, and at the same time enhance the latter's role as facilitator of the learning process. Second, there must be an increase in the rights of pupils. Effective citizenship in a democracy must begin at school. Though welcome, the extent to which the new citizenship component in the National Curriculum will promote equality is open to question. Third, the school's isolation must be challenged. We must take seriously the concept of a 'learning society' and open up all aspects of social, business and industrial life to educational enquiry (Hatcher, 1995: 3–4) (this makes an interesting counterpoint to the opening up of schools to business and industry – see Allen, Cole and Hatcher, 2000). The combination of these three developments, Hatcher concludes, can place the classroom and the school at the centre of a complex learning network and help create a new popular culture about education (Hatcher, 1995: 4).

Essential to a new popular education is the replacement of the attempted inculcation of 'facts' to be learnt and tested with a genuine dialogic education. Such a dialogic process needs to be differentiated from the post-modernist notion of multiple voices where 'anything goes' (for example, Lather 1991, 1998; for a critique, see, for example, Cole and Hill, 1995, 2001). Rather, dialogic education is empowerment education. It is pupil/student-centred, but not permissive or self-centred. Like all education, dialogic education is not neutral, but aims to incorporate counter-hegemonic themes into the classroom.

This is not to say that schools should replace one propaganda with another; rather that pupils be provided with alternative interpretations of why and how things happen and be constantly urged to ask whose history and literature is conventionally taught in schools and whose is left out, from whose point of view is the past and present examined? Empowerment education invites pupils/ students to become thinking citizens but also to be change agents and social critics (Shor, 1992: 15–16).

### Education for all

Finally, radical movements developed a vigorous and varied educational practice, which was concerned with informing mature understandings and on the education of all citizens as members of a more just social order. In this conception, no large distinction was made between the education of 'children' and 'adults' (Johnson, 1979: 77).

As we have suggested, as a longer-term strategy a new Education Act is required if real equality is to be given the central position in education that it deserves. It is beyond the scope of this book to do more that suggest a philosophy for such an Act. However, in the light of the arguments developed in this book, a central tenet of any new Act should be to provide a public education and training service, serving all citizens throughout their lives, that will promote democratically controlled and accountable education at all levels and will apply the principles of equality and critical reflection to all parts of the service.

This is a future vision that all educators, and all those concerned with education, would surely endorse.

## References

Allen, M, Cole, M and Hatcher, R (2000) *Business, Business, Business: The New Labour agenda in education*, Tufnell Press, London

Brehony, K (1992) What's left of progressive primary education, in *Rethinking Radical Education: Essays in Honour of Brian Simon,* eds A Rattansi, and D Reeder, Lawrence & Wishart, London

Carrington, B, and Troyna, B (1988) Combating racism through political education, in *Children and Controversial Issues: Strategies for the early and middle years of schooling*, eds B Carrington and B Troyna, Falmer Press, Lewes

Central Advisory Council for Education (CACE) (1967) *Children and Their Primary Schools (The Plowden Report)*, Department for Education and Science, London

Cole, M (1997) Equality and primary education: what are the conceptual issues? In *Promoting Equality in Primary Schools*, eds M Cole, D Hill and S Shan, Cassell, London

Cole, M (2000) Time to liberate the mind: primary schools in the new century, *Primary Teaching Studies*, **11** (2), pp 4–9

Cole, M and Hill, D (1995) Games of despair and rhetorics of resistance: postmodernism, education and reaction, *British Journal of Sociology of Education*, **16** (2), pp 165–82

Cole, M, and Hill, D (2001) Resistance postmodernism, in *Marxism Against Postmodernism in Educational Theory*, eds D Hill, P Mclaren, M Cole and G Rikowski, Lexington Press, Lanham, MD

Epstein, D (1993) *Changing Classroom Cultures: Anti-racism, Politics and Schools*, Trentham Books, Stoke-on-Trent

Giroux, H (1983) *Theory and Resistance in Education: A pedagogy for the opposition*, Heinemann, London

Giroux, H (1988) *Schooling and the Struggle for Public Life: Critical pedagogy in the modern age*, University of Minnesota Press, Minneapolis, MN

Giroux, H and McLaren, P (1989) *Critical Pedagogy, the State and Cultural Struggle*, State University of New York Press, New York

Gleeson, D and Whitty, G (1976) *Developments in Social Studies Teaching*, Open Books, London

Hatcher, R (1995) Popular Self-Activity and State Provision: The strategic debate in education, *Socialist Teacher*

Heath, SB (1983) *Ways With Words: Language, life and work in communities and classrooms*, Cambridge, New York

Hill, D (1991) Seven ideological perspectives on teacher education today and the development of a radical Left discourse, *Australian Journal of Teacher Education*, **16** (2), pp 5–29

Hill, D (1994) Initial teacher education and cultural diversity, in *Cultural Diversity and the Curriculum, Vol. 4: Cross-Curricular Contexts, Themes and Dimensions in Primary Schools*, eds G Verma and P Pumfrey, Falmer Press, London

Hill, D (1997) Reflection in Teacher Education, in *Education Dilemmas: Debate and Diversity, Vol. 1: Teacher Education and Training*, eds K Watson, S Modgil and C Modgil, Cassell, London

Johnson, R (1979) 'Really useful knowledge': radical education and working-class culture, 1790–1848, in *Working Class Culture: Studies in history and theory*, eds J Clarke, C Critcher, and R Johnson, Hutchinson, London

Lather, P (1991) *Getting Smart: Feminist research and pedagogy with/in the postmodern*, Routledge, New York

Lather, P, (1998) Critical pedagogy and its complicities: a praxis of stuck places, *Educational Theory*, **48** (4), pp 487–97

Mullard, C (1988) Talk to the Faculty of Education, Brighton Polytechnic, 29 June

Sarup, M (1983) *Marxism Structuralism Education*, The Falmer Press, Lewes

Shor, I (1992) *Empowering Education: Critical teaching for social change*, The University of Chicago Press, Chicago

Young, R E (1984) Teaching equals indoctrination: the dominant epistemic practices of our schools, *British Journal of Education Studies*, **22** (3), pp 230–38

# Index

Printed in the United Kingdom
by Lightning Source UK Ltd.
134229UK00001B/153/A